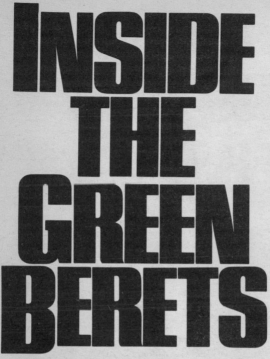

INSIDE THE GREEN BERETS

THE FIRST THIRTY YEARS

A HISTORY OF THE U.S. ARMY SPECIAL FORCES

CHARLES M. SIMPSON III USA (Ret.)

BERKLEY BOOKS, NEW YORK

This Berkley book contains the complete
text of the original hardcover edition.
It has been completely reset in a typeface
designed for easy reading, and was printed
from new film.

INSIDE THE GREEN BERETS

A Berkley Book / published by arrangement with
Presidio Press

PRINTING HISTORY
Presidio Press edition published 1983
Berkley edition / September 1984
Fourth printing / November 1985

ISBN: 0-425-09146-5

A BERKLEY BOOK ® TM 757,375
Berkley Books are published by The Berkley Publishing Group,
200 Madison Avenue, New York, New York 10016.
The name "BERKLEY" and the stylized "B" with design
are trademarks belonging to Berkley Publishing Corporation.
PRINTED IN THE UNITED STATES OF AMERICA

TO THE MEN OF SPECIAL FORCES
past, present, and future,
with my deep gratitude for years of camaraderie, excellence,
and pride at being counted among their ranks.

CONTENTS

FOREWORD

I admire Colonel "Bill" Simpson for many reasons, particularly for this wonderful tribute to the Men of the Green Beret. It took courage and a great deal of personal experience to embark upon an undertaking of this complex and controversial nature.

The intangible atmosphere of authenticity that surrounds this book derives from an articulate, perceptive, sensitive individual who knows intimately the world of his fellow Special Forces soldiers.

It has been my good fortune to have observed Bill Simpson in action in many parts of the world. These areas ranged from the Federal Republic of Germany to a remote section of Khermanshah in Iran and to Okinawa, and the islands of Samar and Mindanao in the Philippines.

I always came away from these encounters with a feeling of pride stemming from the knowledge that where he was in command, the interests of our nation and the reputation of the United States Army were in competent hands.

I am grateful to Colonel Simpson for granting me the privilege of expressing some of my views in this foreword.

I was not the first commander of the Green Berets. To the everlasting credit of the United States Army, a small Special Forces element with a wartime guerrilla warfare mission had been in being for almost ten years before I took command of the Special Warfare Center at Fort Bragg, North Carolina, in January of 1961. Moreover, I was not the architect of the charisma and glamour which surround these extraordinary soldiers, as both qualities stem directly and naturally from the type of man Special Forces attracts and the offbeat missions which they perform.

World War II combat service as a paratrooper and postwar operations with the U.S. Army Counterintelligence in Europe was pertinent to my new command. My great advantage, however, lay in the direct personal support given me by the President of the United States during the period when the world situation seemed to call for an unprecedented expansion of

American irregular warfare capabilities.

In June 1962, in a graduation address at the United States Military Academy at West Point, President Kennedy had pointed out that Mao Tse-tung's brand of war was insidious, new and different and that our preparations to cope with it had to develop along new lines. These initiatives would be aimed at building a force that could reach into conflict dimensions where conventional armies were incapable of operating.

To quote from the President's advice to the newly commissioned second lieutenants, many of whom were soon to see service in Indochina:

"This is another type of war, new in its intensity, ancient in its origins—war by guerrillas, subversives, insurgents, assassins; war by ambush instead of by combat; by infiltration instead of aggression, seeking victory by eroding and exhausting the enemy instead of engaging him. It requires—in those situations where we must encounter it—a whole new kind of strategy, a wholly different kind of force, and therefore, a new and wholly different kind of military training."

As inspiring and prophetic as the words of the Commander-in-Chief were, they did not in themselves prod the Armed Forces into changing their conventional warfare orientation in any significant way.

Because of service apathy and even opposition, the President took the unusual step of arranging a private session with the Joint Chiefs of Staff in the hope that they would urge support for the ambitious training programs that were laboring to get off the ground at Fort Bragg.

Several aspects of the Special Forces Prototype that was being crafted in response to the desires of the Commander-in-Chief were in for heavy going. The reasons were traditional. Unlike the armies of other great powers past and present, the United States Army has always looked with disfavor upon the concept of elite military organizations.

In the early 1960s it was generally accepted in America's high military command and staff circles that there was nothing unique about Ho Chi Minh's war. As far as most of the senior leaders were concerned, the basic training, leadership, organizational principles, tactics and strategy that had won America's wars in the past would be more than adequate for Indochina. Both Special Warfare and Special Forces were terms that raised many hackles among the conventional regulars.

On several occasions public statements by very high ranking Army officers made light of the idea that guerrilla warfare was really important and rejected any inference that an intense political struggle was woven throughout the fabric of Communist military action in Southeast Asia. It was the President himself and not his military advisors who first perceived that the front line of defense against paramilitary aggression had to be in the hearts and minds of the threatened population.

To students of irregular warfare it seemed obvious that refusal by the people of support for underground organizations which spawn guerrilla forces would render guerrilla warfare unlikely if not impossible. There were many ways that even conventional soldiers could influence the population toward support of their government and away from the subversive guerrillas. Mao Tse-tung had proven the obverse side of the principle again and again during his 10,000-mile "long march" across China as he fled before Chiang Kai-shek's conventional forces.

At the Special Warfare Center many of us had become keen students of the irregular warfare phenomenon. We had studied with great interest Edgar Snow's book, *Red Star Over China*, which had been first published in 1939 (Grove Press). It carried his firsthand account of the emphasis which both Mao Tse-tung and Lin Piao had placed upon good discipline and troop behavior as a means of gaining popular support for a struggling revolutionary army. By Mao's order, rules for troop discipline were memorized by the Chinese Red Army soldiers. These all-important guidelines were even set to music and sung daily as an official Red Army song. Six of these rules seemed to bring magical results:

- There shall be no confiscations whatever from the poor peasantry.
- If you borrow anything, return it.
- Replace all articles you damage.
- Pay for everything you purchase.
- Be honest in all transactions with the peasants.
- Be courteous and polite to the people and help them when you can.

There were other rules as well, all designed to make the peasant feel that the Red Army was friendly and benevolent. Chiang Kai-shek's conventional forces practiced no such code of conduct. It was not difficult to see why popular support began to snowball toward the irregulars who lived by the rules prescribed by their leader, Mao Tse-tung.

With this kind of current history as a guide, it was clear that the armed forces, which were visible representatives of the government they serve, must be taught to help win and maintain support for that government through carefully conceived and executed nonmilitary as well as military actions. The first and most urgent requirement was for the highest level of discipline among the troops. This would insure good deportment in politically sensitive areas and result in fair and considerate treatment of the population with whom they came into contact. Furthermore, military supply systems, military skills with civilian applicability, military equipment such as earth-moving machinery, communications systems, field kitchens, and mobile hospitals could do much to relieve civilian shortages temporarily until civil administrative and economic developments made such military help no longer needed.

Conventional soldiers have a scant history of showing great concern for the unfortunate civilians who may be caught up in the tide of war in contested areas. Military leaders as well as the men under their command had to be convinced that the political and psychological fallout from lack of concern for people could negate even the most brilliant conventional shooting victory. In the United States Army, the Green Berets were the first to be taught this lesson formally and to put it into practice as a principle of war.

The Green Berets were interested in many concerns of the villager that other soldiers seldom thought about. They helped him find a more ample source of water by a simple well-digging technique. They worked side by side with him to construct a log bridge which would save making a half-mile detour around a swamp in order to get to his primitive garden plot. They gave him seeds which grew better vegetables than he had ever seen before. Most curious and heartwarming of all, the American Green Berets were interested in him as an individual. They knew a few words of his dialect and around the fire in the evening they improved their vocabularies as they shared his food and drink. It was remarkable that Americans could eat the same things that the jungle people lived on—but these Special Forces soldiers did!

Once friendly relations had been established, the task of training villagers to defend themselves against enemy attacks began. Green Berets traced out village fortification outlines and tribesmen placed row after row of sharpened bamboo stakes in the ground leaning at an angle toward approach routes. Protective shelters were dug inside the village perimeters. An alarm system using an old iron tire rim or an empty artillery shell case provided warning that villagers should man the defenses against attack. Throughout preparations for village security, Green Berets worked shoulder to shoulder with the villagers and when attacks began, they fought side by side with the jungle people who were their friends.

As Special Forces were originally conceived, they were to operate well behind enemy lines in guerrilla areas. There they would help to organize and train irregular forces which might ultimately grow enough in strength and skill to become a problem for enemy conventional units. During their formative period, guerrillas are like soft-shelled crabs—vulnerable. Consequently, they must remain hidden in areas difficult for counterguerrilla forces to penetrate. Dense jungles, rugged mountainous regions, swamps covered with heavy undergrowth provide the kinds of natural environment in which guerrillas can grow.

Day-to-day survival for the guerrilla is often a triumph in itself. He must be rugged both physically and in his determination. If he is sick or wounded, he cannot normally rely upon outside help. His medicines must either be in his pack sack or must be found among the flora and fauna of his environment. Even more important than the medicines his body may require is the medical knowledge necessary to keep him a viable functioning machine. For this reason, Green Beret organizational concepts have always featured medical expertise.

The Special Forces "A" Detachment of two officers and ten troopers contained two enlisted medical specialists, and each of the remaining eight troopers was also cross-trained in medical skills. The training of the Green Beret medical enlisted men involved use of animals. This was undertaken under the most hygienic and humane conditions with the tacit approval of the American Medical Association and under the close supervision of medical doctors.

The enlisted trainees culminated a thirty-eight-week medical training course with their final instruction in the animal laboratory. There, wounded animals were given the same kind of meticulous care that humans should receive. The operating room procedures that would apply to a military aid station in combat were taught to highly selected Green Beret sergeants who would ultimately become enlisted medical members of Special Forces "A" Detachments. Manual skills in performing amputations, in suturing and in general handling of wounds were required by these medical sergeants. But more than that, they were watched closely and continuously to insure that they had in ample measure the qualities of responsibility, compassion, and dedication which would qualify them to deal with vital functions of other human beings. Even though the Green Beret selection process was itself most exacting, a substantial percentage of volunteers who were qualified for other Special Forces skills failed to survive the rigid medical training process. Perhaps most important of all was the requirement for the medical enlisted man to understand his limitations—the Special Forces medical specialist was not a doctor and was warned that he must never assume that he was one. His first commandment was that he should understand, accept, and practice the Special Forces medical creed which described the limits of his right to perform medical services. It was his Hippocratic Oath.

In order to improve our medical intelligence, the Green Beret doctors developed a plan for using Special Forces as medical intelligence collectors. At Fort Bragg, each Special Forces team member bound for Indochina was given a complete physical examination prior to boarding the airplane that would take his entire detachment to its overseas destination. Samples of blood scrum, carefully identified, taken from each man were to be analyzed and compared with serum that would be drawn when he returned with his detachment at the end of a six-month tour of duty. An exhaustive questionnaire administered to returnees by Green Beret doctors was aimed at determining details concerning sanitation, food, insects, climate, rainfall, indigenous customs, living conditions, visible evidence of disease, and scores of other bits of environmental intelligence. This information was then computerized. Little by little a medical map of Indochina began to form. The geographic areas where diseases were prevalent, the times of the year, the times of day or night, the temperatures and relative humidity which marked danger periods were translated into graphs and curves which would be literally a matter of life and death for the Americans who were to come later to Southeast Asia in very large numbers.

It was the Green Beret medical intelligence system that first turned up the strain of malaria passed on by the falciprium mosquito. Falciprium malaria was impervious to U.S. Army malaria prophylaxis on hand for troop use, and research had to be undertaken at once in order to stave off what could have been a major health problem for our forces.

Green Beret doctors, using Special Forces medical intelligence teams, discovered that another dread and rare disease called tropical sprue existed in parts of the Indochinese peninsula. Infected with tropical sprue, the walls of the intestines become flat and smooth and the body begins to waste away from lack of nourishment. Having been warned by Green Beret medics about this disease, the Army Medical Corps addressed it as a potential problem and developed the means to counter it. During my farewell trip to Saigon in 1971, I talked to an American four-star general who was recovering from tropical sprue. The Green Berets had been instrumental in saving his life, among many others.

In early 1963 in company with a Green Beret medical officer, I made a tour of more than two dozen Special Forces camps scattered throughout Vietnam mostly in remote and wild areas. In the course of our travels we put down our helicopter in the Central Highlands in order to look in on a Special Forces medical sergeant whose post of duty was a leper camp. I had never seen lepers before and the initial visual shock was one to remember: leprosy is no respecter of age. The camp held men, women, and children, even babies afflicted with the disfiguring disease. Our Green Beret sergeant had been in the camp almost six months working with these human derelicts.

While the Green Berets continued to carry out the complex mission in Vietnam, they were also active in a number of other parts of the world. On the Eastern Philippine island of Cebu, I saw Green Beret doctors and dentists doing a land-office business among the peasants and their children. Farther inland in Cebu, I ran across a village project on which it seems that every man, woman, and child was working. Some were digging a long ditch which ran into the jungle, others were carrying lengths of iron pipe or mixing cement. Old women were carrying buckets of water to slake the thirst of the workers. The whole colorful scene in this remote, thatched-roof bamboo village was one marked by joyful enthusiasm. Upon making my way back into the jungle in the direction in which the ditch led, I found the explanation.

A spring that was the village's source of water was in the process of being tamed and brought under control. A Green Beret sergeant covered with mud was down in the excavation which had been dug around the spring. He was directing the final preparation of concrete forms which were being nailed together by Filipino farmers and Green Beret soldiers who were sweating, laughing, and talking in a combination of English and Filipino dialect.

In 1971, before it had fallen to the Communists, I was able to revisit the Plateau de Bolovens in Laos. It is a remote area into which few foreigners had reason to go. Communist Pathet Lao troops were ranging up and down the Plateau de Bolovens, attacking the dug-in garrisons of the Royal Laotian Army and preying upon the road traffic. I had been on the Plateau for the first time over a decade before to visit a Green Beret detachment commanded by the gallant "Bull" Simons, which was working with members of the Kha tribe.

The Green Berets lived with the Kha, and consequently they became aware of many things that could be done to improve the generally marginal quality of their existence. Using a great deal of ingenuity, the Special Forces had helped the Kha build a rice mill from salvaged pieces of machinery. The Green Berets had then located a worn-out surplus Army truck in the Laotian capital of Vientiane, had dismantled it, hauled it piece by piece to the Plateau de Bolovens by helicopter, where they rebuilt it and placed it in working order. The tribesmen now had a mechanical means of hauling rice to the mill. Finally, between military training periods the Special Forces soldiers helped the Kha organize the first cooperative market they had ever known. Here simple tools, food, and supplies could be exchanged.

When the Green Berets left Laos in 1961 as a result of the Geneva Agreement, there was real concern among them as to what might then happen to their Kha friends.

During the invasion of Southern France as at Anzio, Italy, I fought alongside the magnificent soldiers who made up the Canadian-American outfit, the First Special Service Force. There has never been a more highly motivated nor more gallant group of fighting men—but there the similarity with the U.S. Green Berets ceased.

It was indicative of the U.S. Army's basic misunderstanding of what Special Forces really are, that official lineage of Special Forces is traced back to the First Special Service Force. The OSS was a much more legitimate ancestor of today's Green Berets, but the problem with U.S. Army recognition of that fact is a syndrome that has wider implications. OSS was a hybrid with a strong political and intelligence flavor.

The United States Army has traditionally tried to steer clear of political involvement either at home or abroad.

It is for this reason that to give Special Forces an expanded role in a world environment where neither conventional nor nuclear forces are appropriate may require them to be launched, guided, and controlled by some echelon outside the Armed Forces. Given the spotty history of the CIA in the conduct of irregular operations and the doubtful stable of experts at other levels of government, it is difficult to say where the reins of control should lie.

On the hopeful side, the early 1980s has seen the rise to the highest positions in the U.S. Army of two individuals whose grasp of the intangibles of irregular warfare is in marked contrast to their predecessors of the past two decades. Both the Secretary of the Army, the Honorable John O. Marsh, Jr., and the Chief of Staff of the U.S. Army, General Edward (Shy) Meyer, are quietly and effectively checking the mechanism and inventorying America's assets for "subterranean" warfare.

Meanwhile, the Green Berets are beginning to stir again

after a long sleep. Interest in their unique properties is on the rise not only in the Pentagon but at even higher levels.

They are an extraordinary strategic tool waiting for the hands of mastercraftsmen.

William P. Yarborough
Lieutenant General, USA (Ret.)
Southern Pines, North Carolina
December 1982

PREFACE

This story of the United States Army Special Forces, written in the year of its thirtieth anniversary, will, if it succeeds in fulfilling my intentions, serve three purposes. It will inform the American public of the accomplishments of the Forces, without going into the sort of detail found in unit histories. It will provide additional information for those with more than a passing knowledge of, or interest in, the Forces. The families of members, for example, have been deprived of any detailed knowledge by the high security fence that invariably surrounds Special Forces Groups. Finally, it will provide future members of the Forces with a guide that will help them avoid past mistakes and realize future potentials and goals.

This account is admittedly an apologia written by a man with a deep affection for SF and one who had long service in its ranks. This is not to say that it is entirely uncritical. Mistakes have been made, and I have tried to identify them without bias.

Any book on Special Forces must of necessity discuss the theories, tactics, and practices of insurgency and counterinsurgency since this is necessary for an understanding of the nature and purpose of SF missions. I have tried to do this so that even the non-military reader would be engaged, and I have included some of my own experiences where relevant.

This book has been twelve years in the writing—that is to say, it was started twelve years ago by Col. Robert B. Rheault, who did much of the research and wrote a first draft of the manuscript. When he submitted the manuscript, however, the publisher wanted him to provide an inside scoop on that 1969 incident which resulted in the detainment and investigation of seven men assigned to 5th Special Forces Group in Vietnam, one of whom was Bob himself. He refused to do this, and instead he put his box of research references and the draft manuscript on a closet shelf and forgot them.

In May 1981, on the Plain at West Point, awaiting an alumni review, Maj. Gen. George S. Patton, a classmate, asked me

xix

about Bob, his book, and the possibility of its being published. It was common knowledge in the class that Bob and I were close friends going back many years, and had served together half-a-dozen times. I told George the status of the manuscript. Later George came to me rather excitedly and said that another classmate, Bob Kane, the publisher of Presidio Press, was present and that he might be interested in publishing Bob's book. It turned out that he was. When I contacted Bob Rheault, I learned that he was not interested in further attempts to publish, but he said I was welcome to all the material he had if I wanted to carry the project forward. This book has my name as the author, but owes a huge debt to Bob Rheault. However, I alone am responsible for its contents, and Bob does not necessarily agree with everything I have said in this version.

What are our credentials to write a book about Special Forces? I volunteered for SF in 1959 while a student at the Command and General Staff College. At that time I was an infantry major, Ranger qualified, a senior parachutist, and had fourteen months of combat in Korea and two years of company command in the 82nd Airborne Division. I then was sent directly to Germany to join the 10th Special Forces Group (Airborne) in Bad Tolz, without benefit of special training for SF. In the 10th SFG, I served as a B Detachment commander, Group S-3 for two years, and as organizer and first commander of C Company (now called a battalion).

In 1960, partly as a result of my glowing descriptions of the 10th SFG, Bob Rheault volunteered for the same unit, taking over my old B Detachment. He also followed me as Group S-3, returning to the States with me in 1963 to attend the Armed Forces Staff College together. Bob went to Vietnam in 1964 to be the Deputy Commander for Operations and Intelligence of the 5th SFG. We came together in 1965 once again as students at the Army War College. I then went to Vietnam as Deputy Commander of the 5th SFG, while Bob went to the Joint Staff. He then took command of the 1st SFG on Okinawa in 1968, moving down to command of the 5th SFG in Vietnam in 1969. I replaced him as commander of the 1st SFG, with the understanding that I would also replace him at the 5th SFG after a year. Bob's assignment was terminated early by the incident alluded to later, and he returned to the United States in October 1969 to retire voluntarily. I was not put in command of the 5th SFG due to General Abrams's (Commander of U.S. forces in Vietnam) personal involvement, remaining instead with the 1st SFG until 1971, when I joined the faculty of the Army War College in charge of Unconventional Warfare studies. I retired from that assignment voluntarily in 1973. Many officers have had more years in SF than my nine and Bob's six, but few have had as much experience at all levels of Special Warfare.

The use of the term "Green Berets" to denote Special Forces is an acknowledgment of the media's usage and widespread acceptance of the term by the American public. A green beret is a *hat,* while a member of Special Forces is a highly motivated and trained expert in conventional and unconventional warfare who wears the green beret. In this book, except for the title, the term *green beret* refers to the hat, not the soldier wearing it. Another term not present in this book is *ex-SF.* There is no such person, for once in Special Forces, a soldier is always SF, although he may retire or be assigned duty out of the Forces. We are an exceptionally clannish group of men (and women

LTC "Maggie" Raye performing for her boys, Nha Trang

such as Lt. Col. Martha Raye, known affectionately as "Maggie" to thousands of SF), and we have a Special Forces Association numbering thousands of members in over two dozen chapters in the United States and Korea.

Although this book is about U.S. Army Special Forces, it does not pay tribute to those superb partners, the women and families of SF members, who have had to put up with so much for so many years—long absences of husband and father, secrecy, countless duffel bags full of dirty clothes, and long hours of shop talk. Likewise, it does not provide adequate plaudits to the Navy Seals, Air Force Commandos, Marine Reconnaissance Forces, Army helicopter pilots, Army and Air Force transport pilots, and the countless others who have provided marvelous support over the years. The special forces of allied armies deserve a book of their own; so many of them were based on and trained by USSF. The Australians and the now-defunct South Vietnamese, who fought and bled beside us, deserve special mention. Finally, there are many outstanding individual members of Special Forces not mentioned in these pages who deserve to be.

Nothing has been said about mercenaries because of the simple fact that few retired SF men take up that avocation. In my experience, retired SF men are an extremely peace-loving group with no desire for further combat. Occasionally, newspapers or paramilitary periodicals headline the participation by "Green Berets" in crime or mercenary combat, but I discount those accounts. Certainly, any group that comprises thousands of men who have been highly trained for violent combat can be expected to have a few bad apples. The SF is no exception, but the renegades are rare and atypical.

Little has been said about antiterrorism by SF, as that is a highly classified topic. It might be a proper subject sometime in the future, but not now.

The topics I have covered will, I hope, shed some light on what the Green Berets are all about.

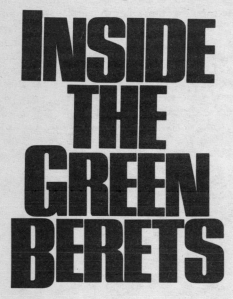

1. GUERRILLA WARFARE

The United States Army Special Forces was thirty years old in 1982. Perhaps no other military organization in history has, in so short a period of time, generated a greater aura of mystery, been more generally misunderstood, or found itself so frequently neglected and ill-used. The organization survives today with a misrepresented past, but with an increasingly optimistic future.

Special Forces provides the United States with a unique capability that could help bring peace and stability to many troubled areas around the world. Unfortunately, little is generally known of the accomplishments and contributions of Special Forces to national policy. This lack of knowledge probably results from the fact that the basic missions of Special Forces, while easily stated, are difficult to grasp and very difficult to carry out successfully. Briefly, the missions are these:

- To seek out, train, and support men capable of becoming effective guerrillas.
- To seek out, engage, and neutralize guerrillas.

These roles are not contradictory. Whether Special Forces develops guerrilla troops, or challenges and ultimately eliminates them depends on *whose* guerrillas they are.

A purpose of this book is to examine these two roles: to discuss how Special Forces was brought into being to perform them; to determine how well or poorly that has been done, and why; to identify the political, diplomatic, moral, and other problems arising from their implementation; and finally, to forecast their implications and potential for the future. In order to accomplish this purpose, we must first learn more about that murky, imprecise form of combat known as guerrilla warfare.

It is one of the paradoxes that, although American experience with guerrilla warfare began even prior to the Revolutionary War, Americans have neither practiced nor understood it very well. It runs counter to our sense of fair play, our conviction that politics and the military should not mix, our impatience and our love of neat, quick solutions. It frustrates us because it does not permit us to bring our wealth, our industrial might, and our technological superiority successfully to bear. It offends the sense of "good order and discipline" of conservative and conventional-minded soldiers. Nevertheless, guerrilla warfare is a vital force in domestic and international conflict. It is not going to go away simply because Americans don't like it, don't understand it, and don't want to become involved in it.

Guerrilla warfare has a long history, perhaps as long as the history of human conflict. Despite these ancient roots, the guerrilla has been given scant attention in most accounts of past wars. Perhaps the great captains wished to hide their impotence against those irregular bands, or, in a winning cause, to play down the importance of the contributions of the guerrillas. Historians give little credit to the Spanish guerrillas whose activities crippled the French in Spain. Wellington and his British regulars are properly enough heroes of the Peninsular Campaigns, but why was so little said about the guerrillas who supported them? One might raise the same question over the division of the laurels between Allenby and his conventional forces, and Lawrence and his Arab guerrillas. Had Lawrence not been a writer himself, would anyone recognize how much he accomplished? The Czarist Russian high command tried very hard to minimize the role of Russian partisans in defeating Napoleon. In America, Confederate Gen. Jubal Early tried to disband the rangers of Mosby, McNeil, and Woodson. Although those raiders plagued Northern troops for years, later researchers found it difficult to find material about them. Only since the Communists began to claim they invented guerrilla war do we find the guerrilla's importance emphasized. Only recently has the guerrilla become a central figure rather than a support player, and guerrilla warfare been a chosen course rather than a measure of desperation. The significance of this important change has penetrated slowly, and in some cases not at all, the minds of too many conventional straight-line soldiers.

The truth is that though early examples of guerrilla warfare are interesting because they show what can be accomplished with few resources, but with great daring and imagination, they are otherwise not very significant. Those earlier conflicts were far less "total wars," and, therefore, the importance of the rear areas and population was not as great.

It was not until World War II that the full potential of guerrilla warfare began to be recognized. That history is worth reviewing for several reasons. First, it is recent enough to be meaningful in a technical as well as in a purely theoretical sense. Second, the war was widespread and varied geographically, politically, militarily, and materially. Third, and most importantly, the aircraft, the long-range radio, and the parachute brought a new dimension to guerrilla warfare. Rather than the hit-or-miss, uncoordinated activities of desperate men dissatisfied with the state of affairs in their own country, operating with no outside help, resistance movements of World War II were supported and even managed from the outside. They could be characterized as coordinated actions designed to assist an overall strategic effort.

Teams of specialists with radios and other sophisticated equipment dropped behind enemy lines to help organize, train, supply, and direct the resistance. France, Russia, Yugoslavia, Greece, China, the Philippines, and Burma were but a few such locales. Russian partisan activity behind the German lines was directed from the Kremlin itself, closely coordinated with the moves of the Red Army. On one occasion, in support of a major Russian offensive, partisans in one sector planted almost 15,000 demolition charges in a single night. Russian guerrillas are said to have killed more than 300,000 German soldiers. While the body count is as usual uncertain, the critical and unquestioned point is that tens of thousands of German combat troops were diverted from the front to protect supply lines and rear installations. Ultimately, the Germans found themselves simply unable to sustain operations in Russia. In another sector, Tito's guerrillas could never have won the war in Yugoslavia alone, but many thousands of German troops were tied down there trying to deal with them. The same was true in Greece. The Polish underground, primarily active in urban and industrial sabotage, working with little or no outside help, damaged almost 7,000 locomotives and 20,000 railroad cars, and destroyed 4,300 military motor vehicles and over 4,600 tons of fuel. More subtly, but every bit as effectively, they built 4,700 faulty aircraft engine parts and 200 faulty cannon barrels. A different approach was followed by the French Maquis whose biggest single accomplishment probably was support of the Normandy landings. "Plan Vert" resulted in 3,000 confirmed rail cuts in the first three weeks. "Plan Violet" disrupted German wire communications, and "Plan Tortue" hit their road nets. At that key juncture of the war, General Eisenhower rated the guerrilla contribution as being equal to that of twelve conventional divisions.

No one claims that guerrillas "won the war" for the Allies or were even a major factor when weighed against the might of the committed military and industrial forces. It is only when one looks at the small numbers of guerrillas involved and the relatively tiny expenditure of funds and materiel, and weighs this against the results achieved, that some idea of their importance begins to dawn. The Greek resistance movement of some 20,000 to 30,000 guerrillas was sustained for more than eighteen months at a total cost of only $4.5 million—$2.5 million for supplies and $2 million in gold sovereigns. At no time did the number of British and American supporters committed to that venture exceed 400. Yet that force was able to tie down large German combat forces, seriously disrupt critical rail traffic through Greece, destroy important quantities of enemy equipment and supplies, and provide a psychological rallying point for the entire nation.

Since the end of World War II, the world has seen 50 to 150 serious insurgencies, depending on the criteria. Guerrilla warfare has been, and will continue to be, a fact of life, not only in Southeast Asia, but in Africa, the Middle East, and Latin America as well. The Communists, from Mao Tse-tung to Ho Chi Minh and Ché Guevara, claim and often seem to be masters of both theory and practice. They made no secret of their plans to use insurgency as a tool to achieve their objectives. A better grasp of the principles of such warfare would thus seem to be in this nation's best interest.

The primary, not often recognized characteristic of guerrilla warfare is that it is a tool of the weak. Until relatively recently it was never the *chosen* form of conflict, but rather a measure of desperation adopted by men who wished to oppose, evict, or destroy those in power. Often those men were the remnants of a defeated army fighting against their country's occupiers, or they represented the early stirrings of political opposition against an unpopular regime. In guerrilla and counterguerrilla war, therefore, there is always a tremendous imbalance of means and resources. On the one hand are the "outs," the small, widely dispersed, lightly armed ragged bands of insurgents, living outside the law in the most rugged and inhospitable regions, responsible for little but their own lives. On the other are the "ins," the government in power, with its police force, army, navy, and air force, its economic and industrial bases, its transportation networks and communications complexes, with the awesome responsibility of securing it all and keeping it all operating. It is the guerrilla's lack of responsibility, more than anything else, that gives him such great operational flexibility. It is ridiculously simple to cut a railroad or destroy a section of power line. These are the traditional "training missions" given by older insurgents to build the confidence and morale of new guerrillas, if for no other reason than the near impossibility of protecting these targets against such attacks. It is easy work for a few guerrillas to destroy the barn of an uncooperative or collaborationist farmer, for what army is large enough to protect *all* of the farms *all* of the time? The strategically weak guerrilla can thus assume the tactical offensive when, where, and how he chooses, waiting until circumstances are in his favor. He acts when the risks are small and the physical and/or psychological effects are greatest. The damage he wreaks may not be great, but it can be a major harassment for the "ins." It is designed to convince many people that the government cannot protect them, and thus that they dare not oppose the insurgents. It may force the government to take disciplinary and repressive measures involving all the population—search patrols, curfews, roadblocks, travel restrictions, food rationing—all of which antagonize the people. It also certainly will force the government to create and deploy ever larger security and military forces.

The effect of this will be costly and frustrating to the "ins," but it seldom, if ever, is of itself decisive. Ultimately, the guerrillas will have to change their style and take over in a near conventional manner, as Mao did in China, or an outside force will have to come in and do so, as the Allied armies did in World War II. Castro's revolution in Cuba proved to be the exception, but mass hatred of the Batista regime plus the Latin Americans' love of charismatic characters made the guerrilla movement an almost instant success. In Vietnam, the Republic of Vietnam had the guerrilla movement well in hand by 1975, when the conventional North Vietnamese Army invaded with artillery, tanks, and jet aircraft to achieve what the guerrillas could not achieve.

Mao Tse-tung's metaphor of the "fish" and the "sea," in reference to the guerrillas' need for popular support, may be a cliché, but is valid nevertheless. It is this basic fact of guerrilla life that has doomed the North Korean attempts to create a guerrilla movement in South Korea. Nothing daunted, the North Koreans have created a large unconventional force of approximately 70,000 trained in air, sea, and ground infiltration (to include the use of tunnels) to infiltrate South Korea to conduct guerrilla warfare in ROK rear areas. The Arab *fedayeen* are likewise doomed to the use of commando raids rather than true guerrilla operations against Israel. The entire population need not support the guerrillas. All a successful insurgency needs is a small "activist" percentage, willing to serve full-time as guerrillas, or part-time in one of the support mechanisms. The rest of the population need be no more than sympathetic, or even apathetic. T.E. Lawrence (of Arabia) set the required ratio of active to passive at only 2 percent to 98 percent. Experience elsewhere has borne him out. However, this in no way diminishes the importance of the population—*it will always be the key!* The guerrilla needs the people for both moral and physical support, for everything except the few special items he may receive from outside or capture from the enemy. Food, clothing, recruits, information, occasional transportation and shelter must be locally available. This is why every counterguerrilla or counterinsurgency effort has sought so urgently to separate the guerrillas from the population. Some have tried terror, others have imposed elaborate measures of population and resource control. That was the rationale behind the creation of the "strategic hamlets" of Vietnam and the endless succession of more euphemistically named successors. If guerrilla bands can be effectively cut off from the people, the guerrillas must either become a conventional army with a conventional rear area and support system, or they will wither and die.

Although less critical, outside support is a highly important ingredient for guerrilla success. Its absence or loss can be fatal to the guerrilla cause. Witness the defeat of Communist guerrilla movements in postwar Greece, the Philippines, and Malaya. In each case, the borders could be and were sealed off, and the insurgencies died. In contrast, successful World War II resistance movements such as those in France, Russia, and Yugoslavia received consistent outside help and ultimately, of course, were joined by the liberating Allied armies.

Closely related to the need for outside support is the value of contiguous territory for sanctuary. A classic case is that of postwar Greece, where loss of an adjacent Yugoslavian refuge and supply line led to the collapse of that extensive guerrilla movement. In Vietnam, the enemy's sanctuaries in North Vietnam, Laos, and Cambodia were the source of endless American frustration, and there were major covert efforts to deny them.

The guerrilla also needs difficult terrain for rural guerrilla warfare. In any given country, he will naturally gravitate, or be forced, to the great swamps, deep jungles, high mountains, and deep woods, where terrain becomes the "equalizer" between the two mismatched opponents. The great swamps and forests of the Soviet Union, the mountains of Afghanistan, the *maquis* from which the French resistance took its name, and the jungles of Burma, Malaya, and Vietnam were all used as guerrilla bases. High performance aircraft, motor vehicles, or armor have relatively little utility there. Even the helicopter, pioneered by the French in Algeria and brought to full flower by the Americans in Vietnam and now the Soviets in Afghanistan, has been no panacea.

To the natural concealment of rough terrain he knows intimately, the guerrilla adds his ability to blend with the local populace. The frustrations of trying to deal with the "rice farmer by day, killer by night" are well known to all veterans of counterguerrilla operations. This inability to identify the enemy often leads to repressive or violent countermeasures classically represented by My Lai in Vietnam. The Nazis and Japanese were notorious in the use of wholesale execution of hostages suspected of having aided guerrillas, but they certainly did not invent the technique nor were they the last to use it. Another method used widely by the British, French, and Americans has involved large-scale population resettlement. The repressive measures, however they may differ in detail, share a common characteristic: they create as many problems as they solve. Certainly those techniques designed to scare the population into refusing to help the guerrillas have often proved counterproductive. It is a paradox of guerrilla warfare that terror tactics have been generally successful for the guerrilla, but usually fail in the hands of the counterinsurgents.

How guerrillas make effective use of selective terror can be illustrated in Vietnam. Picture a hamlet (the scene could easily be switched to Algeria, Latin America, or Thailand) in an area not totally controlled by either side, inhabited by simple, poor people, who, as is so often the case, are ideologically or emotionally committed to neither side; in this case neither Saigon nor the Vietcong (VC). They would simply like to be left alone. The hamlet is occasionally visited by Vietnamese or American troops, who perhaps give away a little candy or medicine, steal a chicken or two, and who definitely ask where the VC are. At night a small group of perhaps no more than five or six VC come into town. They assemble everyone, or at least the key adults, and start off with a propaganda talk. It generally goes something like this:

> We are the noble liberators who are fighting for your freedom from oppression. Our goal is to rid the country of the imperialist Americans and their lackeys, your countrymen who have sold out to the foreigners for their own personal gains. Once our inevitable victory has been achieved, you will no longer be plagued by greedy, absentee landlords or corrupt government officials who live by the sweat of your labors. You will be the master of your own fields, and Vietnam will be free.

Next comes the hooker:

> But, of course, the battle is not yet won. We will need the help of every right-thinking citizen. We will expect the following from you: tonight, when we leave, we will take with us four strong young men who will have the privilege of participating directly in the glorious people's struggle. Next week we will pay another visit, at which time your donation of eight bags of rice will be ready. Each family will whittle two bundles of punji stakes. Any movements of American imperialist troops or their lackeys will be reported immediately to us, and I will give your designated

messenger his secret instructions. Mr. Hamlet Elder, what are your comments on this simple but vital program?

Should the hamlet elder reply in a negative way, the VC will rapidly and efficiently disembowel him, along with his wife and children, and then calmly ask the people to point out the next-ranking man. Indeed, it is likely that the newly designated hamlet chief will see a logic in the VC arguments not perceived by his late predecessor, and an apathetic neutral or even pro-government hamlet has become a VC hamlet. They are not ideologically committed, perhaps, but they are committed, and they will not be won back by candy bars or sick call. It is not the guerrillas' preferred method, but it is one that is widely used and generally effective. Such use of terror can force aid to the guerrillas' cause or merely prohibit aid to the enemy. The VC also used terror to systematically destroy the local government, administration, and leadership. It takes relatively few assassinations or kidnappings of village chiefs, schoolteachers, health workers, or police chiefs to persuade all but the most highly motivated and dedicated that such positions are too dangerous to accept. Terror is a dangerous weapon and, carelessly used, has sometimes backfired on guerrillas, but, on the whole, it has been brutally effective.

Employed by government forces or armies of occupation, however, brutality only alienates the population. Germany's SS was not squeamish about using wholesale execution to stamp out resistance activities in Russia, Yugoslavia, France, and Greece, but this only stiffened the anti-Nazi resolve. The Japanese were equally brutal in the Philippines, but guerrilla leaders found that the aftermath of a Japanese bloodbath was a more deeply committed population.

Excursions into more selective methods have yet to prove themselves. In Vietnam, in the mid-1960s, the CIA launched the so-called counter-terror units (CTUs). This was essentially a Vietnamese operation, but was trained, paid for, and run by the CIA. In simple terms, the concept was to identify and then capture or kill members of the Vietcong political or support personnel living undercover in disputed villages, or even in so-called pacified areas. Press inquiries and concern over unfavorable public reaction to this irregular type of warfare led to a change of name to the less frightening provincial reconnaissance units (PRUs), and a euphemistic explanation of their duties as "neutralization of the Vietcong infrastructure." When the military took over the operation, it was also given the code name "Operation Phoenix." It was largely taken out of the hands of the Vietnamese, whereupon it lost most of its effectiveness and died a lingering death. It is difficult to assess accurately the effectiveness of that program. Certainly the scorecards show a large number of individuals "neutralized," but the problem was always positive identification. Was the individual tagged as "infrastructure" really VC, or merely a personal enemy of an informant? Even if carried out with great skill and discrimination, however, such a program is extremely risky and never yields the wide psychological impact that ensues from a guerrilla terror attack.

In sum, then, these are the distinct strengths and weaknesses of the guerrilla:

- He has ready information and intelligence because he is *of* the area and *of* the people.
- He can strike or not strike when, where, and how he pleases, withholding action until the odds are heavily in his favor.
- He can destroy and terrorize with little concern or responsibility, for he has no need to defend, protect, or secure.
- How effective he is will depend on his ability to exploit these strengths and thus offset his strategic weaknesses— his lack of means and real mobility, his inflexibility once an action is launched, and his susceptibility to compromise from within.
- He must have the support, or at least the indifference, of the population, some outside help, and a "cause" around which to rally his men and his supporters.

His enemies will succeed or fail, not on the basis of their physical numbers and technological strength, but according to their ability to separate the guerrilla from the population, cut off his outside help, cast doubt on the validity of his cause, and convince the population of the worthiness of the government.

The extraordinary increase in the use of guerrilla warfare in recent years is also linked to the advent of superweapons. Guerrilla warfare defies the possessor of superweapons by operating among the people. It thus challenges the strong to use weapons against an uncertain target, doing damage to the very people the strong do not wish to alienate. Other factors like communications, aviation, and improved light weapons change the face of guerrilla warfare itself, upgrading its potential to do damage.

Today, guerrilla warfare and unconventional warfare opportunities and missions abound—in the communist countries, in Western Europe, counterinsurgency in the third world, and intelligence and counterinsurgency training missions in friendly non-third world nations. It requires only coherent U.S. foreign policy and resolution to capitalize on these situations.

2. PREDECESSORS OF SPECIAL FORCES

Guerrilla resistance movements have not been a part of the American experience. In World War II, with the exception of the Philippines and certain other Pacific islands, no U.S. territory fell under enemy domination. Even the courageous few who remained in the Philippines to wage guerrilla warfare were essentially the foreign advisors or leaders of a basically Filipino resistance movement. But there was another kind of American participation in guerrilla warfare—the colorful and short-lived activities of the Office of Strategic Services (OSS).

The OSS existed from 1942 to 1945, sparked by a remarkable leader, Gen. William J. ("Wild Bill") Donovan. In view of the resistance Special Forces later encountered from conventional military and intelligence agencies, it is interesting to note that General Donovan formed his command against strong opposition from the Army, the Navy, and the FBI. If it had not been for his close personal relationship with President Roosevelt, it is unlikely that the OSS would ever have been born. The direct pipeline to the president provided a route through the red tape and service jealousies, though it scarcely endeared the "fair-haired boy" to his critics. Bill Donovan had to fight continuously for the survival of his agency, only to lose the final battle in 1945 after FDR's death. General MacArthur never permitted the OSS to operate in his theater (some say because an OSS briefer was noted by MacArthur to be wearing argyle socks with his uniform). To many in the regular establishment, the OSS was a bunch of screwballs, or worse. In retrospect, it is easy to see that the type of man who gravitated to the OSS in 1943 had much in common with those who signed up for Special Forces ten years later. Columnist Stewart Alsop, who served with them at that time, recalls the presence in OSS of "missionaries and bartenders, polo players and baseball pitchers, millionaires and union organizers, a human fly and a former Russian general, a big game hunter, and a history professor."* Gen. Ray Peers tells of gathering a customs collector, a West Pointer, a watchmaker, four infantry officers, two engineers, a court stenographer, a Korean patriot, and a former American advisor to a Chinese warlord for his unit in Burma.** The very characteristics that made these men valuable to the OSS were those that made them chafe at the rigidity of the regular services.

OSS, as a new and inexperienced organization, worked closely with and leaned heavily on the expertise of the British Special Operations Executive (SOE), particularly in Europe. Two particularly valuable operations, the "Jedburghs" and the Operational Groups (OGs), were undertaken jointly by SOE and OSS in Europe.

The Jedburgh operation was, by unconventional warfare standards, a large and successful one. It is a classic example of exploiting the radio, parachute, and aircraft to make the most of guerrilla resources. A number of three-man teams were formed, consisting of an American or British officer; a Dutch, French, or Belgian officer; and a radio operator. Some eighty-seven of these teams were parachuted behind German lines to join with the resistance forces, providing a link to the Allies. They called for airdrops of arms and supplies and coordinated the guerrilla attacks with the action of the advancing Allied armies. They also trained guerrillas in the use of weapons and equipment dropping. When necessary, they led them into action. It would be impossible to measure the effectiveness of the Jedburghs, and certainly the bulk of the credit goes to the brave Frenchmen, Dutch, and Belgians who carried out the missions. Certainly the Jeds were in no small part responsible for Eisenhower's statements regarding the great value of the resistance to the Allies.

The OGs were larger teams of about fifteen, parachuted into France to carry out specific operations either alone or in conjunction with Maquis elements. They blew up bridges, blasted

*Alsop, Stewart and Braden, Thomas, *Sub Rosa, The OSS and American Espionage* (New York: Harcourt, 1964), pp. 22-23.

**Peers, Ray and Brelis, Dean, *Behind the Burma Road* (New York: Little Brown, 1963), pp. 25-28.

the rail lines, ambushed convoys, blocked mountain passes, harassed retreating German units, and provided reconnaissance and intelligence. Donovan's report to the Joint Chiefs of Staff claimed 928 Germans killed or wounded by nineteen OG teams, which lost only seven killed and six wounded.

In Northern Burma, the exploits of Ray Peers's* OSS Detachment 101 were equally impressive. Starting from scratch with only 25 men, and growing finally to 131 officers and 553 enlisted men, Peers organized and led an irregular force of Kachin tribesmen that ultimately numbered nearly 11,000. They operated deep in the jungle as individual agents, in small groups, or in battalion strength. They kept the Japanese under surveillance, raided, ambushed, attacked, and harassed without cease. The high command in the theater credited almost 90 percent of its intelligence to Detachment 101, and 85 percent of the Tenth Air Force's targets were designated by them. Detachment 101 counted 5,428 Japanese known killed, and a fair estimate of the real total is closer to 10,000. Once Gen. Joseph ("Vinegar Joe") Stilwell, the commander of the CBI Theater, asked Peers and the leader of a successful "Kachin Ranger" guerrilla unit how they could be so sure of the large and exact number of Japanese killed in a particular engagement. The Kachin opened a bamboo tube, dumping a pile of dried ears on the table. "Divide by two," he told Stilwell. Peers soberly recounts that it took six months to bring that practice to a halt. It is doubtful that it ever ceased completely, but it would seem that the Kachin "kill" figures were based on sound mathematics. Detachment 101's own casualties were remarkably light: only 22 Americans and 184 Kachins killed. ** More important than casualties, however, was the intelligence, the continuous pressure on the enemy, and the creation of a psychological rallying point for the Burmese.

*Peers joined 101 at its beginning in 1942 as a captain and finished the war in 1945 as commander, wearing colonel's eagles. His career is a case history of how a good man can succeed in spite of the system. He retired wearing three stars, though he wears neither a West Point ring, parachutist wings, nor Korean medals. He spent World War II with guerrillas and some later years with the CIA. It was to this immensely competent man that fell the unsavory task of investigating the Army's handling of the "My Lai Massacre" and of recommending courts-martial for a major general and several other high-ranking officers.

**Peers & Brelis, *Behind the Burma Road*, pp. 153-54, 200.

For all their daring and imagination, the exploits of the OSS pale when compared to the tonnages and body counts of the "big war." For this and other reasons, in 1945 General Donovan finally lost his fight for survival, but most were not of the breed to find peacetime military service attractive and returned to civilian life, some to reappear later in the CIA. Thus it was, that with the OSS gone and the value of its efforts overshadowed by the big battles or hidden under classification, the U.S. Armed Forces found themselves no better off in the business of guerrilla warfare at the end of World War II than they had been at the start.

World War II introduced the era of the "big bang," the nuclear age. The United States had a nuclear monopoly right after the war which would keep the world safe for a time, or at least scared into peace. Army strength was miniscule compared to the eleven-million-man Army of World War II. The occupation Army in Germany and Austria composed of constabulary regiments had the combat power of a police force. Even when the once-elite 1st Infantry Division was reconstituted in 1949, it was a pitiful imitation of a wartime combat division. There were simply no spaces for elite units, such as the once-proud Ranger battalions.

At any rate, the Army was going through one of its cyclic phases of anti-elitism almost invariably associated with peacetime. The theory is well known and simple: *An army cannot afford to skim off its best people and put them into one or two elite units. These same people if disseminated throughout the service, will raise the quality of* all *of the army.* Even the briefest survey of the composition of the Ranger battalions of World War II shows that it did not work that way. Most of the enlisted members of the Rangers were mavericks who couldn't make it in the conventional units. They enlisted in the Rangers to find something different from conventional soldiering, and indeed they found it.

In wartime, necessity provides the road to new ideas, and special, elite units tend to flourish. The small Ranger companies that were created after the start of the Korean War were truly elite units, composed of volunteers recruited from the airborne units, carefully selected for their professionalism and fine military records. The U.S. Army had never seen elite units of such quality, where a light company was the combat-power equivalent of a conventional infantry battalion. Unfortunately, their power was squandered when they were committed to perform as conventional infantry. Lack of replacements doomed those fine units well before the end of the Korean War.

The late 1940s were bleak days for all of the U.S. Armed Forces, with the exceptions of the strategic bomber and early missilemen. Fortunately, a few of the nonconformists refused simply to fade away. Col. Russell Volkmann, the wartime leader of the Filipino guerrillas on Luzon, was at work on two field manuals on guerrilla war at Fort Benning, though it was doubtful that there would be a readership for them. A small band of unconventional thinkers was trying with little success to be heard in the Pentagon. Then two unpleasant international developments brought their ideas to the fore: greatly increased Soviet pressure on the allies in the newly formed NATO in Europe, and the outbreak of the Korean War in June 1950.

In Europe, military planners were highly alarmed over the dangerous imbalance. The Soviets broke the nuclear monopoly, NATO was scarcely a military reality, and the Berlin blockade highlighted the difference in firepower between the U.S. 1st Infantry Division and three light armored cavalry regiments and some 100 Russian divisions across the iron curtain. Top-level intelligence was convinced that Stalin would attack no later than 1954. In some desperation, the Army at long last turned to guerrilla warfare concepts as a possible "equalizer." The captive peoples of eastern Europe were the target of American hopes to neutralize at least some of Stalin's divisions.

While this was happening, the Korean "police action" began. The atomic bomb appeared neither politically feasible nor militarily useful, and the war was fought conventionally in many ways like World War II, even approaching the stalemated trench warfare of World War I. With thousands of North Korean guerrillas harassing the Eighth Army's rear, behind-the-lines activity on the part of the United States became a tempting course of action in an effort to retaliate in kind. But the OSS was gone, the CIA did not have a similar capability, and Special Forces was not yet born. It was necessary to paste together in some haste an organization to do the job of unconventional warfare.

Russell Volkmann was uprooted from his manual writing at Fort Benning and ordered to report to MacArthur's Tokyo headquarters. There he was told that he was to be responsible for the conduct of behind-the-lines operations in North Korea. When he asked for plans, training programs, manpower, logistical support, and other reasonable capabilities, he was told that there were none. It is not surprising that starting from scratch, Volkmann was never able to get beyond the planning stage before he was evacuated for illness in December 1951. His successors, however, scratched up a whole kit of units, designations, and acronyms: FEC Liaison Detachment, CCRAK, CCRAFE, the 8,240th Army Unit, the 8,157th Special Operations Detachment, UNPIK (United Nations Partisan Infantry Korea), and many others. Records of their activities are sparse and many are still undoubtedly classified, but veterans of the operations are nearly unanimous in their assessment that there was little success. Their accounts are filled with terms like "lack of professionalism," "amateurish," "commander relieved," "ineffectual," "poor planning," and "lack of coordination." Good, brave men fought and died in those largely amphibious operations, but through no fault of their own they largely failed, due to lack of professional expertise. Only Gen. Mark Clark, in his book *From the Danube to the Yalu*,* writes of pinning down Chinese and North Korean troops with partisans and a well-organized guerrilla system. It is nearly impossible to find anyone else at the action level who would support that rosy view.

UNPIK mustered some six regiments which conducted waterborne raids from motorized junks on the enemy coast. Those were small in-and-out actions, not the efforts of a true partisan force living and functioning in enemy territory. The troops were not comfortable behind enemy lines, as most of them had been recruited in South Korea from North Korean POWs and South Korean draft dodgers. That was not a true guerrilla operation.

Those so-called partisan operations were supplemented by behind-the-lines agent activities and escape and evasion assistance for downed airmen. Those efforts were not very successful. It eventually became apparent to all but the rigidly conservative military that in order to carry out special operations successfully, we have to prepare *before* the advent of a

*Clark, Mark W., *From the Danube to the Yalu* (Westport, Ct.: Greenwood, 1973).

war. This preparation should include selecting and training men in special units with unique equipment, doctrine, and support.

The genesis for such a concept existed in the Pentagon. Concealed within Gen. Robert McClure's Psychological Operations Staff Section was a new Special Warfare Division, in which McClure gathered a small group of men who had seen, during World War II, the value of guerrillas and guerrilla activities. Wendell Fertig, the American guerrilla leader on Mindanao in the Philippines, was in command. Volkmann headed plans. Aaron Bank, who had jumped three times into France and once into Indochina with the OSS, was operations chief. There were also Joe Waters of Merrill's Marauders and OSS; Robert McDowell, who had been with the OSS in Yugoslavia; and other veterans of extremely unconventional warfare. Gradually, their mission was defined: to develop a concept and guerrilla warfare plans for the expected World War III, which in the immediate postwar years seemed all but inevitable. Thus was born, among other plans, one dubbed "Rudolph, the Red-Nosed Reindeer," a concept for guerrilla interdiction of Russian reinforcements moving to the front in central Europe. Others varied in mission and detail, but none was more incongruously named.

Within the Army itself there was, of course, the usual opposition to special warfare, particularly in G-2 (intelligence) and G-3 (plans and operations). Fortunately, the Army Chief of Staff, Gen. J. Lawton Collins, was receptive, and General McClure had a special pipeline to the White House through C.D. Jackson, a wartime associate who specialized in psychological warfare and now was a special advisor to President Eisenhower. After many bitter Pentagon battles, Fertig, Volkmann, and their team were finally able to sell their concept. In early 1952, thanks to a little help from a West Point classmate of Volkmann, the Army reluctantly allotted 2,500 personnel spaces to the program.

Selling the Army, however, was only part of the problem. There was more serious opposition to be met from the newly formed CIA and the Air Force, which had only recently broken away as a service separate from the Army. Some old OSS types, who wound up in the CIA, were also pushing for a *civilian* action agency for the conduct of guerrilla warfare. They were being given quiet support by the State Department which still smarted over its years in the backseat during the war and the reigns thereafter of the military proconsuls overseas.

In the Air Force, the extreme air-power advocates visualized the Army reduced to the role of a Marine Corps, while massive air power provided the big punch as guerrillas finished the enemy off in the ensuing rubble and confusion. The CIA and Air Force had quietly agreed to move in on the unconventional warfare piece of the pie. The Air Force would have five ARC (Aerial Resupply and Communications) Wings to drop agents and supplies and to provide the communications, both ground and air. Those Wings would be capable of conducting psychological warfare as well. The CIA would run the guerrilla war on the ground.

All these Air Force preparations and plans had been accomplished without the knowledge of the other services or the Joint Chiefs of Staff. When the Army submitted its own contingency plans for the conduct of unconventional warfare in Europe with Army Special Forces, the Air Force and CIA hands were forced. An interservice and interdepartmental donnybrook ensued.

The Army emerged with Special Forces and the guerrilla mission, and the ARC Wings were drastically clipped. Some deep scars remained, and many within the CIA were opposed to Special Forces for a long time. Army versus Air Force squabbles were still in their infancy and would not be limited to the narrow field of operations behind the lines.

But the Army Special Forces was alive. It was born out of a fear of the universally expected World War III and Soviet strength in Europe, bitter experience in Korea, interservice rivalry, and the beliefs and determination of a handful of proponents. Next would come the growing pains.

3. THE KIND OF MAN IT TOOK

In the early spring of 1952, the United States was a nation neither at peace nor at war. The strange police action in Korea had settled down to dull trench warfare, and the truce talks at Panmunjon had been dragging on for more than a year. Americans were finding it hard to understand that the possession of great power does not necessarily mean it can be brought to bear. The huge defense budgets of the early 1950s were rapidly rearming the hitherto neglected armed forces.

Russia was still the big worry, for it was the Soviets who were bankrolling the Korean War without risk to a single Russian. It was also obvious that they would soon have an H-bomb of their own. Monolithic communism was still a fact, and Senator Joe McCarthy played on the nation's fears.

President Truman had announced that he would not stand for reelection, and who the Democratic candidate was to be was still uncertain. General Eisenhower had announced as a Republican who would "accept a call," but the bitter primaries and the campaign itself were still far off.

Down at the Army's huge airborne infantry training center at Fort Bragg, North Carolina, the emphasis was still on big war and tactical nukes. The 82nd Airborne Division was making training jumps out of the huge, two-level C-124 aircraft, and paratroopers kidded about a new jump command: "Everybody downstairs, outside! Everybody upstairs, downstairs!" The Airborne was still looking back to the mass parachute jumps of World War II, or forward to the big battles of the potential World War III. Korea had been, and still was, a frustrating affair where the airborne role was minor.

In an obscure corner of the sprawling post at Fort Bragg, a Psychological Warfare Center had been established, very much outside the mainstream of airborne infantry life. It was there that Col. Aaron Bank was assigned in April 1952 from his Pentagon desk in General McClure's special operations office.

Aaron Bank, First Group Commander of an SF Group, 10th SFG, 1952

The Army had decided to hide the new Special Forces embryo in the Psy War Center, but had done so over Colonel Volkmann's objections. He felt, and others agreed, that "there was a stigma connected with Psychological Warfare that we didn't care to rub off on Special Forces. Behind-the-lines operations and the 'dirty tricks' game had enough opposition amongst conventional military minds without adding additional problems."

Bank set to work from scratch, gathered the nucleus of his cadre, and drew up his plans. On 20 June 1952, the 10th Special Forces Group (Airborne) was formed at a strength of ten. More OSS and Ranger veterans were gathered, along with a sprinkling of paratroopers looking for something new. All, of course, were volunteers, all were parachute-qualified, and all were in the Army by choice.

Leaning on OSS experience in World War II and historical accounts of other resistance activities, they wrote and ran their own programs in consonance with the newly developed doctrine for unconventional warfare. There was by no means wide acceptance, or even awareness, of this activity. Most of the Army was concerned with how the big battalions of the combat arms were going to fight in the "nuclear environment." Such was the right road for serious-minded officers with ambitions of attaining the rank of general. The fact that a few maverick paratroopers were playing around with something spooky at Fort Bragg was not to be taken too seriously. What's more, they were tied in with Psychological Warfare, and everyone knew the psy war longhairs were not to be trusted. However, there is an "old boy network" among professional airborne noncommissioned officers, and the grapevine soon resulted in other highly qualified soldiers volunteering to join a small elite unit of their peers.

Very few regular officers went to Special Forces before the days of its great popularity in the 1960s. There are various reasons for that. Career management advisors in Washington steered ambitious youngsters away, and still do today. The entire concept and existence of Special Forces was so secret that few officers knew either of them or what they did. Most recruiting was word of mouth among friends. The noncoms would talk to those officers whom they thought would be good at the business; the handful of officers opted in by Bank also explained the situation to their friends and acquaintances. So Special Forces in the early days got a few castoffs and less than a normal percentage of quality career officers. It also got some freethinkers who had never adapted to the spit and polish of the peacetime, palace-guard, 82nd Airborne Division. It got the innovators and imaginative people who wanted to try something new and challenging, who chafed at rigid discipline, and who didn't care what the career managers at the Pentagon said or believed. Many were reserve officers who had no notion of wearing stars and hence never designed their careers around the idea of getting certain vital "tickets punched." An amazing number of those early Special Forces officers went on to a full thirty-year career, serving in the final years as full colonels, not a few of them commanding one Special Forces Group or another. They were an incredibly tough and competent little group of officers who knew how to fight and did so at the appropriate times. One of the early officers, "Blind Mike" Healy, retired in the grade of major general. Another, Dave Grange, was recently still serving as the three-star commanding general of Sixth Army. A sprinkling of regular officers began to request assignments, but sometimes found they were not welcomed by the freewheeling reserves. Some left with a bad taste in their mouths, while a few found their niches and stayed.

Although outstanding officers are necessary for Special Forces excellence, the Army discourages repetitive SF tours for officers, with some justification. An officer needs a good, solid base of conventional soldiering to be able to put unconventional operations in perspective. He needs it, too, in order to be accepted and respected by the other line and staff officers with whom he has to deal. Many of the reserve officers who chose to stay continuously with Special Forces hurt their careers. Many left the service after twenty years, and some merely crossed over to comparable jobs with the CIA or AID.*

For noncommissioned officers, the situation is different, and has been from the start. They can stay in Special Forces as long as they can find a slot that fits their rank and military occupational specialty (MOS), and many have done just that. It is a tribute to the excellence of the SF noncoms that such a high percentage of them have been promoted to the top enlisted rank in the Army, sergeant major. The Sergeant Majors' Academy at any one time has enough qualified students to fill the ranks of several SF Detachments. During the Vietnam War, a number of them were given battlefield commissions in the grade of captain and subsequently served outstandingly. Capt. Bob Maples, commissioned after a dozen years as a SF noncom, turned in a virtuoso performance when he cleaned up Phu Quoc Island of its entire population of some 385 VCs.

But it is the noncommissioned officer who stays at detach-

---

*This easy interchange back and forth between Special Forces and those two civilian agencies is somewhat indicative of the nature of their operation and the type of men involved. AID has a charter for advice and assistance to foreign police forces, and CIA to paramilitary forces, particularly if the activity must be undercover. These jobs require dedicated and competent professionals, willing to work in remote, difficult areas using imaginative, expedient methods to compensate for the lack of a formal structure or a sophisticated support system.

ment level who is so important to SF. There are some minor drawbacks to the establishment and maintenance of such an ingrown corps of NCOs, but the advantages far outweigh them. In the early days, the organization was so small that a high percentage of men knew one another. Those who could produce, those who could hack it, were known. So were the phonies and those who had avoided the tough duty at the operational detachment level and had "never toted the rucksack." The hardcore built and developed slowly, growing from approximately 600 in 1960 to perhaps 1,000 today. Serving both overseas and stateside, these men not only became real experts in at least one specialty, but, as the years passed, became more and more familiar with the skills of the other team members and with the application of the entire art.

Although SF noncoms come in a wide variety of sizes, colors, and personalities, they must have certain attributes in common if they are to be successful. In the words of one SF group commander:

Let's say adaptability. In other words, he's capable of adjusting to new and changing situations and stresses, and he bears up well under pressure. He has ambition, seeks and welcomes additional, more important responsibility. He is cooperative—works in harmony with others as a team. And dependable—consistently accomplishes the desired action with a minimum of supervision. The very nature of our business is that we're completely on our own with indigenous forces. We have no one to turn to. We do it ourselves. And we must be able to count on a man working with a minimum of supervision. He has got to have enthusiasm; he's got to motivate others with his zeal. He must have force, execute his actions vigorously. Ingenuity—the very basis of SF operations is the ability to make something out of nothing. He's got to have initiative—the ability to take necessary and appropriate action on his own. Intelligence goes without saying. Judgment—he thinks logically and makes practical decisions right down the line. Loyalty, moral courage. Self-discipline. Self-improvement. In other words, he is willing to take action to improve himself constantly. Stamina—he performs successfully under constant physical and mental stress. Tact—he says and does what is appropriate without giving unnecessary offense, understanding and appreciating another's viewpoint.

All successful SF soldiers are team players, having no use for heroes who might get them killed or injured. Their primary allegiance is to their detachment, a small group of six to twelve men with whom they train daily and upon whom their lives depend in combat. Their peers bestow approval, give support, and can impose severe sanctions on a member who fails to perform.

Because of the qualities necessary for SF soldiers, they also have a high degree of self-confidence, sometimes verging on arrogance. They like each other, and they are constantly in one another's company, even after-duty hours, not going out of their way to be with non-SF. As a result, they have acquired a reputation as snobs who ridicule less gifted men while having too high a regard for themselves. Many a barroom brawl has erupted when SF and non-SF are mixed in the presence of alcohol, and some term of approbation (such as "leg," i.e., nonairborne-qualified soldier) is overheard.

The first NCOs to join the Forces came largely from the airborne units, for being jump-qualified was—and still is—a prerequisite for SF. Paratroopers know better than anyone else how easy it is to jump, but they also know that the elements of fear and danger are always present. They have the common heritage of having suffered through the man-made hell of jump school, and they enjoy the fraternity that exists among men who have been tested and survived. Furthermore, all airborne troopers are volunteers, and the NCOs who had served in airborne units knew how important this was. They had gone airborne because the airborne was an elite, only to find that the airborne divisions were too big to develop the special esprit and professionalism they sought. Special Forces opened the possibility of a true elite organization, because it was, at least initially, very small. Men had to be triple volunteers: they had to volunteer for the Army (no draftees), they had to volunteer for airborne, and they had to volunteer for duty with Special Forces.

There were a few exceptions. One was Sgt. Paul Ettman, who, in spite of his many years in Special Forces, had never volunteered for anything but the Army. Ettman and his family, like many Polish refugees, wound up in France after World War II. The new government in Poland enticed many to return home, and young Ettman went back to have a look while his parents remained in France. Finding the Communist regime not to his liking, in 1950 he escaped from Poland and began to work his way west. In Prague, however, he was captured and imprisoned for eight months before he escaped from a work detail and continued his flight. He finally reached West Germany in 1951, and wound up in a Displaced Persons Camp where the prisonlike environment led him to take a job in a U.S.–hired Labor Service Battalion. There he found a chance to enlist in the U.S. Army and was sent to Fort Dix for basic training. Things happened quickly after that. Soon after basic, he found himself on orders to Fort Benning for parachute training, for which he had definitely *not* volunteered. "Hell," he says, "with all the troubles I'd had, I didn't volunteer for nothing." Further, he did not like it. "All the time push-ups." He adds thoughtfully, "But I was too scared to quit." After having made two jumps during the last week of jump school, someone discovered the error and told him he would either have to volunteer or quit. Having gone that far, he signed on. He won his wings and, to his puzzlement, found himself assigned to Special Forces. No one told him he had to be a volunteer, so without volunteering, he went. Apparently he liked it, for he stayed on for many years.

Ettman was one of a large group of men who found a place in Special Forces that suited their temperaments and special abilities. All were foreign-born. Most had entered the U.S. Army under the so-called Lodge Bill, legislation which provided a route to American citizenship through military service. In the early days of the Forces, a heavy concentration of such men gave the outfit a Foreign Legion flavor. The team rooms were heavy with foreign accents, and the rosters looked like those of Notre Dame football teams. Those men found full acceptance in the Forces. A Czech, who might have felt a bit set apart in a platoon of all-American men, became a key figure in a SF Team destined to drop behind the lines, organize resistance, and conduct guerrilla warfare in Czechoslovakia. He already had the language and area knowledge the other members of the detachment were struggling to learn. The team knew how important he would be if they had to go for real.

Stefan Mazak was one of those—a tough, little fireplug of a man, no more than five-feet-two inches tall, but all muscle, stamina, and courage. Born and raised in Czechoslovakia, a veteran of the Maquis and the French Foreign Legion, he spoke native Czech, Parisian street-gang French, passable German, and execrable English. He was an expert demolitionist and weapons man, was unshakably cool under stress, had indomitable good spirits in adversity. Although he was weak in the areas that required much English reading or writing, his team loved him, and knew that if Detachment B-1 ever parachuted into a forest east of Prague, Stefan would be the biggest man they had. His courage and perseverance were outstanding, but weren't tested in the U.S. Army until 1960, when he and two others performed incredible feats on a classified mission in the Congo (see Chapter 8). In Vietnam, he proved himself again and again, only to be killed on one of the more hairy classified operations during his second tour in Southeast Asia. Mazak, and many others, volunteered repeatedly for that lonely and dangerous game called "recon," where small teams of two or three Special Forces noncoms, with half-a-dozen natives, prowled the denied areas heavily infested by the enemy. Some of the most courageous, totally unpublicized feats of the Vietnam War occurred on those deep penetration operations where men fought and died alone under the triple-canopy jungle of that forlorn peninsula.

There were many others: Edald Duttlinger, a certified ski instructor and mountain guide from Austria; Julius "Bear" Reinitzer, a big Czech who had escaped from a Communist prison camp; Sully Fontaine, a Belgian who made his first parachute jump behind enemy lines at age sixteen with the British Special Air Service (SAS); Herb Brucker (New York–born and *not* Lodge Bill), who left France in 1938, but went back again by parachute for the OSS in 1944; Henryk "Frenchy" Szarek, a Pole who had served under four flags; Jan Novy, a Czech forest ranger who organized escapes for political refugees from Czechoslovakia and then had to flee on skis; Aito Keravouri, a battalion commander of infantry in the Finnish Army who retired a colonel in the U.S. Army; Danny Brosnan of the Irish (Eire) Army; an Israeli; several ex-British paratroopers; a Dutchman or two; and many more.

There was also a large contingent in the Forces representing

Asia, particularly the Hawaiians. The rosters are replete with names like Haleamau, Wong, Kim, Ahuna, Kalani, Kawakami, Kamalu, and Hayakawa. Dick Kim was one of the greatest Special Forces officers to date. His father, of Korean origin, was a Shanghai-based doctor when the Japanese invaded China. Dick and his brother walked out of Shanghai and were picked up by an escape and evasion net run by Americans. He was sent to Chungking, where he was virtually adopted by American airmen. They sent him to Dickinson College, from whence he was commissioned in the infantry. He is fluent in Cantonese, Mandarin Chinese, Japanese, French, German, Tagalog, and English. After many years of SF, he retired to become an Episcopalian priest.

A certain aura of secrecy surrounded the early days of Special Forces, based both on its mission and the identity of the troopers. Little or no publicity was permitted, and they liked it that way. Many of the "Lodge Bill" men still had families behind the iron curtain and wanted neither their pictures nor their names widely published. Many changed their names, some for pronounceability, but most for protection. The 10th Special Forces Group's album for the period 1953 to 1956 is filled with pages in which one or two faces have been blacked out, the caption reading "unknown." The close-mouthed security among those who had lived under Communist rule rubbed off on the American-born team members and remains to this day among the old-time SF NCOs. They do not talk to one another about anything that is remotely classified, nor do they tell their wives. Most of the mobile training teams that were sent were classified, but the wives knew only that their men were going off on a mission somewhere, returning in six months.

In many ways, tight security was all to the good, for later publicity was only to exacerbate the frictions between the Special Forces and the regular Army. Ask any long-time SF noncom what has hurt Special Forces the most, and he will invariably reply, "Expansion and publicity."

The small teams and the high degree of professionalism of their members allowed for an easy informality. The job could be done without the rigid discipline and careful supervision needed to whip large units of young recruits into efficient fighting machines. Individual initiative was prized and stimulated, and independent action by two or three men or a small team was the rule. The line between officers and NCOs was blurred. An easy camaraderie and the mutual respect of professionals replaced the rigid hierarchy of line units. Teams were too small to make the Army's conventional "you ain't paid to think" approach workable. Captains and majors were team leaders, and master sergeants were team sergeants, but when it was time to move out, everyone grabbed a load and started moving.

Cross-training was done within and by the team. A junior demolitionist or communications sergeant would be in charge of training one day, the senior medic another, and the team leader another. Teams would take their rucksacks into the hills to do their training on their own, escaping the interferences of garrison life. The mountains back of Bad Tolz in Bavaria were strewn with secret SF Detachment huts made out of C ration cartons, concealed on hillsides where the detachments would go to hide and train.

Thus the Forces began to take shape, to take on a stamp of their own. The bums and phonies were weeded out, and those who had come for the wrong reasons left because the demands were too great. If anyone wanted to leave he had only to file the ubiquitous Form 1049, a quit slip. A certain breed stayed and attracted more of its own kind.

4. THE RUCKSACK, BOOT, AND BERET

Differences in mission, organization, outlook, and modus operandi began to set Special Forces even further apart from the conventional units. Notable differences in external symbols began to appear.

The Forces carried the Bergen Mountain rucksack rather than the standard Army field pack. The reason was simple: it could accommodate the larger loads required by troops whose supply dump was on their backs and whose transportation was their own two feet. In West Germany's Bavarian Alps, the men soon did away with the spit-shined Corcoran jump boot, the mark of the U.S. Army's airborne units, and started wearing a mountain boot made by little cobblers in Bad Tolz. These ugly, heavy boots consisted of a double upper which rendered them warm in snow and ice and, if oiled with goose grease, were effectively waterproof. With their thick cleated soles and brass eyelets, they were the most practical field boot possible for that climate. They became a trademark of the 10th Special Forces. The first thing the sponsor of a newcomer did was to take his protégé to town to order and be measured for the handmade boots.

The best-known departure from the Army norms was the beret. Ask any Special Forces man about the beret, and he will belittle it, complaining that it is hot in summer, cold in winter, absorbs water like a sponge, and takes three days to dry out. Give him half a chance and put him in a situation where no one else is looking, and he will stuff it in his pocket and go bare-headed, get a field cap with earflaps for the cold, or a brimmed, floppy jungle hat in the heat. But officially deny it or forbid him to wear it, and you have hit him where it hurts.

For some perverse reason that has always escaped even its friendliest critics, the U.S. Army has generally refrained from making use of simple techniques to foster tradition and build unit pride. Instead, the Army has indulged in a seemingly indiscriminate activation, deactivation, and shuffling of units and their designations. Identity has been focused at the division level, which is too large. There has been an absolute abhorrence of distinctive uniforms. Many professional officers and NCOs, with a deep understanding of the value of unit pride, deplore this situation. Many have taken steps on their own to try to correct it, but ultimately most have been brought back into line by the disciples of uniformity.

The saga of the green beret began when the early members of Special Forces were anxious to have something distinctive to set themselves apart from their conventional brothers-in-arms. It was scarcely original, as the beret has long been the headgear of various special foreign military organizations, including French and British airborne units, British Commandos, the French Foreign Legion Paratroopers, and many of the foreign armies that evolved from the colonial forces of these two countries.

Stories of how the beret started in Special Forces are legion, and there are many conflicting, undocumented claims. Retired Maj. Herb Brucker says that in 1952 he doodled a drawing of a soldier wearing a beret. Col. (then Lt.) Roger Pezzelle saw it, liked it, and submitted a request through official channels for the issue of berets for a "field test."

In the meantime, probably the first berets worn in Special Forces were worn by Capt. Roger Pezzelle's Operational Detachment FA32 in very late 1952. They were black and were purchased in Fayetteville, North Carolina. Roger bought one for each member of the team, with an extra one for Colonel Bank in the event that he caught them wearing the unauthorized hats. The berets were only worn in the field, where a hat was desired to replace the flat-topped, billed cap worn throughout the 82nd Airborne Division. A team's field headgear often became its trademark; certain teams wore wool field (Ernie Pyle) caps, while others wore watch hats (black Navy wool caps), and still others wore marine field caps. Roger chose the beret because it was unique and linked to the OSS and British SOE, direct predecessors of Special Forces. The black color was selected because it was the only masculine one in town. Although Colonel Bank did discover FA32 wearing the berets in the spring of 1953 while the team was in the final phase of testing from its graduation field-training exercise after thirteen weeks of SF training, his reaction is not recorded. Apparently, it did not seriously affect Pezzelle's career, for he transferred to Germany and purchased green berets from a Munich tailor. He also designed the Trojan Horse silver hat badge to be worn on the beret. That was the unofficial badge until 1962, when an official hat badge and colored cloth "flash" for each group was authorized.

After nearly a year of being passed around supply offices all over the United States, Roger's request for field-test berets was honored, and a few boxes of berets arrived at Special Forces headquarters at Fort Bragg. By this time, Brucker and Pezzelle had shipped out to Europe, so no one knew the source of the new headgear. Since the berets arrived through official supply channels, it was assumed they were authorized. As the berets looked good, men started wearing them, more or less openly. Since there were not enough berets to outfit the entire 77th SF Group, oldtimers tell of buying berets locally around Fort Bragg which looked like a Girl Scout beanie. It was fondly known as the "headshrinker," due to its propensities in the rain. In Germany, where the beret is not indigenous, the berets that were designed locally and made up by German tailors for the 10th Special Forces came out looking like pancakes.

Finally, by early 1953 someone, recalling that the Canadians wore berets, unofficially established contact with the Dorothea Knitting Mills in Canada. Teams chipped in their own money and sent away for Dorothea's "Rifle Green" model, the true forerunner of the beret worn today.

The first large-scale public wearing of the green beret probably occurred at the retirement parade of Lt. Gen. Joe Cleland, commander of the XVIII Airborne Corps, the senior headquarters at Fort Bragg. A unit of Special Forces marched in the parade wearing berets, causing many spectators in the stands to comment on how nice it was that someone had gone to the trouble of bringing in foreign troops for "The Great White Father's" retirement.

It was not long before the 77th Special Forces Group at Fort Bragg had published its own orders authorizing the wearing of the beret. In Germany, men of the 10th continued wearing it on the sly. The Army, of course, had not approved officially and looked askance at that strange breach of uniform regulations.

Special Forces men who lived through that era vary in their

Brig. Gen. William Yarborough introducing John F. Kennedy to beret in 1962, Ft. Bragg, NC (U.S. Army photo)

versions of what happened next, or why. Most veterans, however, believe it was Gen. Paul D. Adams, then commanding Fort Bragg, who put the beret in temporary eclipse. They say, further, that he did so in revenge for having his tactical field headquarters penetrated and his operations disrupted by SF raiders during a major field exercise in 1956. In one of the first exposures of the stateside U.S. Army to irregular warfare, Special Forces were enormously disruptive. Convoys were misrouted, false orders were issued on the radio, fuel and chow trucks were commandeered, and, in general, hell was raised. The degree of chaos and confusion reached such a point that everything had to be stopped. Special Forces were summarily ordered out of the maneuver.

In 1956 Adams prohibited the wearing of the beret at Fort Bragg. Most Special Forces troopers had a beret in their locker, but it was a courtmartial offense to be caught wearing one at Bragg. In the field, the berets sometimes reappeared on a clandestine basis. In Germany, outside of Adams's jurisdiction, they were worn most of the time. Of course, everyone had regulation headgear handy, and when certain generals came into the area, the berets disappeared. This ludicrous situation continued for another four or five years.

By 1960, General Adams was gone from Fort Bragg, but his edict banning the beret remained in effect. The early Special Forces advisors in Vietnam were wearing berets, but in those days Vietnam was as remote as the other side of the moon. Col. Don Blackburn, who led "Blackburn's Headhunters" on Luzon during World War II, managed to get special local permission for a one-time wearing of the beret at a Special Forces change-of-command parade. Even that was such a controversial move that a visiting four-star general declined an invitation to attend out of fear of the repercussions—he sent his wife in his place.

Finally, in 1961, at the dawn of the era of counterinsurgency, the commander of the then Special Warfare Center at Fort Bragg, Col. William P. Yarborough, took a calculated risk and wore the beret for the presidential visit. It worked. Everything about the elite troops impressed John F. Kennedy, including the berets. He returned to Washington and sent a message describing the green beret as the symbol of excellence, the mark of distinction, the badge of courage. Shortly thereafter, Army Regulations prescribed the color, shape, angle of droop, authorization to wear, and the insignia.

5. SF PREPARES FOR GUERRILLA WARFARE

As we have seen, the limited war in Korea demonstrated the need for, and led to the creation of, the Special Forces. (The original units were formed for and targeted at a distinctly different theater: to fight World War III in Europe.)

The first of the original units was Col. Aaron Bank's 10th Special Forces Group, assembled and activated at Fort Bragg in the summer of 1952. Its highly secret mission was to exploit the resistance potential behind the iron curtain in the event of the expected Russian invasion of western Europe. Should war break out, it was visualized that clandestine contact would be established with resistance groups. Upon their agreement, small teams of Special Forces would be infiltrated (usually by parachute, though conceivably by water, or even by ground infiltration) to join them, help them organize and train, call for equipment by radio, and try to guide and influence their activities so as to enhance the overall war effort.

Military planners are often accused of preparing to fight the last war better. The classic example of such thinking was the Maginot Line, that super World War I fortified position which had so little to do with World War II. The guiding concepts of the original Special Forces charter, which leaned heavily on World War II experience, fell into the same error. Perhaps that was inevitable, since World War II was the U.S. Army's only experience in fostering resistance activity on someone else's soil. The old saw, "I hope you will forgive my reference to personal experience, but that is the only kind I have had," was applicable. Once the threat of a conventional war in Europe was accepted and the known existence of resistance potential behind the enemy's lines was added to the formula, the idea had considerable validity. Furthermore, at the working level, the idea was not to challenge the logic of a strategic concept, but to get on with the business of creating a viable capability to carry out the mission—a classic and perhaps inescapable attitude with strengths and dangers of its own.

The basic Special Forces in Europe in the early 1950s remains little changed to this day. It was the A Team, or to be technically correct, the Special Forces Operational Detachment A. The A Team, as it will probably always be called within SF, consisted of eight men (one officer and seven NCOs) when 10th SFG was deployed to Germany; now it contains twelve men (two and ten). The original FA Teams were authorized fifteen members, including two officers, with a reduced strength of thirteen. Reductions in strength later brought the number down to as low as six members (one officer and five NCOs).

The early A Teams were called FA Teams, each assigned a number. There was a hierarchy of operational detachments. At the top was an FD Team at group headquarters, designed for deployment in denied areas (areas under enemy control) to control the operations of two or more countries' unconventional warfare activities. There was an FC Team, also in the group headquarters, designed to control teams in a single country. Later the FC Team was the special Forces company headquarters, and there were as many as three, depending on the authorized strength of the SF group. Under the FC Team were two to three FB Teams, designed to control an area command within a denied country such as Slovakia in Czechoslovakia). Under the FB Team were two or more FA Teams, each designed to advise and support a guerrilla regiment of up to 1,500 men. A significant feature was that all these teams were "operational detachments" intended for work in the denied areas. Each level above the FA Team had an administrative detachment that was to remain in friendly territory at a Special Forces Operation Base (SFOB) to administer the requirements of the field detachments. During training and maneuvers, it carried out all administrative functions for the teams in the field.

Each man was highly trained in irregular warfare and in his own military specialty, and cross-trained to a lesser degree in the skills of his teammates. For example, each member of the team was given the goal of being able to orient and erect the radio antenna, assemble the radio set, encode a message on the one-time pad, and send that message in Morse Code at a speed of no less than eight words per minute. Similarly, he had to be capable of receiving an incoming message at a speed of eight words per minute and decoding it, correctly employing the one-time pad. This was a logical requirement, antici-

SF Training. Senior medic practices bandaging wounded, Ft. Bragg, NC

pating the loss of both communications specialists in a situation where the team's very life depended on radio communications. Part of medical cross-training included giving shots and drawing blood from one another, procedures which put quite a strain on team solidarity.

Each team had specialists in operations and intelligence, light and heavy weapons, demolitions, communications, and field medical care. Team members were taught to get along with little or no conventional supply and support, to make use of captured enemy equipment, and to fabricate needed gear from locally available material.

Demolitionist practice, Ft. Bragg, NC

The weapons men studied foreign as well as American weapons. They learned to make zip guns out of pipe and rubber bands, to fire bazooka rockets without a bazooka, and to make simple repairs in the field. The demolitionists acquired special techniques of conserving explosives and concocting homemade explosives and detonators from locally procured materials. They learned to make booby traps and sabotage motors—a refinement of the old sugar-in-the-gas-tank trick. They visited hydroelectric plants, factories, transformer stations, and rail yards to learn to recognize critical points for quick knockout blows. They learned to derail a train and to rig a desk drawer to blow up when opened.

Team communicators had to be able to receive and transmit at least twenty words per minute in Morse Code. They had to understand radio theory and antenna formulae well enough to allow them to coax a 1,500-mile range out of a radio small enough to backpack yet low-powered enough to escape ready detection. They learned ciphers, the use of the one-time pad, and many forms of clandestine communications such as the dead-letter drop or cut-out. They also learned to sabotage radio communications. One night in 1956, a U.S. Army Corps Headquarters in the field went off the air, throwing a big maneuver into chaos because two SF radio specialists acting as Opposing Forces short-circuited the entire corps radio system. These techniques were learned, not simply because they were easy or fun, but because the assumption was that Special Forces would be operating behind enemy lines for long periods of time.

The medical specialists were perhaps the most unique and best-trained team members. As part of their formal school training, they spent six months of intensive study at Brooke Army Hospital in Texas, where they were taught highly advanced first aid, wound debridement, and diagnostic analysis. On maneuvers, injured or sick Special Forces soldiers stayed in the field under the care of the team medic rather than being evacuated to a hospital, except in the most drastic conditions. The medics carried sophisticated drugs and equipment, knew how to use them, and earned the confidence of their teammates. Years later in Vietnam, these medics saved many American lives at remote outposts that had no other medical facilities. They also delivered hundreds of Vietnamese babies and extracted thousands of diseased teeth. In peacetime, they practiced in Army hospitals, rotating through the various wards, on parachute drop zones, on the ski slopes, and in maneuver areas and ranges.

The training for officers, team sergeants, and intelligence sergeants focused on tactics, techniques, operations, planning, and intelligence, starting with the conventional and progressing to the irregular and dirty tricks. It covered raids and ambushes, guerrilla organization; the selection, marking, organization, and sterilization of airdrop and landing zones; underground operations, kidnap and assassination operations, escape and evasion, intelligence nets, agent selection and handling, fingerprint identification, counterintelligence, and security—the list stretched on and on.

Everyone, of course, had to learn how to teach his skill to others, for that was to be his ultimate role—instructor. While stationed at Fort Bragg, teams were assigned to study specific geographic areas of operations in Europe, that study including the language and customs of the area. They studied the national contingency war plans and memorized the top secret locations of potential guerrilla base areas, escape and evasion contact points, and other necessary information for wartime employment. Troops with loaded rucksacks were prepared to make tactical jumps at night into tiny drop zones tucked away in mountainous areas. A high level of physical conditioning was a must, because "humping the hills" with a seventy-pound rucksack was fundamental to any SF operation, and there was simply no provision for stragglers. Nor were there any replacements should a key man be lost, and on an eight-man team, *every* man was a key man. The SF soldiers developed deep pride in their ability to get along with next-to-nothing under tough conditions.

In addition, remaining in Special Forces for any extended period meant receiving training in specialized infiltration means. Free-fall parachuting with military gear, also known as high altitude, low opening (HALO), was developed by Special Forces and honed to a fine art. They were also equipped and trained in rough terrain parachuting, where each man was equipped like a smoke jumper for infiltration into rugged terrain without guidance on the ground or a reception committee. Where appropriate, scuba diving, underwater demolitions, and infiltration from a submerged submarine were taught. Skiing and rock/mountain climbing were especially demanding specialties taught in the 10th Special Forces Group every year. The sensation of hanging on the face of a cliff east of Berchtesgaden some 2,000 feet above the valley floor is one that is guaranteed to induce terror in the stoutest heart. Humping through the mountains on skis with a seventy-pound rucksack is an exercise in endurance totally unrelated to swooping down a ski slope in civilian life. It was tough, challenging, and endlessly fascinating.

After thirteen months of training in the United States, the 10th Special Forces Group was ready to go. The Joint Chiefs

Humping the rucksack, "A" Detachment, Ft. Bragg, NC

of Staff had earlier approved the war plans for its employment, and all that remained was for some incident to trigger the move. In June 1953, that came with the workers' revolts in East Berlin. True, this was but a brief flurry of resistance that was rapidly and brutally put down, but it was enough to show the JCS that Special Forces at Fort Bragg was in the wrong place for rapid employment in Europe. Support of revolution such as in East Germany or Hungary had not been in the original concept, but, in essence, it was the same technique as support of resistance. Rather than to be caught short again with further revolts in satellite countries possible, the JCS decided to ship the 10th to Germany. In spite of the imperatives of this potentially explosive situation, the CIA made one last try to kill Special Forces. Working with confederates in the State and Defense Departments, they leaked the rumor that Special Forces was not ready. So the JCS sent old Burma-hand, Ray Peers, to Bragg to settle the question. "They are ready," Peers reported simply, and the 10th packed its boots and rucksacks.

In November 1953, Colonel Bank and 782 of the newly trained Special Forces sailed for West Germany. Because the program was still secret, when the men formed up on the docks at Wilmington, North Carolina, they were wearing uniforms devoid of stripes, patches, or badges. Already aboard the troop-

Parachute jump training, Ft. Bragg, NC

ship from New York, other soldiers lined the rails, jeering and catcalling at the "recruits." The insults drew no response, but there were some changes made when the professionals of the 10th Special Forces Group came back on deck a few hours out to sea, resplendent in their chevrons and jump badges.

The 10th landed at Bremerhaven and moved by rail to its new home at Bad Tölz. Located directly south of Munich, Bad Tölz was too close to the Communist border to serve as a launch base for any but stay-behind teams. It was ideal in almost every other respect. The garrison itself, a former German officers' training center, was a small, self contained, quadrangular *kaserne* situated near the picturesque Bavarian alpine town. It offered the advantages of a fine gymnasium, a large indoor swimming pool, and a small airstrip across the road, all invaluable for training. The surrounding area was rugged, mountainous, and thickly forested, ideal guerrilla country for war-game resistance operations and for sharpening mountain climbing and skiing skills acquired in the States.

Other American units in Germany, no longer the occupation troops of old but guests of the Federal Republic, were experiencing serious problems on maneuver areas. Their heavy tanks, trucks, and armored personnel carriers could hardly operate without damaging private property. The 10th SF Group, however, found ready access to a 3,000-square-mile swath of territory because its troops could promise "nothing worse than a bootprint." Besides, the SF troopers quickly perceived and put into practice that great key to guerrilla success—getting along with the local populace. Having a large number of German speakers and native-born Germans in the organization undoubtedly helped. More important than language was a feeling and a state of mind, a basic sympathy for other cultures, other ways of life, and other people. The men of the Group got along with the suspicious, close-mouthed mountain farmers and woodchoppers because they genuinely liked and understood them. On maneuvers this paid off, as it was to do in combat elsewhere in later years. The green beret became a passport to help and cooperation over a wide area around Bad Tolz. The men of the 10th Group would lurk in hiding in the mountains, training their guerrilla bands of young German soldiers. Americans, based in the flatlands and rolling hills of the pre-Alps, would be the Aggressors or, as they are now called, Opposing Forces. They customarily found it almost impossible to get information about the SF from the local population. More often than not, they were sent on wildgoose chases up the wrong, steep mountain when they asked, "Where are the Americans in the green berets?"

On one field exercise, a Special Forces Team's supply bundle was erroneously dropped from an aircraft about a minute early. Since it was night, and a minute translates into a long way at 150 knots, the bundle was not found, and the team struggled and improvised without the badly needed equipment.

In the meantime, maneuver commanders launched a search for the government equipment, which included a valuable radio and dangerous demolitions. Questions about the bundle directed to the local people drew only blank stares and head shakes. Waiting until the exercise had ended, the team radio operator set out to find the gear. In the first village *gasthaus* near the drop zone that he visited, he mentioned the problem to some locals over a stein of beer and was told, "Oh, ja, the bundle that was parachuted about two weeks ago—Schmidt has it." At Schmidt's farm, a smiling, conspiratorial Bavarian led the soldier to his barn, where the bundle and its parachute were concealed under the hay.

"Those other guys in the field caps were nosing around looking for this and asking lots of questions, but no one would tell them anything. We knew it belonged to Special Forces and that you'd be around to pick it up." There wasn't a man on the team who failed to absorb that lesson.

Maneuvers are just war games, but Special Forces played them hard. Mistakes were naturally part of the learning process. One SF captain had just moved into a good mountain hideout with his team of about fifty guerrillas. They were tired after a long climb with heavy packs, but the area looked good for their purposes. That evening the local game warden (*jagermeister*) came into camp to talk to the commander. He explained that this was a prime hunting region and that the troops would frighten deer out of the area. He suggested a nearby alternate area, promising assistance and cooperation if the troops would move. "Look, Buster," said the captain, "I'm here and I'm staying. If you give me a hard time, I'll start setting off demolition charges, and there won't be a deer left in this whole *landkreis* within a week." The *jagermeister* picked up his rucksack and rifle, ambling off down the mountain without a word. His next stop was the headquarters of the Aggressor forces. He not only showed them in detail the guerrilla positions, but helped organize the cordon and led the final assault. At the end, he even had to be restrained as the Aggressors closed in for the attack. They were firing blanks, but the enraged *jagermeister* was using live ammunition.

So the men of the 10th learned by trial and error and by improvisation. There were few books and no field manuals, and, best of all, no experts from higher headquarters to supervise or harass. Without reading it in a book or hearing it in a classroom, they learned the strengths and weaknesses of the guerrilla. In numerous exercises against conventional army units, they found what worked and what didn't for guerrilla, as well as counterguerrilla.

The American Seventh Army in Germany in those days was no patsy opponent. It was, in fact, probably the finest army the United States ever fielded. It was loaded with professionals who sought good duty with good troops found in Germany. Seventh Army personnel enjoyed the continuity of three-year tours with extensions, good equipment, good morale, and high standards of training.

But the professionals of the Seventh Army got a taste in Germany of the frustrations many of them would later experience in Vietnam. Many were the complaints of how SF and their guerrillas were cheating or not "playing fair." Guerrilla bands set up shop on the mountains overlooking the enemy headquarters and watched with amusement the mobilization of armored road patrols and large unit sweeps. As the Aggressors lacked accurate intelligence about the guerrillas and did not understand their tactics, the results were usually failures to find guerrillas.

At night when most of the tired conventional troops were back in their bivouacs, the guerrillas would sneak down the carefully reconnoitered trails, striking the lightly defended targets they had selected and carefully rehearsed. Next morning, reports would filter into Aggressor headquarters: "Two critical bridges blown; the rail switching yard at Holzkirchen destroyed; a supply convoy ambushed; a fuel dump in flames; and three wheels gone off the 'old man's' jeep." Or a Special Forces soldier with his hair grown long, dressed in the *lederhosen* of the Bavarian peasant, would saunter into a headquarters command post (CP). If the U.S. security was good, he would take along that foolproof ticket to American trust, a cute kid. The kid would leave with his pockets full of C ration candy. His "father" had the layout of the CP in his head. One wonders how often the Vietcong did the same to us in Vietnam!

Special Forces also learned of the disdain of many conventional commanders for all things remotely sneaky or irregular. One Aggressor battle group commander was provided with a full detachment of German-speaking Military Intelligence (M.I.)

SF Light Weapons Specialist, 10th SFG, pre-1962, Bad Tolz, Bavaria

agents, driving German rental cars and living in *gasthäuser*. The commander of the M.I. Detachment was a major, fluent in German and well trained in guerrilla warfare. The battle group commander forced the major to pitch his command post well away from the commander's CP, refusing to talk or listen to his intelligence expert, for he thought intelligence operations were beneath the dignity of a good combat commander. That M.I. major, by the end of the exercise, had the boundaries and names of all ten guerrilla sectors, the locations of the guerrilla base areas, and all other information that would have enabled the battle group to scarp up the guerrillas and end the exercise prematurely. As it turned out, the exercise ended as scheduled, but with the entire battle group surrounded the last night by 800 guerrillas attacking with blazing rifles and machine guns.

The Special Forces men learned that while big sweeps were laughable and headquarters security was often leaky, guerrillas also suffered from many real weaknesses. Some of the smarter Aggressor commanders did use native-born German intelligence agents to operate clandestinely in the villages, often entering the maneuver area a month before the Aggressor troops were introduced. Those intelligence operations severely hampered the freedom of the guerrillas. Other commanders initiated small, long-range patrols operating quietly, in and around the most probable guerrilla base areas. Equipped with radios, they summoned large formations of Aggressors when they discovered the locations of the guerrillas. Special Forces soldiers discovered that they were vulnerable to that sort of penetration. They found out that once they were on the run to escape from the Aggressors, they were capable of accomplishing little else, and they lost their essential and carefully built civilian support networks. On the run, supply is a serious problem, and food runs short. Internal communications were slow and primitive, and care of the sick and injured was enormously complex. Thus, over and over again they learned and relearned that support of the population was the key.

As time passed, the 10th SF Group came to know the familiar Bavarian hills almost too well, and efforts were made to branch out into other countries in and around Europe. The special warfare planners from the European Command and the commander and staff of the 10th Special Forces Group made visits to France, England, Norway, Italy, Turkey, Greece, Iran, and Spain. The reception to the idea of exchanging training and conducting exercises together was generally received with great enthusiasm. Soon detachments from the Group were conducting training and field exercises with their counterpart organizations throughout western Europe and the Middle East. Some armies had no special forces as such, but some had similar units for commando and Ranger-type missions, such as the British Special Air Service. The old pros in the French 11 Demi-Brigade de Parachutistes de Choc had a wealth of experience in guerrilla warfare.

Such training exchanges were invaluable to the Group and to the U.S. Army as a whole, although it is doubtful much of the top command realized it. The training was not costly, as the small detachments carried all their equipment on their backs and were inexpensive to transport and support. Not only were skills and techniques being exchanged, but solid liaison was being established with the likely nuclei of any "stay-behind" resistance forces of future conflicts.

Men of the 10th Special Forces Group trained and exercised with airborne, commando, ranger, raider, special forces, militia, and clandestine organizations in England, France, Norway, Germany, Greece, Spain, Italy, Turkey, Pakistan, Iran, Jordan, and Saudi Arabia. They adapted more and more to the

Winter, Bad Tolz

problems of working across cultural and linguistic barriers, learning how to get along on native food, how to avoid giving offense by the unwitting or careless violation of a taboo.

In Norway, they learned how difficult it was to operate against the Home Guard which effectively mobilized the entire population against them. Used to a friendly population in Bavaria, maneuvers in Norway came as a shock. An A Team, having executed a flawless infiltration from submarine to rubber boat to a deserted shoreline during the dark of the moon, soon found itself hounded by opposition troops. The team that dropped in by parachute fared no better. Why? Any Norwegian catching even a fleeting glimpse of unusual activity or strange doings reported immediately to the Home Guard.

With the British SAS, a small elite unit of incredible toughness and selectivity, different techniques were practiced. The SAS were not guerrilla warfare operators, but teams whose operations visualized *no* contact with the population. They were masters of concealment, clandestine movement, and land navigation in the toughest terrain. Small detachments were sent to Hereford, Wales, the SAS home base, to practice escape and evasion and learn their techniques for combat in houses, while the SAS members came to Bad Tolz in company strength to learn skiing and mountain climbing from the men of the Special Forces. The one-time commander of the 22nd SAS, Lt. Col. Sir John Slim, son of Field Marshal Slim, also set the example of the perfect British officer, able to ingest incredible quantities of Scotch while remaining the perfect gentleman.

In the rugged mountains of Greece, SF exchanged ideas and training with men who had fought as partisans against the German invaders and later as opponents to the Communist guerrilla movement. The headquarters and its base communicators learned how to load fast and move out rapidly several hundred miles by aircraft or truck, set up a base, and then brief, launch, resupply, and direct the activities of teams operating all the way from Norway to Turkey, directing as many as sixteen separate teams simultaneously. Liaison and cooperation with Navy and Air Force elements improved, and submarine and aircraft crews from those services became proficient in the touchy business of clandestine night infiltration.

At Headquarters, U.S. Army Europe, in Heidelberg, however, staff officers looked at their plans for World War III and asked how many men the 10th Special Forces Group would put on the line on D day, the day all those Russian mechanized divisions came rumbling west. The answer, of course, was "none." The 10th was to evacuate deep into France, set up its base, and start parachuting teams into the nations of eastern Europe. It would be months before effective guerrilla operations could start. Most planners saw the war being over and done with in short order. Guerrillas could not be ready in time to affect the outcome. With the end of the Korean War and the advent of the Eisenhower/Dulles administration, military strength in Europe was drastically cut. U.S. military strategy relied heavily on the strategic deterrent and the strategic air defense of the United States, at the expense of ground conventional combat strength. Although the 10th Special Forces Group was a strategic theater unit, it was under the command of the Commander in Chief of the United States Army, Europe, who was principally concerned with the conventional defense of Europe. Thus Special Forces in Europe found itself fighting for its life.

In the mid-1950s the SF strength at Bad Tolz dropped from over 800 to less than 400. All over Europe, Army planners, to save money, consolidated units in fewer German installations. At Bad Tolz, an unhappy marriage of convenience joined the 10th Special Forces Group with the Seventh Army NCO Academy, which was Gen. Bruce Clarke's pride and joy. The Academy, as could be expected, leaned heavily on those West

Point virtues of short haircuts, spit-shined boots, starched fatigues, discipline, and dismounted drill. Here, in microcosm, the frictions that marked Army-Special Forces relations everywhere became evident.

The first NCO Academy graduation parade provided an interesting example. Inside the quadrangle shared by the Academy and Group, the Academy students were lined up in impeccable ranks at rigid attention. The band played and General Clarke, resplendent in his multiple ribbons and four stars, was on the stand. At his side was the Academy Commandant (also the C.O., 10th SFG). As luck would have it, just at that inappropriate time, Sgt. George Yosich of Special Forces arrived outside the *kaserne* with his troops, an A Team with about sixty acting guerrillas, just in from thirty days in the field. Dirty, bearded, dressed in a hodgepodge of uniforms and civilian clothes, loaded with rucksacks, blanket rolls, and every kind of weapon, hungry as bears, they were a far cry from the troops drawn up inside the *kaserne*. Hearing the martial music from within, Sergeant Yosich, with an old soldier's pride, lined his troops up and marched them in. Around behind the reviewing stand, they performed a smart column left, arriving at the left flank of the parade ground. He then commanded "Halt, left face" and then dismissed them in a flurry of cheers in front of the snack bar. Yosich later recalled it as "just plain beautiful." General Clarke's reaction is not on record.

After Aaron Bank, few senior officers had experience in irregular warfare, so command of the 10th Special Forces Group went to old airborne colonels with no particular interest or experience in the mission. In Bad Tölz during the "economy" years, they were given dual command of both the Academy and the Group. It is not surprising that a good many commanders felt more akin to the well-ordered ranks and classrooms of the Academy than to the strange nighttime doings of SF.

One early commander concluded it might enhance the "good order and military discipline" of the SF if its noncoms were to emulate the cadre of the NCO Academy and carry swagger sticks. It was so ordered. The next day SF noncoms appeared with their swagger sticks—rifle cleaning rods, broomsticks, pool cues, blackjacks, even a six-foot-long piece of two-by-four. The innovation died a swift, natural death.

"Iron Mike" Paulick—a feisty, tough, short, bald West Pointer with an aggressive manner—took over the job. He took advantage of the bimonthly NCO Academy graduations, with a different general officer each two weeks, to drag them to the 10th SF briefing room for a briefing on his unit's activities. At the end of the briefing, he was to place a green beret, replete with the correct number of stars, on the general's head as a token of the unit. Not all generals either liked SF or wanted to hear the briefing, but they got it anyway, as Mike Paulick was a very intimidating man, even with generals. At one briefing he had Lt. Gen. Paul D. Adams, who did *not* like SF (see Chapter 4). The mixed expression of incredulity and rage on his face when Paulick reached up and plunked a green beret with three stars on his head defies description. He snatched it off and threw it across the briefing room, then stomped out to his car. The fact that Mike later made brigadier general is a tribute to his military attributes, not to his tact and diplomacy.

As the 10th Group trained and maneuvered in Europe, the 77th Special Forces Group was activated at Fort Bragg and soon was engaged in similar stateside activities. SF troopers, especially NCOs, transferred back and forth between the two units. The 77th, however, suffered somewhat from being in the States and on a big Army post. It lacked the ready availability of foreign troops and new terrain to explore, and found itself a bit more "under the gun" of the rest of the Army. Nonetheless, its members still managed to train in the arctic cold of Alaska, the mountains of Colorado and North Carolina, the swamps of Florida and Camp McCall, North Carolina, and the Atlantic. They trained with the Air Force and with Navy submarines and Frogmen, and maneuvered against the troops of the Stateside Army and Marines.

With the 10th and the 77th in good shape, attention turned to the Far East. A detachment of three officers and thirteen NCOs was handpicked from the 77th, redesignated the 14th Special Forces Operational Detachment, and in June of 1956 shipped to Hawaii. There their arrival triggered such headlines as "Killer Army Paratroops Will Make Jumps Over Oahu." But they did not stay long enough to enjoy the beaches or Hawaiian hospitality. They were soon committed to missions in Thailand, Taiwan, and Vietnam, in each country providing training for Ranger- or SF-type units. Not long thereafter, an-

Rigger check before first jump, Airborne school, Okinawa, 1st SFG

other small unit (five officers and seventeen NCOs), the 8,231st Army Special Operations Detachment, was formed at Bragg and shipped to Camp Drake, Japan.

In June 1957, the two detachments moved to Okinawa. There they were consolidated to form the nucleus of the 1st Special Forces Group, which was to be in the Far East what the 10th was in Europe. In those early years, they too had only a hot war mission: conducting guerrilla warfare behind-the-lines in such places as China, Korea, or Indochina. They, too, soon found the value of circulating their teams throughout the area to train with native units.

Korea, Taiwan, the Philippines, and Malaysia all offered troops with which to train, uncharted boondocks to explore, and best of all, continued exposure to Asian people, languages, food, cultures, and all the accompanying problems. There was ski and cold weather training in Northern Japan, jungle school in Malaysia, and new Special Forces units to train in Korea and the Philippines. Needless to say, these new SF units were clones of the 1st SF. The Chinese were building a huge Special Forces outfit on Taiwan for their dreamed-of return to the mainland. Submarines called at Okinawa from time to time, and their commanders could be talked into running some lock-in-lock-out* training for the scuba teams.

The southern part of Okinawa had plenty of tough jungle terrain, and the notorious parachute drop zone at Yomitan (an old ex-Japanese airfield) was a challenge to the best paratroopers. Yomitan was crisscrossed with old fighter runways and aprons, dotted with piles of coral rock, and ringed with cliffs and power lines. At the prejump briefing, the marshalling area control officer would often give up in frustration when he came to the part covering "obstacles on the DZ." "Hell, it's all one great big obstacle. Good luck! If you jump into that compound over on the left, even good luck won't help you—that's a war dog training center. The dogs are loose inside, and it is surrounded by barbed wire." The commanding officer of the 1st SFG broke both legs in a Yomitan jump within days of the creation of the unit. A later colonel earned the nickname of "Splash" for his preference for jumping into the soft waters of the South China Sea, a form of parachuting usually reserved for the already injured and casted.

That was a period when the hard-core NCOs of the 1st and the 10th Groups were able to remain for three years on Okinawa or at Tolz, extend for longer if they could, and usually start angling for return overseas as soon as they hit the States. Many of the SF wives in Tolz were German; just as many on Okinawa were Japanese or Ryukyuan.

As the 1950s came to a close, the three Special Forces Groups—the 10th in Germany, the 77th at Bragg, and the 1st on Okinawa—were in good condition, even if small. Overall SF strength stood at around 2,000 men, but that was no ordinary mixture. There were absolutely no second lieutenants, and all first lieutenants and captains had considerable time in grade, for promotion was slow in those days. In the enlisted ranks, there were no privates, PFCs, or first enlistments in the operational teams, and hence there were no "kids." Many teams

---

*Lock-in-lock-out refers to the tricky and dangerous technique of exiting or entering a submerged submarine. To avoid flooding the sub, of course, requires placing the swimmer into a compartment (or lock) and then flooding (for exit) or pumping dry (for return). It is not for the faint-hearted or the claustrophobic, but is useful for putting swimmers ashore and recovering them under clandestine conditions without surfacing the sub.

averaged thirty years of age and ten years of service, though some of that service had been with a foreign army.

The men were tough, intensively trained, proud, and competent specialists in guerrilla warfare. So far, no one in the U.S. military establishment, including those in the SF, had given much thought to the other side of the coin—counterinsurgency.

6. REVOLUTIONARY WAR AND COUNTERINSURGENCY

World War III and the nuclear holocaust—these were the principal preoccupations of U.S. military planners and thinkers during the 1950s. It was no accident that during the same decade, the Special Forces were trained for and thought of themselves as guerrillas/resistance fighters behind the lines of a major conventional conflict.

In the communist world, however, a subtle but important difference in thinking was emerging. It involved guerrilla warfare, but in a context substantially removed from the World War II resistance movements upon which U.S. Special Forces doctrine was based. It more clearly subordinated military to political action; paid greater heed to the interaction in any prolonged conflict of economic, psychological, political, and military factors; and pounded endlessly on the theme that support of an indigenous population was the key to success.

Thus did "Wars of National Liberation" and "Liberation Fronts" blossom in the communist lexicon. The French, who had unsuccessfully faced up to this little understood, multidimensional threat in Indochina and Algeria, called it simply "Revolutionary War." Americans, then further removed from the immediate challenge and reluctant to attach to it any phraseology even remotely related to the "Spirit of '76," cast uneasily around for other terms, finally settling on "insurgency."

As the 1960s dawned, such conflicts threatened existing governments in a startling number of countries around the world, most of them in the underdeveloped areas of Africa, Latin America, and Asia. Those struggles varied in detail from place to place, but shared at least three important characteristics:

- They were basically indigenous.
- They were rooted in the deep dissatisfaction with the existing form of government, and in some cases, in the sheer misery of a substantial part of the population.
- They were sponsored or supported by the Communists.

Greece, Cuba, China, Malaya, Vietnam, and the Philippines were only some of the more striking examples. The British, French, Portuguese, and Dutch empires were disassembled, one by one. The Soviets openly supported the insurgencies. On 6 January 1961, Khrushchev openly announced that while the Soviet Union and other communist nations opposed world wars and local wars, they recognized and would support "just wars of liberation and popular uprisings." This focused the attention of President John F. Kennedy and led his administration to begin searching around for effective tools to counter Communist-supported insurgencies. While the Special Forces was one of those tools, a vast new study of the insurgencies themselves was instigated. To a certain extent, that study continues to this day.

While insurgents use guerrilla tactics to carry out the military part of their program, they bring at least equal skill, dedication, and resources to political action. In the simplest terms, their goal is to wrest control of the people from the existing government. They shrewdly recognize that an *appearance* of an inability to govern and to provide basic services and security, can be as important as an actual inability to govern. Thus, while the conventional military thinks in terms of the seizure of a piece of critical terrain, or the control or destruction of a major industrial or transportation center, the insurgent thinks first, last, and always of the population.

The importance of this simple concept cannot be overstressed. It is fundamental to the revolutionary problems of today's world, and to the very reason for the existence of Special Forces. Unfortunately, it is an easy concept to articulate, but an extremely difficult one to grasp and hold, especially for the American military mind, steeped as it is in images of big battles, front lines, and a century and a half of military victories. Soldiers, diplomats, journalists, and politicians have all paid it increasing lip service in the last decade, but like the layman, most are not quite certain of what they mean, or if they do know, are unwilling to accept its overwhelming importance. The reason for this is quite clear: conventional military victories provide quick, clear-cut "solutions" to troublesome problems, while political action is painfully time-consuming, the body-count type of statistic difficult to determine, and political action distasteful and not held to be the role of the military.

It is this American tendency to see all problems and all solutions in our own terms and to grow impatient when problems drag on that has allowed the Communists to capitalize on various insurgencies. As in Vietnam, the enemy was able to remain relatively fixed in pursuit of long-term objectives, willingly absorbing short-term setbacks if necessary, and making few moves, military or otherwise, without considering their political impact.

Communists have also been able to make highly selective and effective use of terrorism, recognizing, to repeat, that the appearance of a government's inability to govern and to protect its people may very well be as important as the real thing. Thus kidnapping, assassination, or simple terrorizing of minor officials of a government have become vital tools for the revolutionary. This is why today the KGB supports schools for terrorists in Czechoslovakia, Cuba, and North Korea attended by thousands of third world future terrorists.

In the words of the late Bernard Fall, ". . . subversion is literally administration with a minus sign in front of it." Fall, the French-born American scholar who made a specialty of the conflict in Vietnam, noted that in one year, April 1960 to April 1961, during the "quiet" days of that struggle, the Vietcong killed some 4,000 minor officials of the Diem government. How could a Vietnamese peasant, with no strong attachment to either side, be convinced the Diem government could survive and provide security for him and his family, when he saw officials of his own hamlet murdered with impunity? In Algeria, the FLN (Front for the National Liberation) directed its terror, not against the French Army, but against those Arabs who helped or supported the French. It was an approach taken from the French themselves; in World War II, the Maquis concentrated their attention not on German soldiers, but on their French collaborators, until the opening hours of the Normandy invasion when they were ordered to attack military targets.

The passing years have changed matters very little. In Vietnam, the victims of terrorism, assassination, and kidnapping were the village and hamlet chiefs, schoolteachers, health officers, and government tax collectors. There has been a good deal written about Vietcong terror directed against Americans, but any competent observer of the scene knows that this was not a VC policy, except for that short period in 1964-65 that resulted in American intervention in strength. Saigon in the mid-sixties was teeming with unarmed Americans in search of pleasure and relaxation; imagine how easy it would have been to carry out a policy of "kill Americans." One has only to look at the scorecard to know that this was not the party line. Certainly, there were occasionally a few grenades thrown into the bars, but that was more likely irresponsible hooliganism or disgruntled lovers showing resentment to B-girl activity. As for such incidents as the bombing of the Brink Officer Quarters, any terrorist worth his salt could have killed ten times as many Americans with a fraction of the explosives used in that instance. The VC did not waste many such efforts on Americans; the political effect was not worth it. The mutilated body of an American victim of a VC terror attack would have little effect on the target audience, the Vietnamese people. Spread across the pages of American newspapers, it might even produce an undesirable political effect in the United States.

Perhaps the conventional military's difficulty in accepting the primacy of political action in revolutionary wars accounts for the fact that so few successful insurgency leaders were professional soldiers. Giap was a history teacher, Mao was a librarian, Castro was a lawyer, and Ho was a cook. Though lacking in formal military training, they understood politics and none became fascinated with such statistics as body count, number of structures destroyed, or tons of explosives detonated.

Those men and their tens of thousands of followers and disciples around the world gradually pushed the threat of a new world war off the center of the stage, and as they did, the other side of the insurgency coin came into view. If the head of the coin was insurgency, the tail was obviously counterinsurgency. Just as guerrilla warfare is by no means the full thrust of insurgency, counterguerrilla operations will not of themselves defeat the insurgent. Once again, we come to a proposition that is easy to articulate, but hard to accept, hold, and implement. It is easy to understand why U.S. military leaders focused on what they best understood—counterguerrilla operations—and paid uneasy lip service to political action. To this day, some still point to the Russian successes in quelling the Hungarian revolution of 1956 and the brief welling of Czech independence in 1968 as proof that the purely military "bomb-them-back-to-the-Stone-Age" approach is best. This argument, however, does not take two fundamental considerations into account: most civilized people are not willing to take such extreme measures, and in the long run, as may still be proved in Hungary and Czechoslovakia, they simply do not work.

If he is to have any real chance of success, the counterinsurgent must strike at the roots of the population's dissatisfaction and do so quickly enough to wrest the initiative from the revolutionaries. Extreme poverty existing side by side with ostentatious wealth, corruption in government, unfair taxation, high inflation rates and prices, lack of opportunity, and a population growth rate that wipes out what little social progress is made—these are the seeds of revolution in much of the under-developed or developing world. For the revolutionary leader, all that is necessary is to exploit those problems, underline them to the people, and promise alternate options under their leadership in the future. The government's, and thus the counterinsurgent's, position is far more difficult. They must show positive progress in the correction of grievances, and they must do it fast enough and well enough to prevent the insurgents from taking credit for any change for the better. This is a difficult task at best. To do so in the midst of fighting a war approaches the impossible. Ideally, then, the solution is to eliminate the causes of rebellion *before* active fighting begins. That has seldom happened in the past, and it is no more likely to occur in the future.

Thus the counterinsurgent, whether working on his own or in support of an existing government, faces the herculean task of trying simultaneously to fight an enemy from within and to build a complete political structure from the ground up. The weaker, more ineffective, corrupt, or repressive the existing government is, the tougher the task will be.

This is precisely the staggering load the United States and the government of South Vietnam tried to carry out in that torn country. Among the things we have learned—or at least it is to be hoped we have learned—is that in such a situation, there are no quick and easy solutions. Technological advances and massive doses of modern materiel introduced into a near-primitive society do not guarantee progress, and are, in fact, counterproductive. A corollary lesson has begun to emerge: since "revolutionary war" is, by the definition of its most successful practitioners, a protracted war, so, unfortunately, must be counterinsurgency. Whether the endurance, commitment, and single-mindedness required for such an effort can logically be expected of a society as impatient, success-oriented, and open as America is a question beyond the scope of this book.

Another harsh lesson likely to find slow acceptance in the Western world is this: in a counterinsurgency effort, military leaders must either fully understand and accept the importance of *all* dimensions of such warfare, or they must be subordinated to someone who does. *Counterguerrilla* operations, a military function, must not be allowed to overshadow the other, vital expressions of a *counterinsurgency* effort; the former is only a part of a much larger whole.

In Vietnam and elsewhere, it was not enough to mouth old clichés about "winning hearts and minds" while placing all the effort on "kills" and weapons counts. There have been, and perhaps remain still, too many high-ranking American officers who only half in jest repeat such old, sick jokes as "Give us your hearts and minds or we'll burn down your goddamn village," or "If you grab them by the balls, the hearts and minds will follow." With no intention of assessing blame, let us examine just one example from Vietnam of the results that such an attitude can yield. Not long after U.S. combat troops had been committed to the war, a U.S. Marine was shown in a widely distributed television film setting fire to a thatched hut with a cigarette lighter. The simplistic justification offered, and worse yet widely accepted in the U.S. command, was that the Marines had been fired on from that hamlet, that it was therefore a Vietcong hamlet and should be destroyed. But what were the political consequences of that purely military action? First, those residents of the hamlet who were not Vietcong or Vietcong sympathizers before the burning, almost certainly were after it. Second, the airing of the incident on television led to a widespread revulsion against U.S. tactics, both in and outside of the United States. The long-term loss, which any successful insurgent or counterinsurgent leader could have predicted, was incalculably greater than the short-term gain.

On the other hand, mere good deeds—the supremely ineffective acts of passing out candy, patting kids on the head, and perhaps conducting sick call before the visiting American or Vietnamese Army battalion withdraws from the hamlet once more, or the more difficult accomplishments in political, social, and economic reforms—are alone not enough to meet the threat of an insurgency. The guerrilla himself, and the all-important organization that supports him, must be destroyed or at least neutralized.

Ideally, the objective of a counterguerrilla program is not to kill or even capture the guerrilla, but to convince him to abandon a hopeless or worthless cause. A credible amnesty program, backed by visible reforms in the existing government, can be worth many battalions.

Nevertheless, once a revolution has reached the stage at which the insurgency has armed troops in the field, battalions *will* be required by the government in power. Essential, in purely military context, is a properly balanced structure. One part should be a highly mobile, highly trained strike force, its units dispersed in such strategic locations so as to make it possible for elements to move rapidly to the relief of local troops, capitalize on the enemy's tactical lapses or misfortunes, and pursue intelligence leads.

The other part of the balanced military structure should be local or territorial forces. These units should be "of the people," locally recruited and trained, and based not only on the political structure of a given area, but responsive to its political leaders. Operating in or near their hometowns, they have a real stake in providing security for their village, their families, and their property. It is one thing for a trooper from one part of Vietnam to be asked to protect a schoolhouse built by Americans, until recently guarded by Americans, which, if destroyed, will probably be rebuilt by Americans, and, above all, attended by the children of people he does not know. It is quite another to offer him a chance to protect a schoolhouse built by friends and relatives which, if destroyed by the Vietcong, must be rebuilt by those same friends and relatives, and, last, attended by his own children. In the first instance, the trooper understandably becomes little more than a bemused onlooker when the enemy attacks. In the second, he is almost as often converted into a tiger—a dogged, tough, and resourceful fighter.

How large a force will be required for optimum results? How many troops in the mobile reserve, and how many in local forces? There is no precise answer, but another harsh truth about insurgency warfare is that the counterinsurgents must enjoy vast numerical superiority. It requires but a few determined men to infiltrate an airfield, a supply dump, or a village on *one* dark night *once* in six months. How many men does it take to protect all those dumps, airfields, and villages *every* night?

In the Philippines, the late Ramon Magsaysay employed 60,000 troops and backed them with masterfully executed political, social, and economic reform programs in order to defeat no more than 8,000 Huks. Cuba's Batista, with 25,000 troops arrayed against Fidel Castro's 800 revolutionaries, enjoyed a far greater numerical superiority, but offered little else, and inevitably lost. In Malaya, it took 70,000 British Commonwealth troops, backed by 180,000 local forces, twelve years and perhaps $2.5 billion to stifle an insurgency waged by 8,000 guerrillas drawn from a clearly identifiable ethnic minority, the Chinese.

So the ratio of insurgents to counterinsurgents will vary from country to country, and situation to situation. But there is a constant: few, if any, governments can field enough troops or provide enough equipment to get the job done without good intelligence. The swamps, jungles, and mountains in which the insurgents live will gobble up, over and over again, thousands of soldiers floundering through the morass or bogged down with their heavy gear on endless wild-goose chases. The guerrilla knows this, and takes full advantage of it. He also knows, if he has been in his trade for any length of time, that while he lives by surprise, he can also die by surprise. He knows that he *will* die if the local population tells the counterguerrilla forces what they need to know in order to locate him, and that he *will* die if counterguerrillas succeed in infiltrating his own organization.

These approaches—the winning of accurate information about the enemy from the people among whom he moves, or the infiltration of his ranks—always have and always will provide the best intelligence. The best intelligence comes from human beings, not from such elaborate gadgetry as electronic sensors, infrared detectors, "people sniffers," or aerial photography. This is not to say that scientific and technological sources of intelligence should not be integrated with human intelligence—they should.

The best source of all is the agent who gets himself recruited into a guerrilla unit or one of its supporting organizations. But whether the source of intelligence is the infiltrated agent or the people on the sidelines of the war, it must be accepted that such information does not come easily and is particularly difficult to acquire for foreign troops, or even native troops from other regions.

The oft-told tales about such-and-such U.S. Army or Marine outfits moving into a village, conducting sick call, passing out candy and soap, and then being given a full and accurate rundown on the enemy are vastly overstated. The development of a meaningful intelligence network in the environment of a revolutionary war, like all the other steps of a successful counterinsurgency movement, requires professional, painstaking, and very patient effort. Without it, the counterguerrilla forces, as we learned in Vietnam, are doomed to endless, frustrating, and exhausting "walks in the sun."

With good intelligence in hand and at least some military successes being noted by counterguerrilla troops, insurgents, and the uncommitted population, the next difficult step may be within reach. This is the destruction or neutralization of the organization supporting the guerrillas. The task of the military has been to destroy or neutralize the guerrillas themselves—those who carry guns and explosives, and execute raids and ambushes. The supporting organization, or infrastructure, is equally important, but is far harder to identify and deal with effectively. Its members live apparently normal lives as part of the civilian community. Behind that facade, they provide food, shelter, transportation, hiding places, information, messenger services, financial support, medical care, manpower, and countless other services and resources. Without this support, the guerrilla must either have substantial outside help, or shrivel and die.

The leaders of the infrastructure are likely to be professionals themselves, and are often ruthless, hard-bitten men. One story in Vietnam tells of a three-man team recruited in Saigon to help carry the benefits of the South Vietnamese government to an area in Tay Ninh Province, then largely under Vietcong control. The government workers, a teacher, a health worker, and a clerk, were specifically trained for work in that province.

Amid appropriate fanfare and backslapping, they departed in high spirits. Delivered by helicopter to a landing field near a South Vietnamese Army base, they made their way afoot to a hamlet barely three miles away. There they were greeted with enthusiasm and great politeness. The hamlet chief presided at a welcoming festival in which most of the residents participated. The government workers went to sleep that night tired, but happy, certain they would be able to make a real contribution to the future of the village. The next morning they were awakened by a man whom they had met the day before, but had not singled out as very important. He was not the hamlet chief, nor did he bear any emblems of authority. But, although he was very polite, he was also firm. He explained that the three were in a Vietcong village, and that being the case, they were free to return to Saigon if they so wished. But, he suggested, there were three reasons that might lead them to choose otherwise. First, since they had come to the hamlet to help the people, why not stay on and pursue that worthy goal? Second, since they would be on Saigon's payroll, and the Vietcong would also pay them for their services, why not take advantage of the dual remuneration? And, third, if they set out for Saigon, it was likely, in these tumultuous days, that an accident would befall them on the way. All three nodded, contemplated, and stayed. Thus were three recruits added to the Vietcong infrastructure. An apocryphal story, no doubt, but still an insight into the complexities of counterinsurgency warfare, and the need for professionals to wage it.

Separating the guerrilla from the willing or unwilling support of the populace is not easy. To make matters worse, most of the measures designed to accomplish that end involve the imposition of unpopular restrictions on *all* the people. Food rationing, curfews, travel restrictions, roadblocks, searches without warrants, endless interrogations, and night arrests are all likely to antagonize further an already disgruntled population. Over the years, these and other drastic actions have been employed in an effort to locate and neutralize the guerrilla's shadowy supporters. French paratroopers in Algiers used brutally repressive measures, and even torture, to roll up the Liberation Front underground in the Casbah. On the spot, it worked well; back home, it was a catastrophe. The cost was the alienation of most of the French citizenry. The French Army beat the insurgents, but lost Algeria.

We are driven once again to the fundamental point—the population is the key. Whether the guerrilla himself or the infrastructure that supports him is the target, neither can be dealt with effectively and permanently unless the local population *wants* it that way. It is not likely that the majority of the people will move on its own in one direction or the other. It is an active, determined minority that will determine how the mass will act. In Vietnam, for example, the populace of many, and perhaps most, villages was split three ways: a large and relatively passive majority bracketed by two activist minorities, one pro-government, the other pro-Vietcong. In various situations, leaders of the two factions may move the majority first this way, then that.

In the dirty and dangerous business of revolutionary war, the motivation that produces the only real long-lasting effects is not likely to be an ideology, but the elemental consideration of survival. Peasants will support the Vietcong if they are convinced that it offers them a better life, and, more important, if they are convinced that failure to do so will result in death or brutal punishment. They will support the government if and when they are convinced that it offers them a better life, and it can and will protect them against the Vietcong—forever. Forever is a long time, but so is death.

That is a terribly difficult and dangerous decision for the peasant to make, so elemental it is very hard for anyone who has never been exposed to the harshness of such a struggle to appreciate. When the decision has been taken, and if the peasant's decision is to cast his lot with the government, then a critical breakthrough is achieved. There is no way to change the decision; the peasant is now committed to fight and inform against the Vietcong. If he fails, the chances are all too good that he and his family will wind up disemboweled object lessons for others who might toy with the idea of going over to the government. The road to such a breakthrough is tortuous and long. Shortcuts have usually turned out to be dead ends. But this is success at the grass roots in counterinsurgency, and it tends to be contagious. It has worked in many places, even eventually in Vietnam. The South Vietnamese government had the insurgency well in hand by 1975, but lost to an invading North Vietnamese Army which virtually had no popular support.

From the position of the United States, the concept of counterinsurgency becomes even more difficult and complex. We are not faced with a major insurgency at home. The reason for any overseas involvement in counterinsurgency stems from a foreign policy objective: to foster the development of a community of free nations and to frustrate communist ambitions to create a community of communist nations. This means, among other things, that an already formidable task becomes more so. The United States must try to carry out, by proxy, in someone else's country, the complex political, psychological, economic, and military tasks of counterinsurgency.

The job, according to doctrine, will be done by providing U.S. economic and military aid and advice to the threatened nation. In theory, the aid will be used correctly, and the advice will be heeded. Needed reforms will be undertaken, the citizenry will find new hope, and the insurgent and his infrastructure will be correctly identified and properly neutralized.

It has seldom worked that way, of course. Indigenous military commanders all too often see little need for restraint or concern for the peasantry. Wealthy landowners defy attempts to break up their holdings or dilute their power. Local political leaders are interested in their own survival, and reform looks like a more chancy course than repression, particularly if the armed forces are in the politicians' control. All these elements existed in Vietnam, not only during the Diem regime, but in the brief reigns of the leaders who came and went in revolving-door fashion after his assassination. The military victory by the North Vietnamese Army ended that greedy self-interest in South Vietnam at the point of a bayonet.

It adds up to an unpleasant and difficult dilemma, one made even more painful by the emergence of another question about counterinsurgency: should the United States participate at all? Regardless of the soundness of operational concepts, regardless of how skillfully they might or might not be implemented, should the United States involve itself so deeply in the affairs of another people? Does the United States have the moral right to interfere? These are tough questions with massive implications for the future of this country and much of the rest of the world.

As the 1960s began, in the early days of the New Frontier, counterinsurgency was a new word and a new concept. Counterinsurgency was to be the answer to communist expansion and growing threats of subversion and of wars of liberation. Those were the considerations that caused the Special Forces to do an about-face from their original role as guerrillas toward the far more difficult mission of counterinsurgency.

Green Beret at Eternal Flame, JFK's grave, Arlington Cemetery

7. NEW MISSIONS AND BIG PUBLICITY

The late President John F. Kennedy is thought of by many as a sort of patron saint of the Special Forces, and there is more than a germ of truth in the theory. There was a not surprising affinity between the Forces and the new young president who talked stirringly of what a man should do for his country. The SF men appealed, perhaps, to Kennedy's sense of the romantic and the elite. They, in turn, were flattered to find an advocate at the top who had understood the symbolism of the beret and had overridden the traditionalists. Special Forces' detractors were unhappy with that development, but could do little but refer slightingly to SF as "Jacqueline Kennedy's Own Rifles."

There was more to the attachment than superficials and symbolism, however, for Kennedy was deeply interested in the underdeveloped world and its problems, and perceived the threat that insurgencies posed to free political processes in many nations. The United States, at that moment in history, still felt an unquestioned moral obligation to challenge the spread of communism wherever it might occur, and Kennedy sought a way to challenge that new danger. With characteristic vigor, he had barely assumed the presidency before directing his new Secretary of Defense, Robert McNamara, to improve U.S. capabilities for the conduct of paramilitary operations and unconventional war. "We need a greater ability to deal with guerrilla forces, insurrection, and subversion," he told Congress in a special message, "and we must help train local forces to be equally effective." He also carried the message straight to the military establishment, counseling the 1962 graduating class at West Point that they must help their country find a way to "counter wars of liberation." He suggested to the cadets that to do so would require a "whole new kind of strategy, a wholly different kind of force."* When the results he wanted were not quickly forthcoming, Kennedy followed his original directives with a flurry of pithy memoranda, the essence of which was simply to "get going."

Nothing stings the Pentagon quite so much as direct attention from the very top, and by this time, it was clear the new president meant business about counterinsurgency. The word took on a magic of its own, employed with great familiarity and frequency by all sorts of people, civilians and military alike, who understood almost nothing about it. There was a run on the Pentagon bookstore to acquire almost anything in print—the British experience in Malaysia and elsewhere, the French experience in Vietnam and Algeria, and anything else pertinent to putting down insurgencies. Inside the Pentagon, new staff sections and special assistants were created in each of the services and on the Joint Staff. New faces appeared, and a few careers received jet propulsion.

A young and promising Army brigadier general by the name of William B. Rosson was designated special assistant to the Army Chief of Staff for special warfare. Today Rosson has four stars, having been deputy commander of all U.S. Army troops in the Pacific. Marine Maj. Gen. Victor ("Brute") Krulak, a Kennedy favorite and a feisty little scrapper with a grasp of the overriding significance of political action in irregular warfare, became the first SACSA (Special Assistant for Counterinsurgency and Special Activities) to the Chairman of the Joint Chiefs. He later retired with three stars. Col. William B. Yarborough took over the Special Warfare Center at Fort Bragg, and moved up quickly to the rank of major general, retiring in 1971 as a lieutenant general.

Everyone rushed to get into the act. The Navy created SEAL (sea, air, land) teams and trained them to parachute into the sea wearing scuba gear, at least theoretically ready to emerge from the water ready to fight. They also converted old Regulus missile-carrying submarines to carry troops and miniature four-man submarines for sea infiltration of special warfare forces. The Air Force came up with Air Commandos, decked out in

---

*Of the 600 graduating cadets listening to him that day, 21 would be killed in action in Vietnam within five years. Eventually over 400 of them would serve in that war.

jaunty Australian-style bush hats, and, to the utter consternation of the Army staff, ordered thousands of rapid-fire Armalite rifles. However, their primary weapons were dozens of old T-6s, T-28s, C-47s, and old naval Corsairs. They also selected some of the hottest pilots in the Air Force and put them behind the sticks of those old prop antiques.

The services rushed new field manuals into print, and the commercial publishing market brought out new books on resistance, insurgency, and guerrillas. The writings of Mao, Ché, and Giap neared best-seller status, although it remains doubtful that many of those who acquired the books actually read them, or that of those who did, many grasped their lessons. The nation's "think tanks," from Santa Monica to Washington, joined in the chorus with a great rash of new studies. If there was a surfeit of information about the subject, there was also a genuine enthusiasm, one reason for which was that, on paper, counterinsurgency seems both logical and practical. Practice, of course, was and is something else.

It was in such a flurry that the Special Forces found themselves pushed suddenly front and center onto the counterinsurgency stage. Why Special Forces?

First, the SF troopers' guerrilla experience could be decisive in analyzing the strengths and weaknesses of enemy guerrillas. The antiguerrilla maneuvers in Germany were now altered to provide Special Forces advisors to the conventional Aggressor commanders, with chaotic results for the guerrillas. Moreover, Special Forces detachments were small, self-contained, and capable of operating independently in remote areas for extended periods of time. The teams had language capabilities and were oriented to and trained in the cultures and backgrounds of other peoples. The skills already possessed by the teams lent themselves to counterinsurgency, or at least counterguerrilla, operations. Why couldn't a team developed and trained to organize and advise a guerrilla battalion be used to organize and advise a paramilitary counterguerrilla battalion? Here was a group of mature and motivated professionals ready and eager to help develop indigenous potential wherever it might be found. And, last, the Forces were not only good, but they were ready and available.

Orders thus flowed from the Pentagon to expand the Forces rapidly and drastically from the three understrength groups.

The 10th in Bad Tolz, the 1st on Okinawa, and the 7th (the redesignated old 77th) at Fort Bragg were increased in authorized strength to approximately 1,500 men each; that was over a fourfold increase. Other new groups were planned to take responsibilities for the Middle East, Africa, and Latin America.

More important, perhaps, the security wraps came off, at least partly, and the Forces became the darlings, not only of the White House, but also of the press corps. Publicity flowed like wine, too much and of inferior quality. It left headaches and a bad aftertaste. It was during this era that the image of Special Forces as a bunch of swaggering killers cast in the John Wayne mold began to emerge—an image which may have done more damage and proved harder to put to rest than almost anything else in the Special Forces' cloudy future.

At Fort Bragg, the Special Warfare School, under the command of newly promoted Brigadier General Yarborough, dutifully shifted into high gear in an effort to meet the new manpower goals. In an army used to cranking out privates through basic training in the millions, no one gave enough thought to the basic problem of training thousands of qualified Special Forces men. Could an outfit whose medics took a full year to train, whose communicators and other specialists required only a little less, whose requirement for professionalism was almost total, be expanded so swiftly? By the end of 1961, the answer was already partly in hand, for Fort Bragg was "behind the manpower curve," where it was to remain for a decade or more.

As missions for SF teams were found, or created, in Asia, Latin America, and Africa, Fort Bragg's Special Warfare School increased its output of graduates from something under 400 a year to almost eight times that. Attrition through training standards had always been a valuable tool when the Forces were small; it served to sort out those who belonged from those who did not. By 1962, attrition had fallen to about 70 percent from its earlier rate of near to 90 percent. By 1964, it was down to 30 percent, and more ominously, the "numbers merchants" at the Special Warfare Center and in the Pentagon were applauding the improvement. In 1965, there were two more milestones of doubtful character: to meet the expansion goals, SF accepted 6,500 first-term Army enlistees (although all still had to be triple volunteers—for the Army, for paratroop training, and for the Forces). Horror of horrors, second lieutenants began to appear wearing the beret!

As if that weren't enough to create stomach pains among the old hands, the Forces went public in singularly flashy ways. At the 1962 annual meeting of the Association of the United States Army in Washington, SF soldiers, in a showy perversion of mountain-climbing techniques that must have turned real mountaineers green, rappelled down the walls from the roof of the six-story Sheraton Park Hotel. At Fort Bragg, the Gabriel demonstration area (named after Sp5 James P. Gabriel, one of the first SF soldiers killed in Vietnam) was created, to show off skills ranging from catching and skinning snakes (thus the sobriquet "snake eaters"), to being snatched off the ground by low-flying aircraft. It was a hell of a show in anybody's book, but like most exhibitions, it was more flash than substance. The old SF troopers contemptuously called it "Disneyland." Their misgivings had small effect; by 1965, the Gabriel Show was being staged an average of five times a month for VIPs and other visitors. A Green Beret Drum and Bugle Corps was formed. Even out on Okinawa, the foolishness continued: the Kennedy Rifles, a drill team, resplendent in chrome plate and white bootlaces, snapped through its paces for visitors and the bemused Ryukyuan local citizenry. In 1969 came the ultimate—a, so help us God, Green Beret Chorus!

Irrelevant trappings and misguided publicity notwithstanding, however, the early days of the Kennedy administration saw Special Forces missions overseas greatly increased in both numbers and scope. It soon became apparent that some additions should be made to the basic SF organization. At first, it had been visualized that the basic Special Forces A Team would be all that was required to conduct counterguerrilla training for an indigenous army or paramilitary battalion. The commanding officer, his executive officer, the team sergeant, and the two weapons sergeants would teach tactics, operations, and weapons. The intelligence sergeant would instruct in his specialty, help develop agent networks, and counter enemy subversion. The medics and engineer/demolitionists would work on small civic action projects, and the radiomen would help improve local communications.

But both in the field and back at the Pentagon, the conviction grew that this was not enough, that a wider range of capabilities was required if the job was to be done effectively. From this conviction grew the concept of the Special Action Force (SAF). Built around the basic 1,500-man Special Forces Group organization with its thirty-six A teams, nine B teams, and three C teams, the SAF became a task force of specialized detachments. A small Civil Affairs Group included specialists in public health, education, sanitation, civil administration, public works, and forestry. A Psychological Operations Battalion had experts in radio and leaflet propaganda, public information, entertainment, and education, all backed up by sophisticated mobile equipment. The Engineer Detachment provided professional experience in all kinds of construction, maintenance, road building, water purification, and well drilling. The all-purpose A team "docs" were now backed up by a Medical Detachment of experts in preventive medicine, dentistry, hygiene, sanitation, and public health, as well as general medicine and surgery. An Intelligence Detachment brought professionals for photo interpretation, agent handling and nets, counterintelligence, lie detection, lock picking, wiretapping, bugging and debugging, and even more exotic enterprises. Some SAFs—to the vast amusement of old-time SF troopers who had been the bane of the MPs in so many situations—even had Military Police Detachments, skilled in riot control, investigative procedures, and population and traffic control. All SAFs had an Army Security Agency unit, with classified capabilities and mobile and man-portable equipment in the field of electronic intelligence.

Out of this wealth of talent, the theory went, a team tailored to almost any counterinsurgency need could be drawn. There were, of course, a few implications to be dealt with. The SAFs would have to be invited by the host country. The ambassador and the U.S. MAAG (Military Assistance Advisory Group) would then have to concur. Other members of the country team would become aware of the operation, many with vested interests of their own which might become endangered, causing them to feel threatened. U.S. AID, for example, had strong claims on such overlapping areas as police work, health, and economic development and assistance. The CIA was jealous of its intelligence role and often dabbled in paramilitary training as well. If the country abutted the communist bloc nations, the CIA would very likely be running a cross-border intelligence net from the country and would fear lest the operation be compromised. The U.S. Information Service frequently was already in place with some information, education, and propaganda programs. In the heat of competition, the question of whether the job was being done, could be done, or even should be done, all too often was obscured by the struggle over who would win the charter to do it. Although the ambassador would have the final say, the dissenters would be on record in the event that anything connected with the counterinsurgency team went wrong.

Four Special Action Forces came into being as the struggle continued—one on Okinawa built around the 1st Special Forces Group for the Far East (SAFASIA); one in Panama around the 8th Special Forces Group for Latin America; and two at Fort Bragg, organized around the new 3rd and 6th Groups for Africa and the Middle East.

In Europe, the 10th Special Forces Group, straining to meet its expanded role in the new climate of urgency and hoopla, assumed functions much like those of the large SAFs, but without their resources. The 10th, as a matter of fact, at this juncture was handed responsibility for an awesome chunk of new geography. In addition to Europe, it became responsible for North Africa, the Middle East, and South Asia as far east as Pakistan. (The 6th, at Fort Bragg, was eventually to take over most of the area outside Europe, but in the early days the 10th had to go it alone.)

I (the author) was in the 10th Group when word of the area of interest was received. I had been in the Group and the Forces two years as a B Detachment commander and later the Group S-3. Here was the challenge of a lifetime, an opportunity which seemed tailor-made for me. I was a bona fide expert on the Middle East, having attended the American University of Beirut and been the West Point Associate Professor of Middle Eastern History for two years. A new company was to be formed, starting from scratch. I wangled command of that company and was the first man assigned to it. Two companies of the 10th were designated to remain responsible for the old European guerrilla warfare role. I was given command of C Company and charged with building and training it to carry out counterinsurgency missions in that vast new area.

The company quickly grew to its authorized strength of 50

General Westmoreland meets troops of 1st SFG Scuba Detachment on Okinawa, 1971.

officers and 200 NCOs, and moved into an intensive training program. Besides the usual Special Forces training, the company gathered intelligence about the countries around the Mediterranean rim and beyond, and started language instruction in such tongues as Arabic, Urdu, Farsi, Greek, Turkish, and Pushto. In company with EUCOM and USAREUR representatives, the company commander toured the new region, explaining counterinsurgency and what SF had to offer countries worried about real or imagined insurgencies within their borders.

It was not long before we were accepting any mission that came to the 10th, or that we could dig up. In some cases, the counterinsurgency aspect was at best obscure. The value to long-range U.S. foreign policy was often doubtful. What I and my aggressive young officers achieved was an initial entrée, whatever the pretext, to an area of interest. Once local rapport had been achieved, evaluations would follow and better-defined missions would hopefully ensue. Meantime, the team members, acquiring firsthand area and language experience, were challenged enough to stay sharp. Even the old-timers in the outfit approved; they already knew the high value of close contact with different people and different cultures, of challenges in new and different lands.

The learning experiences were widly varied. In Jordan, Maj. Joe Callahan and his B team were directed to establish and run a paratroop school. While scouting for a proper location, Callahan asked to see some of his prospective trainees. Consider

Callahan's delight when a group of fine physical specimens breezed through a very tough obstacle course, hardly drawing a deep breath. Four weeks later, the school was opened and a bunch of ragtag, singularly uninspired Arabs showed up for the training. Where, Callahan asked in astonishment and dismay, were his earlier tigers? Well, that was the national soccer team, which the government had run through the paces to create a good first impression. Special Forces teams were used to unexpected obstacles, so jump school started with the new talent. It was rough for both the Arabs and the team, but the mission was a success. King Hussein, as enthusiastic as Kennedy, was on hand for the final graduation parachute drop and had to be dissuaded from donning a chute himself and making a jump. Mission accomplished. No one asked what foreign policy objective had been served—or, for example, how the whole thing looked from the Israeli side of the border.

An even more farfetched assignment for the 10th came early in 1963. The Royalist government of the tiny kingdom of Yemen had been overthrown in a Nasser-supported coup, and a new republican government was installed in Sana under President al-Salal. The son of the old king, Mohamad al-Badr, fled to the hills to fight a guerrilla war, in which he had the strong support of King Faisal of neighboring Saudi Arabia. With what must have appeared unseemly haste to both Mohamad al-Badr and Faisal, and for reasons that are not clear to this day, the United States was among the first to recognize the new republic.

Faisal, whose country possesses the richest oil fields on earth, bridled, and asked Washington for some visible proof of U.S. support for Saudi Arabia. Specifically, he asked that a battle group-sized airborne unit be dispatched to Saudi Arabia to perform public demonstration mass paratroop drops,and that a jet fighter squadron simultaneously perform flybys. Initially, Washington decided to use the Airborne Battle Group of the U.S. 8th Infantry Division in Germany to make the jumps. Clearer heads decided that once the aggressive young troopers were on the ground and in the midst of an utterly alien society, trouble could very predictably ensue. So our veteran troopers of the 10th Special Forces, virtually impervious to all kinds of cultural shock, were picked for the job.

The 250 men of my Company (C) were slated for jumps in Jiddah on the Red Sea and in Riyadh, the royal capital. In each case, we were to jump in coordination with the 800-man Air-borne Battalion of the Royal Saudi Army, an outfit based in Jiddah that had not jumped in over two years. The Jiddah jump came first on a drop zone, as flat and hard as an asphalt parking lot, east of the city. The local population turned out in air-conditioned pickup trucks and ringed the drop zone, but pressed in to gain better observation sites. When C Company jumped from three C-130s, the drop zone was little more than 1,000 yards long. Jumpers caromed off the roofs and hoods of the parked trucks, the lead and trailing jumpers in all-sticks landing outside the ring of vehicles on both sides of the DZ. The Saudis jumped next from nine C-123s, but, unfortunately, their Egyptian cotton parachutes had deteriorated from disuse. Three troopers came all the way in without benefit of deployed parachutes. As they did not wear reserve parachutes, the results were messy.

Somehow the Saudis got those troopers chuted up and loaded for the jump the next day in Riyadh. Having learned from the Jiddah jump, the Saudis had no vehicles near the drop zone, but the crowd was ten to twelve people thick and must have numbered over 100,000. I was the drop zone safety officer positioned in the upper third of the DZ. The C Company jump came off smoothly, forming up quickly and marching to the reviewing stand to be presented to the royal princes assembled there. The Saudi jump, miraculously, this time was also injury-free, despite a snappy wind across the drop zone. Then, un-expectedly, the three C-130s made another pass and dropped six 600-pound bundles of C rations in cargo parachutes with reefers with barometric release devices. The idea was to have the bundles parabola down with the chutes furled, then open 100 feet off the ground and land relatively softly. I watched in horror as the first two bundles came all the way in without deploying their parachutes, landing in the lower one-third of the drop zone. They burst on impact, spewing rations in every direction. The crowd broke ranks, running onto the DZ to scarf up the manna from heaven. The second two bundles landed behind me, in the open again, and again spewed rations, while the crowd ran onto the drop zone. The third pair of bundles, aimed directly at the upwind crowd, failed to deploy until the last possible second when both chutes popped, and the bundles floated over the crowd and landed softly outside the DZ. The crowd raided those bundles, and there was not a ration or scrap of parachute nylon or rigging to be found. Thanks, Allah, but did You have to do it the hard way?

Inevitably, a counterinsurgency mission for a C Company team, headed by Maj. William ("Peanut") Hinton, returned to Saudi Arabia a few months later to train 350 selected officers and NCOs in the very basic counterinsurgency subjects. As happened often in the Middle East, they first had to be taught to read maps and follow compass courses before they could advance to the more sophisticated subjects.

There were many other missions more worthwhile, better planned, and well executed. The 10th was making and developing contacts and establishing friendships that exist today in spite of official government hostility. In Iran, a U.S. MAAG "Otter" aircraft crashed high in the Zagros Mountains in January, killing all four crew members and passengers, officers of the MAAG. Iranian mountain climbers attempted to scale the mountains to retrieve the bodies, but the deep snow was too much for them. Members of the elite German Mountain Division were summoned to accomplish the mission, but they too failed. Finally, the MAAG turned to the 10th Special Forces Group and a twelve-man team headed by Capt. Herb Schandler and the legendary Lt. Larry Thorne (see Chapter 11) was sent to Iran to do the job. In a little over two weeks, they brought out the bodies and some radio equipment. This so impressed the head of the MAAG that he requested a mobile training team (MTT) from the 10th Group to work with the Iranian Special Forces Group, really little more than an airborne battalion employed by the Shah to bash heads in Teheran during the frequent mob scenes. An MTT of one B detachment and three A detachments traveled to the First Army area around Khermanshah for three months to train the barracks-bound First Army in field operations in the Kurdish Mountains. The mission ended with a joint demonstration for the Shah and his senior officers, and was followed by a major training mission every year until the stateside Middle Eastern Group took over the mission.

Capt. Steve Snowden, Lt. Rudy Fromm, and one tiny A team trained the entire nucleus of the Turkish Special Forces, including airborne qualification, Special Forces tradecraft, and scuba diving for selected Turkish officers. Otherwise courageous men, the Turks were terrified of salt water and petrified at the prospect of sharks. It was ludicrous to see the scuba instructors forcibly holding grown men's heads under the water in preparation for teaching them to swim, *before* they began the sophisticated scuba instruction. Never has one A detachment accomplished so much, building the equipment for an airborne course, conducting the course for 350 officers and noncoms, teaching a full-scale Special Forces course in classroom and field, and camping on the beach at Atalya and conducting water training. As was so often the case, they had the skillful and motivated support of a senior colonel at the MAAG in Ankara who provided wholehearted support. Without such support, missions such as Snowden's and Fromm's would have been quite impossible.

Capt. Mike Boos and his Baluchi-speaking detachment went to the hills and deserts of Pakistan to exercise with the highly qualified 19th Baluch Regiment of special warfare warriors. They came back with their tongues hanging out, as that regiment was famous for running from its summer camp back to its home garrison in less than twenty-four hours—that is a distance of 100 miles.

Most important of all, the troops were experiencing new problems in cross-cultural relationships, grappling with them, and coming away better equipped and more mature. They were learning again how important it was to get out in the hills to the people, away from the American advisory missions clustered in the capital cities.

8. SPECIAL MISSIONS: AFRICA, LATIN AMERICA

The program the Special Forces carried into Africa in the early '60s was, on the whole, well executed and well received. In the Congo, Cameroons, Guinea, Mali, Senegal, Kenya, and Ethiopia, teams ranging from one or two men to more than fifty took on a long list of training tasks. Few of the skills assembled for the Special Action Forces Africa back at Fort Bragg were not, in one country or another, called upon.

Some teams worked at conventional military jobs with conventional military forces, such as the seventy-two-man unit which provided basic training for Ethiopian Army recruits for six months in 1965. Another far smaller team of twelve men under the command of Lt. Col. James Vance, a long-time veteran of Special Forces and a totally unflappable officer, achieved a greater multiplier effect in the same country by providing counterinsurgency training for a handpicked group of fifty-two officers in 1968–69. As elsewhere in Africa, the Forces in Ethiopia functioned with little fanfare, often wearing no identifying patches, berets, or other insignia, sometimes remaining in civilian clothes. The deliberate and commendable low profile should not be allowed to obscure completely the story of an earlier, and hairier, SF mission in Africa, one that predated the era of counterinsurgency and the SAFs.

It was the summer of 1960, and in Bad Tolz, Col. "Iron Mike" Paulick, commanding officer of the 10th Special Forces Group, read with growing interest and dismay news stories about trouble in the Congo. On the heels of the former Belgian colony's independence on July 1 of that year, a wave of violence spread across the vast country. Some of it was random, some simply drunken, some occurred as rival groups fought for power, but much was directed at the remaining white community, particularly those in isolated areas and without means of protection or escape, many of them Americans.

There was no hint that the 10th would be involved, but Paulick called Lt. Sully Fontaine to his office. For a lieutenant,

Col. "Iron Mike" Paulick, CO, 10th SFG, 1958–62

Fontaine had a remarkable record of experience. A Belgian by birth, he had parachuted behind the Nazi lines in France for the British SOE during World War II. He spoke French better than English; furthermore, he had been commissioned in the Belgian Army and had served in the Congo. He had so conscientiously maintained his academic interest in the area that only a few nights before he had been a guest lecturer on the Congo at a Bad Tolz night class of the Overseas University of Maryland. Should the 10th be called upon to help in the Congo, Fontaine would obviously be a major asset, and Paulick told the lieutenant to put together a team and get ready to go.

Fontaine's personnel choices were typical of the Forces at the time: Sobiachevsky, a Russian; Yosich, who had led partisans in Korea; "Pop" Grant, an ex-Navy frogman; Stefan Mazak, the tough little Czech and ex-French Foreign Legionnaire; Capt. Jake Clement, sometimes known as "The Snake," a name derived from his jungle survival expertise; and Charles Hoskins, a weapons specialist who later posthumously won the Medal of Honor in Vietnam.

Two days later Paulick's hunch proved at least partly right. The 10th was ordered to send one French-speaking officer to

Leopoldville in the Congo, where U.S. Ambassador Timberlake was hastily gathering together what assets he could to help save American and European lives. By negotiating with USAREUR, the number in the team was increased to three, but no more. The hodgepodge team included three helicopters, the same number of light single-engine airplanes, pilots for all the craft, a couple of Army officers, an Air Force ham radio expert, and the SF trio from Bad Tolz. Fontaine selected Clement and Mazak to fill out his tiny team and flew off to Leopoldville under instructions to be prepared for anything. No one—least of all Clement, who was delighted to be along in any capacity—questioned an arrangement in which a lieutenant was in command of a captain. Such formalities as rank concerned the Forces very little, and besides, Fontaine was the man with the language and area know-how, though all three spoke French.

The mission very nearly came to a disastrous end almost from the start. Their aircraft touched down first at the wrong Congo airfield, one covered at that moment with wildly shooting rebels. They were saved only by the fact that Fontaine had on the earphones and could understand the verbalized consternation of a French-speaking tower operator trying to locate an aircraft that claimed to be already on the ground. Their plane took off in a fusillade of typically wild gunfire. The second time around they got down on the right field.

In a brief meeting with Ambassador Timberlake, Fontaine and his men got their mission precisely defined. Where large, reasonably secure airfields were available, Belgian planes and paratroops would be in charge of evacuation; in areas with minimal airstrips, or none at all, the Special Forces and their little planes would have to do the job.

The little task group worked out a simple procedure. Where possible, the aircraft were to work in pairs, only one being designated to land until the situation was scouted on the ground. If no fire was received, one SF trooper, dressed in civilian clothes and carrying no weapons except concealed grenades, was to get out of the plane and move toward the expected evacuees. If possible, a second trooper would cover the first from the plane with a submachine gun while the pilot remained ready for instant takeoff. Simple signals were worked out for contingencies: "If I take my hat off and scratch my head with my left hand, start shooting." If no shooting was necessary and all else appeared well, the second plane could land and evacuation would proceed.

Despite a few minor shooting scrapes and a few holes in the aircraft, things were going pretty smoothly until a special situation forced a change in procedure. Receiving word of a group of refugees in desperate straits, Fontaine took off in haste to find out what help would be needed. The light plane put him down at a small strip at Gwendje and then took off to orbit a safe distance away. Fontaine, carrying a portable radio and his hidden grenade, made his way on foot to the nearby village. There a white priest told him twelve refugees, including six nuns who had been raped and badly needed medical attention, awaited evacuation. Cutting them off from the outside world were about fifty heavily armed rebel troops, still looting and burning nearby.

Fontaine coaxed enough out of his portable radio to reach Mazak who was ten miles away. His plea was brief: Round up a platoon of Belgian paratroopers and get to Gwendje fast! The two rescue aircraft were to circle the Gwendje strip, but were not to land until signaled. Mazak acknowledged, and Fontaine rounded up the refugees and headed for the airfield.

It proved to be no sanctuary. A horde of screaming rebel troops brandishing weapons of every description and firing wildly at real and imaginary targets immediately descended on them. Fontaine singled out the biggest and meanest-looking, who seemed to be loosely in charge, walked up to him, and asked him to step to one side with him. "Okay," said the self-styled major, "but makes no difference—all whites must be killed."

Fontaine jerked the grenade from his pocket, pulled the pin and handed the pin to the major. "If you shoot me, my friend, I will die, but we will most certainly die together." For two incredible hours, while the refugees and rebels alike stared in tense silence, the confrontation continued. The light pressure of the grenade firing lever against Fontaine's hand became almost unbearable. The bluff was not going to work.

Suddenly there was a tremendous commotion in the nearby bush. Stefan Mazak charged like a five-foot-two-inch bull elephant out of the brush and into the center of the mob, firing his submachine gun into the air and bellowing imprecations in foul legionnaire French. With the major's attention distracted,

Fontaine chucked his grenade toward the mob. With the explosion, the rebels panicked and fled. The refugees were airborne within minutes. Mazak apologized for the dramatics, but explained that he just couldn't wait for the slowpoke Belgian paratroopers to effect the rescue.

Nine days after their arrival, the SF trio had completed their assignment. The count was impressive: 239 refugees had been evacuated without a single casualty.

The Congo mission was obviously neither a guerrilla nor a counterinsurgency job, but typical of the many "special" tasks that the Forces were given because they had a pool of diverse and exotic talent, and because they earned a reputation for getting the job done with imagination and quiet dispatch.

Political warfare, of which guerrilla warfare is one example, has basically been an endless process in Latin America. There is no formal victory as in a total war, nor even an armistice to end the hostilities. It ebbs and flows; tactics, causes, and personalities change. Latin governments have been fragile things, coup-ridden and lacking in any real appeal to the people. This is because the basic loyalty, and hatred, of Latins has been toward individuals rather than institutions or ideologies. "Personalismo" is the word used to describe this orientation, but it explains the fact that the history of almost every country has been a case of one dictatorship after another.

Castro caught the imagination and admiration of the Cuban people, and Batista collapsed. It took only a few successes, and very few guerrillas were involved. Castro remains a threat to all of Latin America as an individual, not because of his communist ideology. But Ché Guevara could not pull off the trick in Bolivia in spite of all the romance associated with his name. He was a foreigner (Argentine), couldn't communicate with the Indians who spoke only Quechua, and he had no successes before he was killed.

The "machismo" the Latins admire was exemplified by a story about General Barrientos of Bolivia. As a young general, he watched a parachute jump put on by a handful of poorly trained parachutists using freefall parachutes. More than one never pulled his rip cord, but instead came all the way in. Barrientos, realizing that everyone was in shock by that tragic affair, went over, took a parachute off one of the dead exjumpers, and made his first parachute jump—successfully— with the chute. That is "machismo" personified!

The insurgent movements in Latin America have been quite small in comparison with that organized by the Vietcong. Further, they have tended to be fragmented, sometimes having communist insurgents oriented toward Russia, China, and Cuba, with no cooperation between the three groups. There are also right-wing insurgents who fight both government and communists. Only rarely is there an infrastructure in support of guerrilla movements. The Asiatic communist organizational genius has been notably lacking in Latin American insurgencies. However, most Latin American armies are old, well-established organizations that have been running their countries since they gained independence from Spain and Portugal in 1810–25. Before World War II, these armies were accustomed to getting foreign military advisors and assistance, usually German, and had some well-trained elements. In comparison to European and Asiatic armies, however, they are relatively small. Many of their problems spring from obsolescence and lack of technical and managerial skills.

The insurgency movements, nevertheless, have been responsible for the deaths of hundreds of thousands of people. In Colombia alone during the 1960s, casualties were estimated at over 250,000 people. They have also been expensive, both in terms of economic dislocations and in the cost to the governments fighting the insurgencies. The recent counterinsurgency effort in El Salvador has set government back in economic terms and in political support from the populace which had high hopes for the new government. U.S. military and economic aid, as well as a very limited U.S. military advisory presence, has been deemed necessary to assist in the stabilizing of that unhappy situation.

In 1961, the Special Warfare Center noted that no Special Forces were operating in Latin America, despite the prevalence of insurgency. To alleviate the situation, the Military Groups in each Country Team in Latin America (except Mexico, Haiti, and Cuba) were surveyed, and detachments were prepared and dispatched from the groups at Fort Bragg, specifically the 7th SF Group. At the same time, preparations were made to activate a new group in the Panama Canal Zone, to be designated the 8th Special Forces Group (Airborne) 1st Special Forces, Special

Action Force.

The 7th Special Forces Group was directed to prepare and dispatch a Headquarters and Headquarters Detachment, Company D and selected augmentation detachments for assignment to the Canal Zone. In January 1962, a Special Forces survey team arrived in the Canal Zone to inspect several potential sites for the planned Special Action Force. Fort Gulick was the logical choice, for it is the home of the U.S. Army School of the Americas attended by Latin American military students. The move was made during the summer of 1962. The nucleus of the new SAF was consolidated at Fort Gulick under the command of Lt. Col. John H. Sawyer. In January 1963, Lt. Col. Arthur D. ("Bull") Simons took command, and on 1 April 1963, was given its new designation. The exploits of the 8th SFG over the following ten years until its demise can be termed as an outstanding success. Although insurgency was not really eliminated anywhere, there was a great reduction in the effectiveness of rural insurgency.

The U.S. government's answer to the challenge of Castro, backed by the promises of support Khrushchev gave was twofold: active support and membership in the Alliance for Progress, and the Military Assistance Program. The 8th SAF was but a part of the overall program which included virtually all federal departments of the U.S. government, as well as other agencies of the U.S. Army, such as the School of the Americas and the 3rd Civil Affairs Group. The 8th SAF played an important part in those activities by sending varying types of detachments to work in member nations of the Alliance for Progress under the auspices and sponsorship of the local Country Team and Military Group. The ambassador of the United States in each of those nations was in overall charge of the U.S. effort and had much to say on the degree of U.S. involvement.

Both in numbers and variety, Special Forces missions in Latin America have been notable. Between early 1963 and 1970, the peak period, nearly 500 SF training or assistance teams were dispatched to nineteen countries. The number of Latin Americans who received Special Forces training was well up in six figures; in 1965 alone, 285 busy SF troopers managed to instruct more than 41,000 military men in Latin America.

There are good reasons for the special responsiveness of the countries of the south. Virtually all contain the seeds of insurgency or revolution: small, extremely wealthy upper classes with ostentatious styles of life and lack of social consciousness juxtaposed against the grinding poverty of the rest of the population, high rates of unemployment, corruption in government, inequitable land ownership, rural areas so backward they have changed little in five centuries, birthrates which consistently outstrip economic growth, and above all, growing demands for progress—the familiar pattern of revolution. In such an environment, it is noteworthy only when some form of resistance to the government does *not* exist. With or without Castro in Cuba exporting revolutions and providing a blueprint, most of the nations of Latin America during the 1960s felt themselves astride individual and collective powder kegs.

Relations between the U.S. Army and its Latin counterparts had been quite cordial during most of that time. Their officers were trained at West Point and other U.S. service academies, at the Command and General Staff College at Leavenworth, and at the School of the Americas. At the joint and international level, they came together at the Inter-American War College at Fort McNair, District of Columbia.

Thus several interrelated factors all but guaranteed that the 8th Special Forces Group and its Special Action Force would find plenty of work and cooperative hosts once they had reached operational readiness in 1963. Before that year was out, medics from the SAF had joined with Bolivian doctors and health workers in alleviating that country's epidemic of hemorrhagic fever, the virulent and mysterious killer which had nearly crippled U.S. units in Korea. The death toll had reached 300, and an entire province was in a state of near panic before SF medics helped implement a drastic and successful program of rodent control and food protection.

Down almost the entire length of the Andes, engineers from the SAF helped their host countries open up previously isolated or all but impenetrable areas. They built bridges, roads, airstrips, and ferries, frequently remaining to instruct in their operation and maintenance. At the other end of the climatic and topographical scale, in sweltering Honduras, what certainly must have been one of the most versatile Special Forces teams of all time played a highly effective part in 1965 in a joint U.S.–Honduran civic action, a vocational and technical assistance program. Consisting of only some thirty officers and men, it offered instruction in agriculture, food processing, veterinary medicine, sanitary engineering, automotive mechanics, diesel engines, radio and television repair, welding, industrial machinery, electricity, and refrigeration. The training was offered without distinction to military and civilian students. Those who demonstrated leadership qualities and instructional ability received special attention and schooling, as well as lesson plans, training aid diagrams, and reference data booklets. On a cost-effectiveness basis, or on any terms, it was one of the best run and most serviceable programs in the history of U.S. aid, military or otherwise.

As editors and publishers, troopers of the Latin American SAF's Psychological Operations battalion also proved effective. To fill a need for such information in Panama, they developed a "Guia Del Campesino," a sort of farmer's guide, aimed directly at the rural populace. It contained lively tips on how to better the quality and increase production of crops and livestock, how to maintain farm tools and equipment, and it provided simple and easily implemented suggestions for first aid, child care, and sanitation. When distributed by the Guardia Nacional, it did an adroit job of helping establish rapport between government forces and the Panamanian peasantry. So successful was this project that eight other Latin American countries later invited Special Forces to develop something like it for them.

More conventional military missions were also served. The Special Forces trained teams of special light infantry units—Lanceros, Cazadores, Rangers—for counterguerrilla operations throughout the continent. It was such a team, Maj. Ralph ("Pappy") Shelton's Ranger training mission to Bolivia in 1967, that, ironically but typically, drew more attention than all the rest of the efforts in Latin America combined. Shelton and his team trained companies of Bolivian Rangers in counterguerrilla operations in the Andes. Eleven days after they graduated, one company cornered the elusive Ché Guevara and killed him during the course of his capture, or shortly thereafter. That single event struck a crippling blow at Cuban-exported revolution in the Americas, though by no means shutting it down.

The peak year for SF activities in Latin America was 1966, when almost 100 missions were in the field. Since then, there has been a steady decline both in numbers and scope, a development traceable in part to a rising sense of both nationalism and anti-Americanism in many Latin American countries. But in many cases, the mission has been accomplished; the Forces, as they are intended to do, simply worked themselves out of a job.

Unfortunately, the reaction against the Vietnam War had shock effects on American involvement everywhere, and nowhere has that shown up more clearly than in congressional appropriations for military aid to Latin America. U.S. military assistance for Latin nations fell from a high of $81 million in fiscal year 1966 to $16 million by fiscal year 1971. While the SF missions come cheap, they still must compete for every dollar they get with other parts of the assistance program, including the purchase of tanks, artillery, and jet aircraft. The fact that most of the nations receiving such weapons have little, if any, real need for them, and must, in fact, divert scarce resources needed for social improvements in order to acquire and operate those expensive toys, has been too often ignored by donor and recipient alike.

So the dollar competition for the low-silhouette, civic-oriented Latin American programs of the Special Forces has been, but is not likely to remain, tough. Only their demonstrated effectiveness, particularly in those countries where the Forces were invited in *before* internal dissidence rose to the active guerrilla or insurgency level, seems to offer a chance for their survival in Latin America in the years ahead.

Of course, the 8th Special Forces Group is off the books today, together with the Asia SAF, the Middle Eastern SAF, and the African SAF. The mood of America in the early 1970s made that an easy decision for the policymakers in the Pentagon, most of whom thought Special Forces a waste of perfectly good personnel spaces in the first place. The job in Panama continues with a battalion of the 7th Special Forces Group carrying on in the tradition of the 8th Special Forces, but the 8th did an impressive job in its relatively brief life span. At this writing, there is a high likelihood of a reactivation of the 8th SFG for duty in Latin America.

9. LAOS AND THAILAND

There is a good deal of Southeast Asia, it is sometimes difficult for Americans to remember, outside Vietnam. And Special Forces has been active in most of it.

The SF commitment in Asia dates back to 1954 when a team from Fort Bragg's old 77th Special Forces Group was dispatched to Thailand. For six months it trained the Royal Thai Rangers, the forerunners of today's Thai Special Forces. The little 14th Special Forces Detachment from Hawaii later carried out comparable missions in Taiwan, Vietnam, and Thailand. By June 1957, the 1st Special Forces Group had been activated on Okinawa. For the next three years, its teams helped develop and expand counterpart special units in the armed forces of Korea, South Vietnam, Taiwan, and the Philippines. In keeping with the military thinking of that day, those were guerrilla warfare units tailored for behind-the-lines activities in an essentially conventional conflict. Despite the writings and success of Mao, despite the experiences in Malaya, the Philippines, and in Vietnam itself, the need for counterinsurgency training had not yet been recognized.

It was in Laos, that misty little kingdom of 3.7 million gentle souls, that Americans took some first tentative steps in counterinsurgency. That effort remains to this day clouded with confusion and secrecy, and in some ways, it is just as well that it is so. In spite of courageous and imaginative efforts by individuals and small groups, the incredible inconsistency of U.S. policy, as well as the tortuous and inept implementations of its decisions, defies description.

The Special Forces' effort in Laos was not immune to the disease. In July 1959, the State Department and the CIA were running the shadowy U.S. efforts to help Lao Royalists or Lao Neutralists fight off the Pathet Lao guerrillas and their North Vietnamese masters. Security was so tight that SF troopers who served in Laos in those early days are still, as a matter of conditioning, reluctant to discuss their mission there. Yet while the citizens of the United States knew nothing about the assignment of Special Forces troops to the little Asian country, their presence was common knowledge in Vientiane, the capital of Laos, and in such other widely scattered spots as Hanoi, Moscow, Peking, Paris, and Fort Bragg.

Elaborate precautions to disguise the identity of the troopers were taken, but clandestine operations have never been a long suit for the United States. They were, to put it in the kindest light, ineffective. Gen. John A. Heintges and all other American military personnel in Laos were dropped from military rolls, and they donned civilian clothes. A fictitious organization, the Programs Evaluation Office (PEO), was set up for them with "Mr." Heintges as director. It was to the PEO that the first SF troopers were assigned in the summer of 1959. They were carefully smuggled into Laos from Bangkok aboard Air America, a CIA "airline," and disembarked in Vientiane wearing sports shirts and slacks. It was a magnificent bust: no sooner were they on the ground than Radio Hanoi trumpeted that "the United States has invaded Laos."

But the charade was continued for two more years, fooling no one, of course, with the possible exception of the U.S. public, which didn't know anything about Laos anyway. At PEO headquarters in Vientiane, one SF veteran recalls that the use of military commands, such as "Reveille, you guys, everybody out of the sack," would have allowed penetration of the PEO cover by somebody less than a sophisticated enemy intelligence agent. Reality arrived in 1961, when the PEO was converted back into a conventional Military Assistance Group. The playacting came to an end, and the troops went back into uniform. That burst of candor did not last long, for in 1962 the Geneva Accords called for the removal of all foreign military from Laos. The shadow war reverted once more to the CIA.

Before that happened, the so-called Special Forces White Star mobile training team enjoyed some success, suffered some failures, and was exposed to many of the frustrations and problems that were later to afflict the Special Forces in Vietnam. The 107 SF troops, who joined the PEO in Vientiane in the summer of 1959, were in Laos primarily to train regular units of the Laotian Army. As the French had learned before them, that was a singularly difficult and exasperating role, for the

Lao, given their natural bent, have little stomach for soldiering and even less for war. They are a gentle and noncombative people who much prefer fiestas and lovemaking to fighting.

The original plan called for a Special Forces A team of twelve men to be assigned to each of twelve Royal Laotian battalions in the field. There they were to stiffen and improve training, generally keep an eye on the military and political situations in their areas, and report to their superiors in Vientiane. They were to prepare to lead the Laotian soldiers in guerrilla roles if overrun by the Pathet Lao, and, last but not least, they were to try like hell to capture a North Vietnamese soldier to prove what everyone in Laos knew was a fact.

It looked all right on paper, but like so many American plans for Indochina, was something else in implementation. For political, military, and economic reasons, many of the SF troopers found it possible to spend very little time with Lao battalions in the field, but a good deal of time training replacements for them in or near headquarters towns. A more serious problem for Lt. Col. Arthur ("Bull") Simons, the first White Star commander, was the fact that he had too many chiefs to please: the CIA, the PEO, the Lao government, the U.S. State Department as represented by the American embassy in Vientiane, and even the French army advisors who remained the only "legal" foreign military mission in Laos. Inevitably, Simons found that when he pleased one master, he more often than not infuriated the others. That he managed to get anything done at all was remarkable.

While the shadow CIA control of the American slice of the Laotian war was one of the complications with which Simons had to learn to live, it is also true that it was the intelligence agency which first identified the potential of such tribal minorities as the Black Thai, the Meo, and the Kha for the fight against the Pathet Lao. Typically, the Communists had moved in that direction much earlier. Souphanouvong, the "Red Prince" of Laos, acquired the services of two great tribal leaders in the early 1950s, but no one on the other side paid much attention to the development. When Special Forces entered the scene, the Royal Laotian Army was still largely ignoring the minorities.

With CIA-gathered intelligence and insight into the tribes in hand, SF half-teams of six men edged out into the highlands

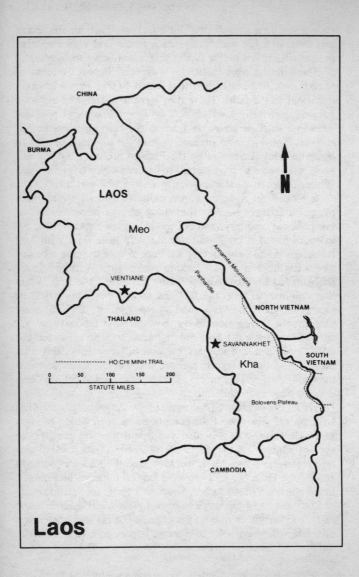

Laos

of Laos, living there under incredibly primitive conditions, to train and organize the Meo tribesmen in guerrilla warfare. The tough little tribesmen, traditionally deeply scorned by the wealthier, more civilized lowland Laotians, took to the training and to their SF trainers. That was the beginning of a long love affair between the "savages" of the Indochina highlands and the men of the Special Forces. Eventually, the highlanders formed an army of approximately 30,000 men under Meo Maj. Gen. Vang Pao. For years, that army was the most effective fighting force in Laos, until the Communists overran the country in the 1970s. It is to the credit of Simons and his successors, as well as the CIA, that the Meo training program succeeded so well despite the complications and contradictions of policy and command in Laos.

A later, somewhat similar program with the Kha tribes, also Simons' brainchild, was started when he returned to Laos in 1961 for a second tour in command of the White Stars. Although not as warlike as the Meo, the Kha occupied a strategically critical area in Laos, their tribal homelands stretching eastward across the Bolovens Plateau to the Annamite Mountains and the border of Vietnam. This is the Laotian Panhandle, the rolling, jungle country that was later to become well known as the location of the southern extension of the Ho Chi Minh Trail. If an effective guerrilla force could be organized from among the 10,000 Kha, Simons reasoned, it might clear the Pathet Lao from the productive Bolovens Plateau, put a stop to the exploitation of the tribesmen as porters or fighters by the Vietcong, and raise distinct hell with the Communist supply lines from North to South Vietnam.

Remembering more painful lessons from his first Laotian stint, Simons asked for and received authority to run the Bolovens show on his own. The CIA would provide support, its Air America planes and helicopters moving men and supplies to otherwise inaccessible areas. Other agencies would keep hands off. The SF troopers were precisely where they wanted to be—on their own. In the remarkably short period of six months, five Special Forces A teams, a total of only sixty men, recruited, armed, and trained about 600 Kha. They formed simple, light infantry companies and developed fast-moving tactics that leaned heavily on surprise. Quietly, without fanfare or notice, they cleared the Pathet Lao from the Bolovens. Simons was ready to push on to the east, toward the Vietnam border.

But, on 23 July 1962, the foreign ministers of the countries represented at the Geneva negotiations on Laos signed a protocol. It set 7 October as the withdrawal date for all foreign military personnel in the kingdom. Out of an estimated 10,000 North Vietnamese soldiers then in Laos, about 40 checked out through the control points set up by the International Control Commission. The North Vietnamese and the Vietcong must have been utterly astounded when *all* the U.S. Military Assistance Group and *all* of the Special Forces in the White Star program packed up and went home.

The Kha program, sadly, died on the vine. The CIA continued to work with the Meo, and although many an old White Star hand joined the Agency and continued to work in civilian clothes, to all effects and purposes the Special Forces program in the kingdom came to an end early in October 1962.

Operation White Star is a classic example of a successful operation run on a shoestring. The multiplier effect has never been more plain. A small number of dedicated professionals produced thousands of effective guerrillas who operated in their native environment, using tactics suitable to the terrain and the enemy disposition. Such an operation does not need the huge logistical infrastructure the U.S. Army erected for the Vietnam War, it does not require hundreds of thousands of American boys who do not know the first thing about jungle warfare, and it does not attract the attention of news-hungry media men in search of the shocking and spectacular.

In neighboring Thailand, the SF role was longer-lived. Since the first small detachment helped train the Royal Thai Rangers in 1954, there was an almost continuous Special Forces presence in the country. As "Bull" Simons was the central figure in the early days of Laos, Col. Bob Bartelt was the chief driving force of the Forces in Thailand. He was a slender, soft-spoken, bespectacled officer whose low-key and almost diffident manner made him tremendously successful in dealing with Orientals. His quiet facade concealed a dedicated, objective professional who became one of the Army's true experts on Southeast Asia. Bartelt, who joined the Special Forces in 1954, first went to Thailand in 1957. He was bitten deeply by the

SGT. Maj. Graham, LTC Beckwith, Col. Simpson, LTC Johnson, CSM Vierck, Thailand, 1970

"Asia bug," and he served in that area almost continuously for twenty years, including tours in Okinawa, the Philippines, Taiwan, Vietnam, and, of course, Thailand. Bartelt returned to the United States for a brief assignment at Fort Bragg late in the summer of 1969, but it didn't last long. By the following May, he was back in Southeast Asia as an advisor to the Thai Division fighting in Vietnam.

Under his leadership, the 46th Special Forces Company for four years provided, with the exception of a few small projects handled by the ubiquitous CIA, all of the counterinsurgency and much of the conventional combat training for Thai armed forces. His SF teams were spread from the Malayan border to the Mekong River in the northeast. One of his biggest projects, though scarcely the type of job envisioned for the SF by the planners, was the training of the Royal Thai Regiment (later expanded to a full division), dispatched to fight in Vietnam.

The old pros who volunteered to accompany Bob Bartelt to Thailand did their diverse and unglamorous jobs well, but always with a sense of anticipation, followed by disappointment. When the outfit had been formed back at Bragg, the word was out that SF in Thailand would have a secret mission back into Laos. It was never revealed in detail, but the unconventional warfare proponents visualized small teams of U.S. and Thai Special Forces joining with tribal elements in Laos to harass and raid the Vietcong supply routes and base areas along the Ho Chi Minh Trail. The 46th Company co-located with the

Thai Special Forces Brigade and erected powerful communications capable of reaching unconventional warfare teams anywhere in Southeast Asia, as well as far into China. The possibility of disrupting the comfortable VC sanctuary appealed to the old guerrilla warfare hands, but the plan died aborning. CIA and the State Department had things sewed up (though not too well under control) in the little kingdom across the Mekong, and Operation Golden Eagle never flew.

Other SF programs in Thailand did. Specialists sent from the Special Action Force on Okinawa to handle the noncombat elements of counterinsurgency gave the program new breadth and depth. Troops from SAFASIA's 539th Engineer Detachment and 156th Medical Detachment, wearing civilian clothes and working under the direction of U.S. AID, trained hundreds of Thais in road building, the operation and maintenance of heavy equipment, public health, sanitation, and medical care. More often than not, the SF teams consisted of two NCOs living in remote villages in guerrilla-plagued Northeast Thailand. With minimum supervision or support, they went about their distinctly unglamorous tasks with singular devotion. Progress was often slow and frustrations were monumental, ranging from governmental indifference and occasional outright interference, to communist assassination of villagers who worked with the Americans. The difficulties seemed to have small effect on SF troopers; there were always more volunteers for the assignments than there were requirements.

Bartelt built a solid foundation in Thailand, but the SF program there was doomed to suffer the same fate as that in nearby Vietnam. The 46th Company was demobilized in place, as was the SAFASIA on Okinawa. Today, Thailand faces enemies outside her borders and insurgent guerrillas within, including the notorious Chinese terrorists on the Malaysian border. Vietnamese troops and artillery line the Cambodian-Thai border with occasional incursions by fire into Thailand. The infamous domino effect has often been discredited, but is alive and visible in Southeast Asia today. Unfortunately, almost nobody cares, a legacy of the biggest American commitment in Asia—Vietnam.

10. VIETNAM: CIDG (CIVILIAN IRREGULAR DEFENSE GROUP); THE KATU AND THE BRU

Of course, it was Vietnam, America's most controversial international adventure, that really brought Special Forces to the attention of the American public. Intriguing and interesting though Special Forces activities had been elsewhere in the world, the American public understandably has rarely been interested in the peacetime activities of the nation's military forces. The Laotian commitment had not appeared in the media of the United States, and even the early Vietnam involvement attracted little attention as Special Forces operated with its customary secrecy. Wives of soldiers serving in Indochina in the early '60s told of being asked, "Oh, your husband is in Vietnam? That's nice. Does he get home for the weekends?" SF still enjoyed a certain anonymity, in spite of the misguided efforts of Pentagon and Fort Bragg publicists. The label "Green Beret" had not become current, and Special Forces was often confused with Special Services (the Army's soldier entertainment organization).

Ultimately, the commitment in Vietnam became too big to ignore, and a few other factors helped catapult Special Forces into the front pages. Capt. Roger Donlon was awarded the first Medal of Honor of the war for his heroic leadership in the defense of a Special Forces camp called Nam Dong. Writer Robin Moore published a fictionalized account of Special Forces' activities in Vietnam, heavily larded with blood, gore, sex, and derring-do. It soared to the top of the best-seller lists and made "Green Berets" a household word. John Wayne and company put Moore's book (more or less) on film, moving yet one step further from reality and putting the action into glowing technicolor amid the pine trees of Fort Benning, Georgia, with a cast of "Vietnamese" extras left over from *Custer's Last Stand*. A young guitar-playing Special Forces medic, Sgt. Barry

Sadler, followed with a hit song, "The Ballad of the Green Beret," which had such lyrics as "Silver wings on my son's chest, Mean he's one of America's best." An obscure Army doctor with antiwar views hit the headlines as the martyr in a trial for refusing to "teach war crimes" to SF medics.

All of this certainly put Special Forces in the limelight, though the image was pretty far removed from actuality. Worse yet, the spotlight hurt SF within the Armed Forces. Many resented the excessive coverage given to "Green Berets," and understandably, though erroneously, blamed SF for seeking publicity. The Chief of Staff of the Army, Gen. Harold K. Johnson, very much of the colorless, moralistic, anti-elitist breed, became a strong foe of Special Forces and made his enmity felt. Many others, some in high places, shared his stand.

Can the full story of Special Forces in Vietnam be told? What is a fair assessment of what they accomplished? Can the SF contribution be evaluated separately, intertwined as it was with the far larger political, economic, and military forces? All of these are valid questions. Naturally some few aspects remain highly classified and may never be revealed. To try to assess the U.S. involvement in Vietnam is certainly beyond the scope of this book. However, the story of SF can still be told, and perhaps because the truth is so far from the popular image, it needs telling.

The first Special Forces missions to Vietnam were not too different from those conducted in so many other parts of the world in the 1950s, before counterinsurgency became both a popular word and an assigned mission for SF. All over Asia, mobile training teams had helped friendly nations develop their own special forces, and it was not surprising to find the tiny 14th Special Forces Detachment committed to such a role in Vietnam. Overall U.S. participation in Indochina, though quiet, had been by no means small. As a silent partner of the French, America had provided very nearly a billion dollars prior to the fall of Dien Bien Phu in 1954.

After 1954 and the Geneva Accords, U.S. aid became direct and started its long upward trend. The early MAAG in Vietnam was not concerned with insurgency or revolution and busied itself instead with repeating a recent success. American advice and money went toward building a conventional army to repel a Korean-style invasion from the north. The SF mission fell in line with this concept and helped to build an offensive guerrilla warfare capability, the Vietnamese Special Forces.

It was on one of those early missions that Capt. "Hair-breadth" Harry Cramer, on temporary duty from 1st SFG on Okinawa, was killed near Nha Trang in October 1957. It was a training accident, but it is interesting to note that the training was on the ambush, specifically on how to ambush, not on how to counter this classic guerrilla technique.

In the late 1950s, too, Sam Amato took a team to Vietnam from the 77th Special Forces Group at Fort Bragg. This detachment and its successors trained the beginnings of the Vietnamese Army Rangers. It was a highly successful program, and in later years, Vietnamese Ranger Battalions proved to be among the best of the Army of the Republic of Vietnam (ARVN) infantry units.

As time went on and the pattern of the war and the U.S. involvement changed, Special Forces in Vietnam were to find themselves in a number of different roles and missions. Far eclipsing all the other SF activities in both size and scope was the so-called Civilian Irregular Defense Group (CIDG) program. In the conduct of that unique program over a period of nine years, Special Forces became involved in every conceivable aspect of counterinsurgency: military, economic, psychological, and political. The saga of the CIDG program involved thousands of U.S. Special Forces soldiers and hundreds of thousands of Vietnamese civilians, millions of dollars, and approximately 100 camps spread from the Demilitarized Zone to the Gulf of Siam. It is the story of countless small skirmishes and some big bloody battles, of carving isolated camps out of the jungle or trying to prop them up out of the delta floods. It is a story of teaching Vietnamese how to shoot, or build, or farm, or care for the sick, or run agent operations, and of dealing with the religious and ethnic minorities of Vietnam— the Montagnards, the Cambodians, the Hoa Hao, and the Cao Dai. It is a story of cooperation and conflict with the CIA, LLDB (South Vietnamese Special Forces), MAAG, MACV (Military Assistance Command Vietnam), AID, SOG (Special Operations Group), Vietnamese province officials, and American combat unit commanders. It has been praised and reviled by Americans and Vietnamese alike. It was on the verge of being destroyed many times, not only by the VC, but by its

Typical CIDG Honor Guard, Vietnam

American creators. Believers and supporters kept the program alive for a long time, but finally in 1970, as planned since 1966, the program was Vietnamized and the Americans later withdrew and returned to Fort Bragg.

In the overall context of the Vietnam War, it was certainly a relatively small operation, at least small in size and in cost, but it had within it the germs of counterinsurgency success. It is a large part of the Special Forces story. More than that, however, it shows in its successes and failures how and why we failed in Vietnam and, perhaps, how we might have succeeded.

The Civilian Irregular Defense Group program was a U.S. Army Special Forces operation from start to finish, but it is the Central Intelligence Agency and not the military that earned the credit for conceiving and starting the program. It was indeed the military who later converted it (or, as some believe, perverted it) and who finally Vietnamized it.

The idea for the CIDG program was born in 1961, at a time when the level of hostilities in Vietnam was still relatively low. The Vietcong (a contraction of Vietnamese Communists) were concentrating their activities on the rural population, and armed

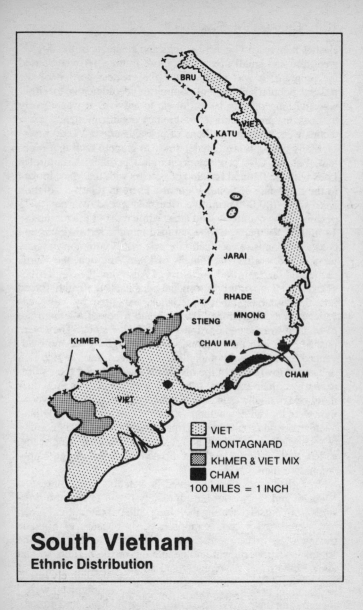

BRU

VIET

KATU

JARAI

RHADE

MNONG

STIENG

KHMER

CHAU MA

CHAM

VIET

VIET
MONTAGNARD
KHMER & VIET MIX
CHAM
100 MILES = 1 INCH

South Vietnam
Ethnic Distribution

clashes between VC guerrilla units and elements of the ARVN were rare and small in size. To those in the CIA who started the program, it was obvious that the greatest portion of the peasant population was not committed ideologically to either side, wishing only to be left alone to survive. It was equally obvious that propaganda, revolutionary organization, and terror tactics were bringing millions of peasants under VC control.

Many concepts were under study to grapple with that problem, but the CIA originators, mindful perhaps of failure in Laos with the flatland Lao and of success with the Meo, looked to the highlands of South Vietnam. There in relative isolation lived some 700,000 primitive tribesmen spread over nearly 75 percent of the country's land area, while most of the remaining 14 million Vietnamese were jammed into the fertile deltas and coastal lowlands. The situation is one that is common in many parts of the world. The Indians of Latin America, the Kurds in the Middle East, the aborigines of Australia, the Naga tribes of India—all are primitive, original inhabitants ultimately forced into the less hospitable hinterlands, exploited by more advanced, later migrations. The highland tribes of Vietnam are of Malayo-Polynesian or Mon-Khmer ethnic stock. They were pushed back into the highlands centuries ago by the more advanced Sino-Mongol populations that moved into the rice-rich deltas and lowlands. In the highlands they retained their primitive ways, their elaborate tribal and social structures, and their thirty-odd mutually unintelligible dialects. Throughout the years, they were looked down upon as "moi" (savages) by the flatland Vietnamese and treated as inferior human beings, to say nothing of second-class citizens. The French, and later the Americans, called them Montagnards, a French term meaning simply "mountain men."

In earlier times they had lived in isolation from the rest of Vietnam and the world, but ultimately began to feel the pressures from outside. During their long colonial reign, the French had established a certain rapport, partly because of humane treatment by missionaries, but mostly because they kept the Vietnamese government and people out of the highlands, and allowed the tribal government and people a certain amount of autonomy. During the Indochina War the French GCMAs (Groupment Commando Mixte Aeroporte), special forces-type teams, enjoyed considerable success in organizing and leading

Montagnard guerrilla units against the Viet Minh.

After the signing of the Geneva Accords and the departure of the French, Vietnamese moves into the highlands caused real problems. First came the refugee settlements of the Diem government which seized the best land, brought taxes, and outlawed the crossbow. Then came the VC seeking sources of food, recruits, labor, and intelligence. The Montagnards saw little that appealed to them in either group, avoided both when possible, and went along when they had no other choice. Too often it was the VC who succeeded in building and developing their guerrilla bases and lines of communication.

The CIA planners saw the threat and the opportunity to step into the role vacated by the French, but they probably overlooked a major difference. The French were engaged in a policy of divide-and-conquer to preserve colonial rule in their own right. The United States was attempting to launch a program to help South Vietnam unite and stabilize all of its diverse political, ethnic, and religious factions. Certainly, the Montagnards did not see the distinction and warmly welcomed these new "round eyes" as protectors from the hated flatland Vietnamese. The Americans found the "yards" enormously appealing and vastly preferred the simple, rugged honesty of the highlanders to the more wily, devious, and inscrutable Vietnamese. In addition, their sympathy for the underdog was aroused. Special Forces veterans of the old 10th Special Forces Group found the same affinity for the simple, stoic, rugged Montagnards who hated Vietnamese that they experienced in Germany among the Bavarian Mountain peasants and woodchoppers who hated the flatland Prussians. Returnees from White Star, both CIA and SF, were only too happy to work again with mountain people.

The top CIA planners, of course, were not interested in likes and dislikes. They were looking at a problem in counterinsurgency. The highland forests and jungles in Vietnam could provide base areas and infiltration routes for the VC and North Vietnamese. The partially alienated Montagnard population in this same area was willingly or unwillingly providing scouts, porters, food growers, and even recruits for the armed units. If that population could be protected, or, better yet, protect itself from exploitation, the VC would be denied much needed support. If the Montagnards could be organized and trained

Montagnard Camp Ban Don on high plateau before it was rebuilt in 1966, II CTZ

beyond self-protection, they could become a source of intelligence on VC activities in that vast area, or perhaps even an offensive force.

Initially, the program was strictly defensive in nature. It was population denial, a real key to counterinsurgency success. In other parts of Vietnam, separating the VC from the population was being tried with strategic hamlets and major resettlement programs—the Malayan blueprint. The CIDG program, or Village Defense Program, as it was initially called, wisely elected to avoid resettlement, thus eliminating the attendant drawbacks: the psychological defeat of abandoning homes, the government expense of building and supporting new villages, and the abandonment of huge strategic areas to the enemy.

With considerable justification, it was felt that Vietnamese-Montagnard alienation was too deep to contemplate an effective program in the highlands that included Vietnamese. It was to be an American show, leaving the problems of integrating the program into the overall effort for later. An initial area and tribal group was selected, the Rhade tribe, who lived mostly in Darlac Province in the Central Highlands around Ban Me Thout and the Cambodian frontier. The Rhade are one of the largest tribes and certainly the most advanced and intelligent. The concept was formed in late 1961, and in January 1962 representatives from the Government of Vietnam (GVN), Rhade tribal leaders, and the U.S. Combined Studies Group (one of CIA's several euphemisms) met and agreed to certain principles. The Rhade would denounce the Vietcong and support the GVN. The GVN agreed that the Vietnamese civilian and military officials would keep hands off. The CIA agreed to run the program, to fund it, and to *coordinate* with the Vietnamese. The Americans and Vietnamese agreed to expand the program from the pilot model if it was successful.

As they had in Laos, the CIA called on Special Forces to provide the troops. On the island of Okinawa, Capt. Ron Shackleton, Commander of Detachment A-113, was alerted for Vietnam. Shackleton and his team were something less than delighted. They did not know what a "special mission in Vietnam" might comprise, and they were told nothing more. The team had been preparing for a mission in Laos, where the action was, and resented being shipped to some tidal backwater. Worst of all, only half the team would go. Though Special Forces A Detachments are designed to operate as two split detachments, they preferred the greater depth of a full detachment. It was hard to pick those who would go and those who would stay, but there was no doubt that big John Slover would be team sergeant. Soft-spoken, burly, a veteran of Korea and of a previous SF tour in Vietnam training Rangers, an expert in all of the Special Forces skills, and a natural leader, he would be Shackleton's right-hand man. Sgt. Manfried Baier was the medic, Charles Lindewald and John Clark the weapons men, Al Warok the demolitionist/engineer, and Lester Walkley and Bill Beltch the communicators. There was little preparation time, but fortunately the team was well trained and in good shape, and had two men who spoke Vietnamese and two who spoke French.

On 13 February 1962, the team, looking like civilians, moved out to Kadena Air Base and were flown to Vietnam aboard an unmarked C-130 aircraft. They were met at Tan Son Nhut, outside of Saigon, and transported to a luxurious villa, welcomed, and given instructions by CIA agents. The mission was simply stated, leaving maximum flexibility. Pointing to a map of Darlac Province, the CIA briefer laid it out:

You will deploy to this area at dawn tomorrow and begin to organize the Rhade tribe to resist the VC. Dave will be your area specialist, inform you of your contacts, and handle the administrative end of the program. You will run the military and operational end. You report to no other military or civilian officials in the area, nor do you comply with any of their directives unless it suits your purposes. This program will be referred to as the Village Defense Program (VDP). If you are successful, it could lead to a major expansion throughout the country, wherever minority groups can be advantageously employed against the VC. We are glad to have you aboard. Good luck.

The next morning an unmarked C-46 piloted by Taiwanese flew the team to Ban Me Thout, the province capital of Darlac.

The concept for the Village Defense Program was quite simple. It was merely to arm and train enough of the Rhade so that they could protect themselves against the VC. Up until that time, the VC had used a relatively mild system to subvert the Rhade. VC cadre moved into Montagnard villages, being careful to abide by all customs and traditions. They helped clear land and harvest crops, talking of the autonomy the tribes would enjoy after the revolution. As they became more solidly ensconced, they began to add a few little requirements: attendance at "orientation" classes, a rice tax to help feed the guerrillas, the establishment of warning systems and lookouts, and, finally, conscription of youths as scouts, porters, guides, and agents. The VC took care not to be too demanding wherever possible, but if there were objections, selective use of terror and assassinations usually sufficed. After all, the tribesmen had little choice, and help from Vietnamese sources could not be expected.

The VDP counter to this did not involve moving people away from the VC, nor engaging in massive combat operations. Neither was necessary nor desirable. The SF team would establish itself in a centrally located village, prepare simple defenses, and recruit and train a small "strike force." This strike force would be the only full-time military force organized and the only paid troops. They would provide soldiers to help a village under attack, to reinforce a threatened area, to patrol between villages, to gather intelligence, and to set ambushes.

These would be young men, preferably without families or fields to till. Next the SF team would train the village defenders. Those men would be taught only the basics of village defense and small arms operation, and would return to their home villages to live and work, fighting only in self-defense. Each defended village would also construct rudimentary defenses, bamboo fences, punji stakes, traps, fighting positions and protective shelters, and develop a local intelligence and warning net. A simple radio would be provided to call for help from the operational base or neighboring village. As soon as a ring of villages had been prepared and defended, the perimeter would be pushed out farther to embrace even more villages. Throughout the entire program from the very first day, small civic action projects were carried out. The Special Forces medic, as he had done in so many other places, proved his worth at establishing initial rapport. To the Montagnards, neglected and mistreated over the years by all save a few French missionaries, this was an impressive display of interest and concern.

Captain Shackleton and his team established themselves at Buon Enao and immediately set to work. The reaction of the Rhade was positive and heartwarming, and the number of defended villages quickly multiplied. The reaction of the VC was not long in coming either. They attacked the village of Buon Tong Sing one midnight and saturated it with automatic weapons fire from three sides. Then they breached the bamboo fence and penetrated the compound, driving the defenders back to their second line of foxholes. There the Rhade stiffened and held, driving the VC back into the jungle. They attacked at Buon Hra Ea Hning with an overwhelming force, and again penetrated the village where a bitter battle ensued. Again they were thrown back, losing twenty-five killed against two Rhade killed and three wounded.

Not all was Rhade success, of course. On the night of 19–20 May, the villages of Buon Cu Bong and Buon Tong Dok fell to the VC without firing a shot. Some thirty-four weapons were lost. Rhade retribution in that case had to be swift and impressive. The villages were burned, and the survivors dispersed to other villages. The psychological lesson was impressive, and there was no repitition of that loss.

In frustration, the VC turned against undefended villages outside the security circle. No longer did they use the mild techniques of before, but terror and arson. Refugees, at one time numbering several thousand, fled to Buon Enao. But here the refugee story differs from those in other areas of Vietnam. At Buon Enao, they were not only cared for and given the means to build homes and raise crops, but they were retained in their original locations—this time with trained defenders. Another unique aspect of the Buon Enao experiment was the handling of VC prisoners, particularly those who were Montagnards. Rather than being sent off to some central prison camp, they were retained in the area, given good treatment, and put on a schedule of half-a-day's labor and half-a-day's classes.

Two of Ron Shackleton's prisoners received encouragement from a rather unexpected source. In the early 1960s, U.S. generals and high-ranking officials were sent on world tours to observe firsthand insurgency and counterinsurgency. Buon Enao was often swamped with VIPs. One day a four-star visitor appeared who had obviously been fully briefed to greet and shake hands with every Rhade he met. At the same time, two newly captured VC were standing in the primitive command post, nervously awaiting interrogation. The result was inevitable. The two bewildered prisoners found themselves being wished every success by an enthusiastic, smiling American general. No one present dared straighten out the VIP, and unfortunately no one recorded the reaction of the two Vietcong.

Not all of Buon Enao's prisoners received such an accolade, but the concept sought to win converts rather than merely incarcerate them. Ultimately, the POWs were given the materials and allowed to build their own village and send for their families. There were no escapes; on the contrary, five VC agents who came to lure them back to the jungle were themselves captured. The Buon Enao team estimated that nearly 90 percent of the prisoners were successfully rehabilitated.

It was not easy work. Shackelton and his men worked long hours and lived in the primitive manner of their Rhade hosts. But the satisfactions of accomplishment were enormous, and by April 1962, 28 villages were in the program, 1,000 village defenders armed and trained, and a 300-man strike force was operational.

Vietnamese government officials began to worry about the speed with which Montagnards were being armed. A radio message was received ordering a hold on the issue of all weapons. Shackleton's solution to this development was one that is familiar to junior leaders in all of the services. Back went the response: "Your message received garbled and undecipherable STOP am closing down this station for twenty-four hours to attempt repairs OUT." By the time communications had been "reestablished," all of the 800 remaining weapons on hand had been issued, and the team had a solid backlog of armed trainees to carry through the period of investigation and arguments.

The Vietnamese never did like the program too much, but its effectiveness could not be denied. The Village Defense Program was, initially at least, a glowing success, and there were not too many of those in Vietnam in 1962. True, problems would emerge due to Vietnamese-Montagnard enmity that had been bypassed in the interests of getting the operation going, but those did not surface until later. Additional teams came from Okinawa to continue and expand the concept. By the time Shackleton and his team completed their six-month tour in August, the program was well under way, as evidenced by an 1,800-man strike force, 280 trained medics, and 129 Rhade hamlets protected by close to 10,000 village defenders.

A second operational base was started farther north at Plei Mrong. Captain Grace, a young West Pointer, and Tony Duarte, a top-notch professional NCO with a Silver Star from Korea and a tour in Laos under his belt, came into Plei Mrong with a light company of seventy-seven Bahnar tribesmen from Kontum and started to build the camp. By December, they had trained the first two companies for local patrolling and defense. They were ready to spread out and train some 700-800 village defenders in twenty-one Jarai villages. The VC here tried a different approach. They infiltrated some of their own people among the new recruits. (This technique was to be forever a thorn in the side of the CIDG program. Many a Special Forces soldier slept nights on end with one eye open, wondering which of his troops would cut the wire, open the gate, turn a machine gun into the camp, or roll a grenade under his bunk. Every smart Special Forces soldier automatically *assumed* that he had VC in the strike force.)

Waiting until Captain Grace and a large force were out on patrol, the VC hit Plei Mrong with a battalion-sized attack. The inside VC did their work well, cutting the wire and sabotaging the 81mm mortar. Calls for help to nearby Pleiku were not honored. ARVN was not happy enough with the U.S. program to help the "savages," and besides the Ranger Battalion at Pleiku was "needed to protect Division Headquarters." It was a bloody and painful battle for the new program. Over 130 men were killed, wounded, or missing, and 104 weapons were lost. In the bitter aftermath, Vietnamese officials again talked of ending the program, but a few believers managed to convince the top brass that that was exactly what the VC wanted.

The effort was kept alive and expanded elsewhere, with Jeh and Sedang tribes at Dak Pek, Mnong at An Lac, Jarai near Cheo Reo, plus a whole series of Rhade camps. Later the program moved into areas inhabited by ethnic Vietnamese or Cambodians, and even into areas amost totally depopulated, but it all started with the Montagnard effort. By the end of 1962, there were twelve A teams in Vietnam, in such places as Buon Ya Soup, Mang Buk, Plei Djerang, and Ban Yum. Nobody in 1962 would have predicted that by 1966 those same little Rhade Yards would conduct a sophisticated parachute assault into the flatlands several hundred miles south of Rhade country!

As time passed and the pace and nature of the war quickened, the village defense concept and implementation changed. The initial idea had been essentially passive defense against an enemy of limited means. Gradually, the concept evolved into one where the A team moved into an area, built a type of frontier fort, recruited and trained three to five strike force companies who defended the camp and patrolled and secured the surrounding area. The village defender idea faded out as the program took on a more military and offensive-oriented flavor. The presence of the A team became accepted as vital for the success of the program. That change in concept was to have serious implications when the Pentagon leaders later debated the question of introducing American combat troops into the Vietnamese War.

Other factors intruded as well. The Buon Enao idea, based as it had been on the fairly concentrated, relatively advanced, and pro-French Rhade, was not always viable to export to other areas of Montagnard country. In Bahnar country, east of Pleiku, there were simply not enough people to recruit extensively. In other areas, the program began to be bastardized. Some military

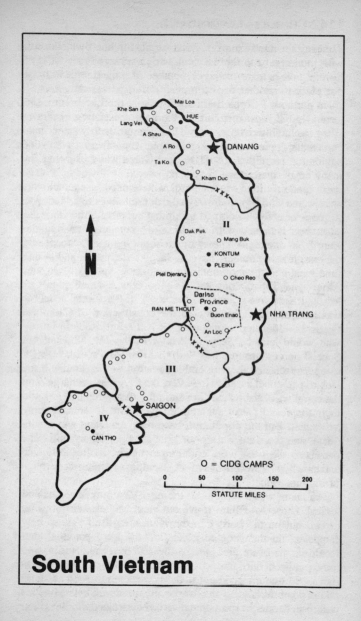

South Vietnam

O = CIDG CAMPS

Khe San
Mai Loa
Lang Vei
HUE
A Shau
A Ro
DANANG
Ta Ko
I
Kham Duc
xxx
II
Dak Pek
Mang Buk
KONTUM
PLEIKU
Piel Djerang
Cheo Reo
Darlac Province
BAN ME THOUT
Buon Enao
NHA TRANG
An Loc
xxx
III
xxx
SAIGON
IV
CAN THO

0   50   100   150   200
STATUTE MILES

authorities wanted camps in certain areas for their own reasons, with little regard to the political or demographic facts of life. Special Forces teams lifted companies of trained strikers from one place to another to accomplish *military* missions.

In northern I Corps, particularly along the Lao border, the terrain is the most difficult in Vietnam, consisting of steep-sided mountains covered with dense jungle, with weather patterns that cripple aircraft and helicopter support. From the very beginning, recruiting for CIDG in I Corps was frustrating. In many areas, there were simply no people at all, or only very sparse and primitive Montagnards who wanted no contact with anyone and who slipped through the dense foliage like shadows. A series of efforts, doomed to almost certain failure from the start, was launched with the idea of "counterorganizing the Katu." No one really knows much about the Katu, except that they are few in number, have no large settlements, and at one time inhabited the mountains in the remote valleys of Ashau, Aloui, and Tabat along the Lao border. A small group of lowland Katu lived closer to the coast in the foothills, and it was here that the CIA ordered the construction of Camp An Diem, an initial step to penetrate the Katu. Sgt. Robert Mattox, who would later be Sergeant Major of the 1st, 5th, and 6th Special Forces Groups, was with that team and recalls how SF troopers protested the vulnerable location of the camp and the lack of personnel assets. However, the CIA was in charge, and the camp was established. For months, they struggled to build their force and patrol far enough westward to contact more tribesmen. But the population base near An Diem was inadequate, and the Katu were poor grist for the military mill. The patrols to the west were endurance marches, often followed and harassed by wolf packs of VC, seldom accomplishing much of military value.

An Diem was a failure, so the next idea may have seemed logical. Close An Diem, move out west, and establish a camp or two out on the border in the Katu area itself. Those new camps would then not only develop the Katu potential, but would do so in an area where the VC bases and infiltration routes existed unmolested. The idea, however, had serious flaws. No one really knew if there were many Katu in those godforsaken hills, and the whole idea of the CIDG program was to put roots in the population. Without people, the effort became a conventional military operation with no real stake in the area, no human intelligence nets, no source of recruits, no hearts and minds to win from the VC.

On the small-scale maps at higher headquarters, two blue dots along the border in the great gap between camps at Kham Duc and Ashau looked impressive. By 1964, SF had been given the mission of "border survelliance," and the push to move camps to the west was in full swing. So camps were established at A Ro and Ta Ko at tremendous effort. At A Ro, a bulldozer was parachuted in and a landing strip carved out of a jungle ridge line. At Ta Ko, such a move was out of the question, as the size of the elephant grass-topped hill would accommodate only a couple of helicopters, and heat and altitude cut their maximum loads down drastically.

The worst aspect of Ta Ko and A Ro was the lack of troops. Recruits were always scarce in the underpopulated I Corps, but recruiting to live in VC areas of the Lao border highlands was nearly impossible. The mayors of Danang and Hue were approached with the problem, and they obliged with forces of teenage hoodlums who had been scraped off the waterfront by methods reminiscent of the nineteenth-century British Navy press gangs. That was a far cry from the original CIDG program. Going on patrol with these recruits was, as the troops say, "something else." Smoking, chattering, holding hands, playing transistor radios, shooting monkeys, sucking on sugarcane, they were a sad bunch. Needless to say, they posed little threat to VC base areas and infiltration routes. As for contacts with the Katu, they were understandably few. A patrol from Ta Ko did meet a Katu family once, but before the two SF NCOs could function, the waterfront hoodlums gunned them down.

In 1965, the camps of Ta Ko and A Ro were closed. A Shau was kept open over the objections of SF, but the VC effectively closed that one in early 1966, as they later closed Kham Duc in 1968.

If one remained long enough in Vietnam, history had a way of repeating itself. In 1969, the planners in I Corps were looking at the small-scale maps again and telling Special Forces to get ready to push out to "new camps" on the border of I Corps. Only the presence of a few old-timers, veterans of the agony of 1965, prevented the repetition of the old lessons. The only other border camp in I Corps was Khe Sanh, which achieved notoriety as a U.S. Marine Corps bastion, but Khe Sanh is a story in itself.

Khe Sanh was the extreme northwestern outpost of South Vietnam, situated only a few kilometers east of the Lao border and south of the Demilitarized Zone. It lay astride the old French Route 9 from Quang Tri to Tchepone in Laos. A French-owned coffee plantation on a high plateau still functioned in the early 1960s, and approximately 10,000 Bru Montagnards lived in the area. Many worked on the plantation or collected cinnamon bark, another cash crop of the area. There at Khe Sanh, the CIDG program was initiated, as originally conceived by the CIA. It still pleased the military leaders who viewed with concern the extensive enemy infiltration through the western part of the Demilitarized Zone, just around its flank in Laos.

The Bru are not great warrior stock, but simple, gentle people who became increasingly caught up in a war they knew and cared nothing about. Special Forces went to Khe Sanh and set up a camp around the old French fort on a hill. For once in I Corps, recruiting was easy, and Khe Sanh flourished. Troops were trained, patrols ran on schedule, security was good, schools were built, health workers and aid men were trained, and, in general, Khe Sanh in 1964 was a CIDG success story. The VC pretty much left the Bru villages alone, and when they did venture in, word was passed to the SF camp at Khe Sanh. Security was such in 1964 that the airfield, some five kilometers away from the camp, could be secured with a squad or so of sleepy Bru.

By 1965, things began to go downhill. Enemy infiltration increased. The decision was made to move the camp to the airfield. Here one could see an example of changes that were beginning to affect the program country-wide. The airfield, of critical military importance, was secured, while the Bru villages and their 10,000 people were of lesser importance, or so it seemed.

In spite of large injections of U.S. ground troops into Vietnam, security continued to deteriorate. Ultimately, the Marines came to Khe Sanh, and for a while the Special Forces A team and its jackleg battalion of little Montagnards and Danang "cowboys" lived together on the growing Marine base. Gradually, they found themselves squeezed out by more and more supplies and equipment, artillery, aircraft, barbed wire, sandbags, and high-ranking American officers. To regain a little operational flexibility and freedom of action, the A team and the Bru picked up and moved out of the oppressive and organized chaos of Khe Sanh. Down the road a few kilometers toward the Lao border, they built another camp at Lang Vei. Initially, it was nothing more than a fortified Montagnard village. Certainly, it was no Khe Sanh, which had burgeoned to a huge, raw, red clay wound around the enlarged airfield.

In one of those heartrending tragedies that somehow hurt worse than the intentional blows of the enemy, a U.S. fighter-bomber aircraft, lost in the fog-shrouded mountains, bombed and strafed the Lang Vei camp. Casualties were brutally high, particularly among the wives and children. The Bru wept, and their Special Forces advisors gritted their teeth. Painfully, Lang Vei camp was rebuilt as a fortified camp across Route 9 from the destroyed village.

By May 1967, an estimated two to three North Vietnamese divisions invested Khe Sanh and vicinity. On 4 May, a company-sized force attacked the camp with the assistance of at least four inside Vietcong CIDG troops. The attack by what was estimated as an enemy platoon was supported by PT-76 tanks and mortars, and succeeded in overrunning the western and southern corners of the camp. With the assistance of fire support from Khe Sanh, the SF and CIDG repelled the attack and ejected the attackers, though half the SF defenders were killed or wounded, as well as ninety CIDG killed, wounded, or missing. Though Lang Vei was successfully defended, it was at a grievous cost to its gallant garrison.

By early 1968, the North Vietnamese had Khe Sanh under virtual siege, and it looked as though Dien Bien Phu was programmed for a rerun. So was little Lang Vei, seventeen kilometers down the road, but it was seldom mentioned in the press dispatches. Finally, in February, the North Vietnamese decided to knock off Lang Vei and again attacked it with troops, tanks, and mortars. No marines came down from the big base in Khe Sanh to help out, but Sgt. Gene Ashley, a thirty-eight-year-old black Special Forces medic, organized a small relief force of Montagnards and led five successive assaults into the camp. Ashley was killed, but his efforts resulted in an escape route

Old Camp Lang Vei (overrun by Soviet tanks in Jan. 1968 Tet Offensive), ICTZ

being carved out for the remaining defenders, some of them trapped in the underground command bunker with a PT-76 tank parked on top. Two years later, Ashley's widow and five children received his posthumous Medal of Honor.

A last indignity, however, awaited some of the battered, loyal Bru, who finally made their way to the wire at Khe Sanh. There they were met by U.S. Marines who disarmed them and kicked them back out into the bush.

The saga of the "poor damned Bru" was not over yet. The remnants were gathered and taken back east to Mai Loc, where once again they built a camp and installed their families nearby. When things settled down in Khe Sanh, they could return home. Mai Loc was never a happy camp. The local Vietnamese were not happy over the arrival of the Montagnards, and the American mechanized brigade couldn't see much value in those little brown men and their "green beanie" advisors. In April 1970, the VC pulled off a masterful sapper attack on Mai Loc. Half the bunkers were damaged and twenty-two CIDG were killed. M. Sgt. Gale Stopher, an old Special Forces pro and "one helluva team sergeant," died while carrying a wounded Bru to medical aid.

When the smoke cleared and the two North Vietnamese divisions withdrew into North Vietnam from the Khe Sanh area, Lang Vei was rebuilt once again, but not for long. By August 1970, MACV's destruction of the CIDG program hit Lang Vei, and Special Forces Detachment A-101 packed up and moved out for good. As for the Bru, who knows? The remnants are no doubt in the hills near the Lao border, and the agony of those terrible years has taken its place in the tribal history passed from father to son. I wonder how they remember their Green Beret friends.

11. EXPANSION: CAMBODES, HOA HAO, AND CAO DAI

Certainly there were problems, frustrations, and even a few failures, but for every Ta Ko or An Diem there were many successes. The concept was basically sound. It was based on an understanding of revolution and the importance of the people. Most of all, it was carried out by men who understood and believed in what they were doing, and who had the patience, imagination, and dedication to see it through. In the early 1960s, in the remote highlands of South Vietnam, Special Forces CIDG camps were virtually the only government presence, the only expanding islands of security, the only sources of intelligence.

Success led to expansion, and the CIDG program pushed out in many directions. If the concept could work with Montagnards, why not with other population groups? Rapidly, the CIDG program grew from mere population denial in the highlands to a country-wide extension of the strategic hamlet program, an effort to push the government presence out beyond the limits of other agencies. By 1963, there were thirty camps; by 1964, over forty, with some in all of the four corps tactical zones. CIDG strength was up to 20,000, and Ron Shackleton's seven-man team had grown to a "provisional group" of over 1,000 U.S. Special Forces. CIDG camps sprang up in the rubber plantations of III Corps, in the desolate Plain of Reeds, and along the canals and rice paddies of southernmost IV Corps.

On 1 July 1963, "Operation Switchback" was completed, putting the CIDG program under the U.S. Army, and thus under the newly formed United States Military Assistance Command Vietnam (MACV). The CIA was removed from the chain of command as an aftereffect of the Bay of Pigs operation in Cuba.

By accident or by design, SF found itself dealing with other religious and ethnic minorities of Vietnam. At least in part, the reasons were the same that had led to contacts with the

Montagnards. These groups were also alienated from the Vietnamese majority and its government, but Special Forces found they could bridge the gap. Further, since the CIDG had no official status with ARVN, recruiting efforts had to seek otherwise untapped resources. Lastly, SF preferred to set up in the remote regions and in the border areas, and it was there that many of the minorities had settled.

In the III Corps area between Saigon and the Cambodian border, Special Forces found an excellent source of manpower among the Cambodian population. Not only did they prove to be good fighters and to have good intelligence from the floating cross-border population, but they could be recruited in entire company-sized blocks with a built-in chain of command. These troops were being fed into the CIDG system by the not-so-secret society of the Khmer Serei, through the "Temple" in Saigon. The Khmer Serei had elements in Thailand and Cambodia, as well as South Vietnam, and counted among its objectives the overthrow of Prince Sihanouk. Sihanouk had long been understandably paranoid about the Khmer Serei and had cut off relations with the United States in retaliation for alleged CIA support of the Khmer Serei secret propaganda radio.

The U.S. State Department, whose Cambodian policy had been primarily based on the precept of "do nothing that might scare Sihanouk into the arms of the Red Chinese, and when in doubt do nothing at all," looked with a very jaundiced eye upon Special Forces' considerable force of Cambodians and, at one juncture, tried to force a dissolution of that part of the program. Fortunately for thousands of Cambodians and Vietnamese peasants living under the protection of CIDG Strike Forces of tough Khmers, this idea was voted down.

Special Forces leaders were by no means unaware of the Khmer Serei involvement and long-range objectives. As a matter of fact, if a company of Cambodians performed badly, a call would go back through SF channels, and one of the Khmer Serei leaders would be brought out from Saigon by helicopter. He would assemble the strike force, deliver a stinging rebuke, perhaps replace a commander or two, and everything would be squared away. The important points, as far as the Special Forces were concerned, were that the Cambodians were good troops who knew the area, who could communicate with the local population which was heavily Cambodian, and who could

Co. D, 5th SFG, Plain of Reeds (Muc Hoa)

get intelligence about what "Charlie" was doing in his sanctuaries across the border. The political leanings of the Khmer Serei made them quite unscrupulous about conducting espionage in "neutral" Cambodia. Special Forces tapped that source and would have been quite remiss not to. To the intelligence chiefs at MACV, this information filled the biggest information gap of all. To the A team leaders along the Cambodian border, it was a simple matter of survival.

Another Cambodian group, the Khmer Kampuchea Krom (KKK), also flowed in and out of the CIDG program with the fortunes of war. The KKK, in spite of an ostensible long-range political goal to restore to Cambodia the lost Vietnamese provinces of the old Khmer empire, were really little more than opportunistic bandits, who fought from time to time for the VC, for the GVN, or simply for themselves. When it suited Special Forces *and* the KKK, they fought in the CIDG program.

The Hoa Hao and the Cao Dai, though ethnic Vietnamese, were two religious groups which had at one time fielded powerful private armies. President Diem effectively broke their power, and since that time, they remained largely outside of the struggle for South Vietnam. General Khanh, during his tenure in 1964 and 1965, was able to effect some rapprochement, and for a while the Hoa Hao area of Chau Doc Province

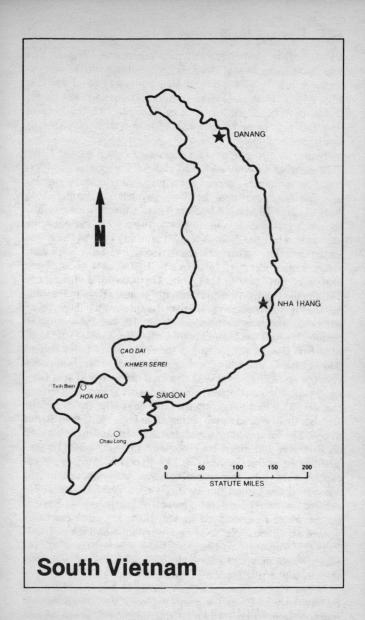

DANANG

N

NHA TRANG

CAO DAI

KHMER SEREI

Tinh Bien

HOA HAO

SAIGON

Chau Long

0   50   100   150   200
STATUTE MILES

South Vietnam

was one of the most effectively pacified areas in Vietnam. The Special Forces camp at An Phu on the Bassac River was effectively run by a Hoa Hao leader and was one of the first from which SF advisors were withdrawn to be used elsewhere. In war-torn Tay Ninh Province of War Zone C, hundreds of Cao Dai proved to be one of the few recruiting potentials available.

Farther south and west, a legendary figure named Larry Thorne, working with odds and ends of Cambodians and Vietnamese minorities, carved out a quiet, unspectacular success in counterinsurgency near the town of Tinh Bien. The incredible story of Larry Thorne is a book in itself. A magnificent physical specimen (his friends winced when, filled with bonhomie, he impulsively hugged them in a great crushing bear hug), he was an expert skier, swimmer, scuba diver, free-fall parachutist, and mountain climber. In the early 1960s, as a middle-aged captain of forty-two in Bad Tolz, Larry could, and regularly did, run the twenty-year-olds into the ground. Born in Finland, he fought six years against the Russians, was three times wounded, and was awarded every medal that Finland could bestow. He won the Mannerheim Cross (equivalent to the U.S. Medal of Honor) for leading a small ski patrol miles behind Russian lines, ambushing and completely destroying an entire convoy, and killing over 300 enemy. During World War II he fought the Russians again, this time with a force of German marines. That unit fought on for three days after the end of the war, but finally managed to surrender to U.S. rather than Soviet troops. Thorne was imprisoned, but escaped, and made his way on foot over 200 miles back home to Finland, where he was jailed again at the insistence of the Russians. After twice escaping, only to be recaptured, he was finally successful and made it to the United States via Sweden and Venezuela. He enlisted in the U.S. Army, naturally gravitating to Special Forces where he continued to add to the legend. He accomplished an "impossible" body recovery mission high in Iran's Zagros Mountains (see Chapter 7) and returned home to Fort Bragg where they still talk about his exploits as the notorious maneuver guerrilla leader, "Charlie Brown."

When Thorne first came to Vietnam in late '63, the camp he took over at Chau Lang in IV Corps was in a miserable position, dominated by two of the legendary "Seven Moun-

Forward observation post in Seven Mountains, Ba Xoai

tains," enemy strongholds since the earliest days of the Viet Minh. It was Larry's job to move the camp to the vicinity of Tinh Bien, a typical delta village, a district capital, spread out along a canal that paralleled the Cambodian border. The town and its commerce were dominated by the VC. Many houses were empty, many fields untilled. The population was apathetic, if not frankly hostile, to occasional government patrols, and the district chief and his meager force of local "civil guards" seldom stirred beyond the walls of their triangular mud fort.

When Thorne, his team, and a small force from Chau Lang occupied the new site at Tinh Bien, they literally had to fight their way in through ambushes all along the way. Almost every night the new CIDG camp "repelled boarders." It was going to be a long, tough battle, for pacification is a slow and tortuous process. When Thorne and his team left Vietnam in mid-1964, every man wearing at least one Purple Heart for wounds, they had not seen any final results. They had only started the trend.

By early 1965, the situation at Tinh Bien had changed dramatically. Under the protection of the strong camp built nearby and the continuous patrols and outposts, Tinh Bien and its people were thriving. No longer did the VC stop sampans on the canal to extract taxes. No longer did VC patrols enter the villages at night to deliver propaganda lectures and collect rice and fish. Houses were no longer empty and deserted, shops were open and stocked with wares, new schools had been built, and a dispensary in town supplemented the medical care provided by SF and CIDG medics out at the camp. Tinh Bien was a "success story"* in the struggle for pacification, and there were many more like it.

The real key to the success, however, was the fact that the security screen behind which all this progress had been made was "homegrown." They were local soldiers whose families lived in Tinh Bien, and who had a real stake in the area. They would not pack up and leave at the whim of some distant general launching an operation in a high priority area. Thorne, the brawling soldier of fortune, who fought communism under three flags, who could never explain counterinsurgency in his heavily accented, broken English, had put all the pieces together—security, population and resources control, civic action, responsible use of firepower, intelligence, psychological warfare, relationship with the people, and understanding.

By early 1965, Larry Thorne was already back in Vietnam. He served in Phuoc Vinh, the Isle de Phu Quoc, and Nha Trang before winding up with one of the hairier reconnaissance operations. It was while on operations over Laos that he disappeared in a downed helicopter in October 1965. Though his body was never found (others in the same chopper were), he was declared killed in action a year later. The many in SF who knew and loved Larry don't really believe that he is gone, and would not be surprised to see him walk out of the jungle someday at the head of a ragged band of Montagnards.

---

*To the keepers of scores and statistics at MACV headquarters in Saigon, the view was not the same. "What's happened out at Tinh Bien?" queried a staff officer. "It used to be a really good camp with lots of body count. Now they hardly ever kill anybody!"

12. THE MOBILE STRIKE (MIKE) FORCES

The CIDG idea was born in an era of little heavy combat, long before the injection of regular North Vietnamese Army units and heavy U.S. Infantry and Air Mobile Divisions. The camps had generally performed well, even though they were never built, equipped, or armed to withstand a large-scale assault. The rule of thumb for camp defense was the ability to stand off an attack by a VC regiment through the hours of darkness. From the beginning, particularly where the program was succeeding, the VC attacked CIDG camps to eliminate them. Most camps were, by definition, in remote areas and difficult to bail out when trouble struck them.

The enemy's all-out efforts to take such camps as Ben Het, Bu Dop, Duc Lap, Dak Pek, and Dak Seang resulted in some of the biggest battles of the Vietnam War. When they were attacked during the late 1960s, the military command could and did throw tremendous firepower, artillery, helicopter gunships, fighter bombers, and even B-52s into the balance. In some cases, ground troops were committed, though it must be noted that MACV became more and more reluctant to commit U.S. ground troops to such actions. Attacks on CIDG camps were invariably initiated by the enemy and usually included careful ambushes of relieving forces. The enemy rarely fought U.S. ground forces unless he thought he could win or inflict unacceptable losses on the American commanders.

In the early days, however, there was little chance of getting help from *any* source. Hiep Hoa and Tan Phu were overrun in 1963, and their survivors marched off to VC prison camps. It was outside of Tan Phu that Capt. Herbert "Rocky" Versace and 1st Lt. "Nick" Rowe were captured in the course of a major ambush. Versace was executed by the VC, allegedly due to his total lack of cooperation with them, while Rowe remained a captive for five years until his eventual escape (see Chapter 20). In 1964, Capt. Roger Donlon and his heroic team at Nam

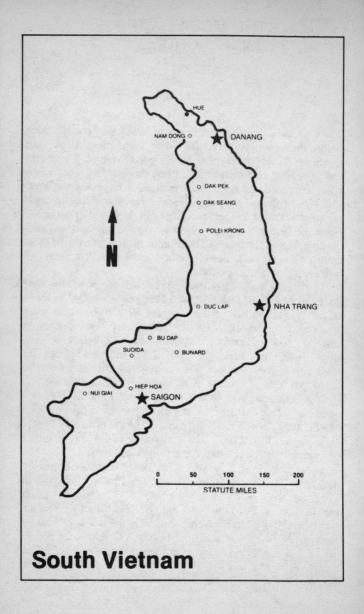

HUE

NAM DONG ○　★ DANANG

○ DAK PEK

○ DAK SEANG

○ POLEI KRONG

N

○ DUC LAP　★ NHA TRANG

○ BU DAP

SUOIDA ○　　○ BUNARD

○ NUI GIAI　○ HIEP HOA
　　　　　　★ SAIGON

0　　50　　100　　150　　200
STATUTE MILES

South Vietnam

Maj. Nick Rowe minutes after he escaped from five years' captivity by VC in LV CTZ

Dong hung on by sheer will. Though Donlon was painfully wounded in the stomach, shoulder, leg, and face, for five hours he was all over the camp rallying his defenders. He survived to win the Medal of Honor, but the Distinguished Service Crosses for Sergeants Alamo and Houston at Nam Dong were posthumous. A few weeks later the VC took the camp at Polei Krong and held it until daybreak—there was no outside friendly help. In 1965, the CIDG held out at Kannack; hundreds of North Vietnamese regulars were found hanging in the wire at dawn, but it had been a long and lonely night.

If things were going to be that tough and the CIDG camps were to survive, hardening camp defenses was not enough. There had to be reaction forces responsive to Special Forces command for the relief of beleaguered camps. On the theory that "if you want something, you better do it yourself," Special Forces started to create its own mobile reaction forces, the crack "Mike" forces of future years. The concept was that these units could be used as mobile forces for any number of purposes—to reinforce a threatened camp, to patrol areas not covered by camp strike forces or other units, to run special missions in remote areas, and, of course, to bail out camps in trouble.

This was a further departure from the original CIDG concept. These new units, though composed of Vietnamese nationals with U.S. Special Forces leaders, had no particular roots in the areas where they fought. In fact, by 1969, one would see examples such as Rhade Montagnards from the 5th Mobile Strike Force from Nha Trang, fighting on the Isle de Phu Quoc or in the swampy Rung Sat west of Saigon. But the tenor of the war was changing, and SF was not going to sit by and watch its camps go under without taking some action.

The daddy of what was to become known as the "Mike Forces" was a battalion of Nungs formed in Danang in 1965. The Nungs are a tribal group originally from the area near the North Vietnamese-Chinese border. During the French and early Diem regimes, there had been an entire Nung Division which earned a top reputation for professionalism and fighting quality. That division was later demobilized, and the Nungs settled in several enclaves in South Vietnam. They were not active again until the CIA and Special Forces recruited them to serve as personal bodyguards for the SF teams in the new CIDG program. Hired at a high pay scale, the Nungs proved their worth on numerous occasions, winning the respect of the Special Forces. The successful defense of Nam Dong, described above, was only possible because of the loyal defense of the inner perimeter by Nungs and Special Forces. In the early days, it was often the Nungs who provided the backbone of training, the defensive capability, and the element of stability on patrol that made the difference between success and failure. They posed some problems, too, because they attached their loyalty to the Americans rather than the Vietnamese, and because their pay scale exceeded that of even the Vietnamese regular army.

The press and even some "official spokesmen" began to refer to the Nungs as "mercenaries," and then the term spread into common use to describe all CIDG strikers. The Nungs *were* mercenaries, but the ordinary strikers in the CIDG program were not, by any stretch of the imagination. The vast majority were Vietnamese nationals who were fighting in the defense of their homes and Vietnam. Many of them (but not all) were paid, as are soldiers all over the world, but that did not put them in the category of Gurkhas who fight for the

British everywhere but at home in Nepal, or the bands of polyglot renegades who hired out to fight in the Congo. Notwithstanding, news reports on CIDG activities almost never appeared without referring to "Green Berets and their hired mercenaries." That was, naturally, a source of endless irritation and frustration to the Vietnamese, as it was doubtless a source of great gratification to the National Liberation Front's Ministry of Propaganda.

A mobile strike force was authorized for each C detachment in July 1965, with another authorized for Nha Trang under the operational control of the commanding officer of the 5th Special Forces Group, making five in all. Each was battalion-sized, with an authorized strength of three 198-man companies, plus a small headquarters, totaling 598 men. By the summer of 1966, none of them had arrived at their full authorized strength.

In August 1966, I arrived in Vietnam, assigned as Deputy Commander, 5th Special Forces (CIDG). While still unshaven and in badly rumpled khakis, I had my first encounter with my new commanding officer, Col. Francis ("Black Jack") Kelly, a huge, Roman Catholic, Irish, ex-Boston cop who spoke with great intensity. Over a period of two hours, he outlined his personal goals as a Special Forces commander. One of his goals, typically emphasized with great gravity, was: "While I am group commander, none of my camps will be taken by the enemy. If one of my camps appears threatened, be it day or night, the Nha Trang Mike Force will be parachuted into that camp to prevent its defeat, and *you* will lead them!" Needless to say, the second thing I did in Nha Trang was immediately to seek out that Mike Force commander, a personable young captain commanding a veteran A team. At that time, the Nha Trang Mike Force consisted of only 350 men, headed by the A team, and only the A team was airborne-qualified. I gave the Mike Force commander orders to recruit immediately to a strength of 850 men, to combat-train and airborne-qualify them by the end of September, and to be prepared to go day or night, trained or untrained, as of then.

In the following weeks, between visits to all my eighty CIDG camps spread over the width and breadth of South Vietnam, I kept an eye on that 5th Mobile Strike Force (airborne) and even had the opportunity to make two parachute jumps with them in the drop zone west of Nha Trang. That drop zone was in contested territory, and the Mike Force always carried ball ammunition on its five qualifying jumps, as the frequency of "jump-up, shoot-back live targets" thoroughly warranted it. Colonel Kelly helicoptered out to watch our last, graduating jump in the rice paddy drop zone. Using the limited steerability of the M-10 parachute, I attempted to maneuver to the relatively dry paddy dike, but failed and ended up soaking wet and muddy, plopping in the flooded field. My administrative enlisted assistant, M. Sgt. Bobby Suggs, with consummate ease derived from several hundred jumps, floated down in his starched fatigues and landed easily on the dike without even a drop of moisture on him. Kelly thought that was funny as hell. At any rate, I had a jump-qualified Mike Force, in the event the worst happened and required a parachute commitment to a beleaguered A camp. It never did, though they later made two parachute assaults at Bunard (III Corps) and Nui Giai (Seven Mountains in IV Corps) that were totally ignored by the press.

Both parachute assaults are worthy of mention, mainly because of the rationale used to get them authorized. Bunard was the site of a new A camp to be opened in Phuoc Long Province, about 100 miles north of Saigon. Company A in Bien Hoa, the parent unit, requested two 5th Mobile Strike Force companies from Nha Trang to secure the area while introducing its own Mike Force (newly airborne-qualified) and the A detachment to take responsibility for the new camp. It would have been necessary to airlift the Nha Trang troops to Bien Hoa, and there transload them to some forty helicopter sorties for movement to Bunard. Since the troops were airborne-qualified, it would be simpler, easier, and above all, cheaper in terms of helicopter sorties, to air-drop them directly into the new camp site. The airdrop was approved by MACV, but delayed until April 1967, to allow the 173rd Airborne Brigade the honor of making the first (and only) American airborne assault in the Vietnam War, in "Operation Junction City" in January 1967. The 173rd's highly publicized airborne assault landed on drop zones already in the hands of other American units. The 5th Mobile Strike Force's airborne assault on 1 April 1967, undoubtedly, had the largest and highest-ranking pathfinder detachment in the history of airborne assaults. Lt. Col. Tom Huddleston, commanding officer of Company A, much of his

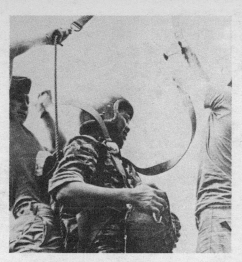

5th SFG Mike Force striker in Airborne training

Col. Francis J. Kelly, CO 5th SFG, 1966–67

5th SFG in VN training

Camp Con Thien

Camp Trang Phuoc

Camp Prek Klok

Camp Tra Bong

5th Special Forces HQ

5th SFG HQ, Sept. 1966, Col. Kelly departing CSM Piloetti Troop line

(battalion) staff, and most of his senior noncommissioned officers, including his king-sized command sergeant major, "Paddy" Flynn, jumped from helicopters some thirty minutes prior to the mass jump of the Mike Force. The only problem that anyone had on the drop zone was twenty-foot-high elephant grass and two-foot-wide elephant turds, one of which I managed to descend on squarely.

The Nui Giai airborne operation probably set a record for a quick reaction parachute drop. The entire operation was conceived, planned, and put into effect in only thirty-six hours. The companies of the 5th Mobile Strike Force were dropped from six C-130 aircraft, flying in trail at an altitude of 700 feet to form a "catcher's mitt" for a much larger operation of CIDG companies surrounding a Vietcong stronghold on one of the Seven Mountains. Dropping on 13 May 1967, the Mike Force troopers remained in combat until 18 May, sustaining five casualties and assisting in inflicting fifty-two enemy casualties, the capture of considerable enemy equipment, and the neutralization of a VC base. The figures are not staggering, but two airborne assaults in six weeks by a group of little Rhades that wore loincloths and used crossbows only four years previously was surely a notable achievement. The little fellows were too short to reach the static line when the order "hook up" was given. Although they had to be lifted by two big Americans moving up the stick, they went out the door like a shot when it came time to "go." Airborne!

In addition to airborne-qualifying and greatly increasing the size of "my" Mike Force, I was also able to affect the size and quality of the other four Mike Forces, one each for C Company (I Corps), B Company (II Corps), A Company (III Corps), and D Company (IV Corps). In short order, A Company matched the 5th Mobile Strike Force strength of five companies, while B, C, and D companies rose to the strength of three companies each. All were airborne-qualified by the end of September 1967.

In early September, while on a liaison visit to Saigon, I learned of the MACV Campaign Plan that was being compiled for the first time. It was to be a blueprint for the calendar year 1967, outlining MACV's goals and objectives. The 5th Special Forces Group was not invited to submit its input, but deemed the time ripe for an uninvited submission. We quickly made a

LTC Tom Huddleston (he also flies the helicopter)

five-year plan stretching out to 1971, and turned it in to the G-3, MACV, somewhat to his surprise. The plan for 1967 was accepted and incorporated in the 1967 MACV Plan. It included, among many other things, a very large increase in the size of the Mike Forces, in fact double in size from the 1966 authorized strength. In addition, thinly disguised, were other units that were very like Mike Forces, but with more specialized missions. In each Corps Tactical Zone, we created Mobile Guerrilla Forces, consisting of a 150-man Mike Force Company plus a 35-man reconnaissance platoon. They were designed to conduct guerrilla warfare in the vast stretches of enemy-controlled territory outside areas of operations (AOs) of CIDG camps. The concept was to infiltrate these company-sized forces, usually by foot, and to operate against the enemy's lines of communications, usually branches of the ubiquitous Ho Chi Minh Trail in the enemy's so-called war zones. The 5th Special Forces Group called these operations "Black Jack" missions and conducted dozens of them from 1967 on. They prowled enemy-used trails, destroying food and ammunition caches, intercepting couriers and small parties of reinforcements, leaving delayed-fused demolitions and booby traps along the trails, and generally spreading chaos and ruin in the enemy's backyard.

Also, the reconnaissance units under the 5th Special Forces Group were actually tripled in strength in 1966 by the addition of Mike Force–like battalions. "Project Delta" was first formed in 1964, and in 1966 was augmented by "Project Omega" and "Project Sigma." Every A camp was authorized two reconnaissance platoons, greatly increasing their trained reconnaissance assets with school-trained Mike Force–like units attached to each camp.

The Mike Forces fought very well under extremely difficult conditions in such areas as War Zones C and D where other troops never ventured, or operated only in massive multithousand-man sweeps. On 2 November 1966, III Corps mobile strike forces in the strength of three companies moved in War Zone C north of Camp Suoi Da. That war zone was the home of the 9th VC Division, which engaged the three companies in eight separate fights, before MACV ordered in the 196th Light Infantry Brigade to relieve the Mike Forces. Eventually, the 1st Infantry Division, the 173rd Airborne Brigade, and a brigade each of the 4th and 25th Infantry Divisions were committed to an operation known as "Attleboro," which involved 22,000 American and South Vietnamese troops. The Mike Force battalion was credited with 85 enemy killed and another 148 probables. Overall, "Attleboro" cost the enemy over 1,100 dead and large amounts of supplies lost.

There were several reasons for the success of the Mike Forces in making contact with the enemy. They were light, highly mobile units that were capable of moving with great speed through the jungle. Like the CIDG, they usually operated outside the "fans" of friendly artillery fire, which was unusual only because the United States and other allied forces *never* operated without artillery cover. The large conventional forces moved ponderously by "cloverleafing" at the rate of only a few hundred meters an hour in order to avoid ambush. The Mike Forces at times literally ran through the jungle when necessary, disregarding security in favor of high mobility. It must be admitted that a primary reason they were effective in contacting enemy forces was that the enemy was not afraid of the Mikes, or the CIDG for that matter. The big conventional units rarely ventured forth in less than battalion-sized operations, always had reserves near at hand, carried heavy weapons, wore armored vests and steel pots, and always had artillery cover and close air support. The enemy just did not win when they elected to close and fight the "Big Americans." They usually had fire superiority over the Mike Forces and almost always numerical superiority, so they had a fighting chance of winning. On numerous occasions, only the close air support available to the Mikes saved them from heavy losses when they were outgunned and outnumbered, but that does not detract from their bravery and the highly effective leadership of the American Special Forces leading them.

Many CIDG camps survived to fight another day because of the timely and courageous intervention of the Mikes. Even General Abrams, scarcely a strong supporter of Special Forces, was quoted in 1969 as stating that the 3rd Mobile Strike Force was doing the best work in III Corps. This opinion was shared by General Ewell, the commanding general of the operations area in question, one in which a large concentration of U.S. combat units was present.

The "Third Mobile" did indeed perform magnificently in the toughest areas of III Corps, digging deeply into War Zones

C and D, finding "Charlie" in hideouts and unearthing his big caches of weapons, food, and ammunition. A large share of the credit for that performance belongs to its commanders, Maj. Jim Ruhlin, Maj. Ola Mize (Medal of Honor), Capt. "Bo" Gritz, and all the others too numerous to name—particularly the noncommissioned officers, that special breed of Special Forces soldier who repeatedly sought out the tough and dangerous work with the Mike Forces, the special projects, and the classified missions.

A special word of praise also goes to a little-known group of professionals, the relatively small band of Australian Special Air Service warrant officers who fought side by side with Special Forces in Vietnam from 1963 until the end. They were always in the toughest slots, serving with great distinction with the Mike Forces in I and II Corps. One of the first to die was Australian Kevin Conway at Camp Nam Dong in 1964, on the same night that Roger Donlon won his Medal of Honor. He was a veteran of years of guerrilla warfare in Malaysia and Borneo, and he was walking, though the camp was under heavy fire, to a mortar pit, when drilled between the eyes by what was presumably a sniper round. The Australians were hard-fighting, hard-drinking, hard-swearing, thoroughly professional soldiers who will forever remain blood brothers of the U.S. Special Forces, to whom Americans everywhere owe a debt.

The Mike Forces of 1966 onward, with their camouflage uniforms, jump wings, steel helmets, and modern M-16 automatic rifles, were indeed a far cry from the simple, unpaid, pajama-clad peasants, armed with Springfield M-1903s or Swedish "K" submachine guns of the 1962 Village Defenders. But the enemy had also changed as much or more. It had been a long time since anyone captured a homemade shotgun, or even an obsolete French MAS-36 rifle. AK-47s, Soviet rockets, and Chicom heavy mortars made it a new ball game. Special Forces had adapted to the change by developing the Mikes, but they had not lost sight of the main objective—the people. The essence of the program was still in the CIDG camps with the people.

Though it can never be proved, the following conjecture needs to be stated. If the Special Forces in Vietnam had developed effective Mike Forces in 1964, when the Vietcong initiated deliberate attacks on isolated detachments of Americans, to include CIDG camps, the need for intervention by American combat troops would not have been necessary. The leaders in the Pentagon were most concerned for the 21,000 Americans spread out over Vietnam when it became evident that the VC were forming into regimental and division-sized units and on the offensive. The ARVN, demonstrably ineffective against the large VC units, was unwilling to risk going to the relief of embattled isolated detachments of Americans. If Mike Forces under American leadership with American air support existed to do the tasks ARVN should have done, the war could have taken quite a different turn.

13. RECOVERY OPERATIONS

From the beginning, Special Forces has been charged with what can be called "Recovery Operations." The precedent goes back in time until at least the closing days of World War II, when the 6th Ranger Battalion made a deep penetration to the Cabanatuan Prisoner of War Camp on Luzon, in the Philippines. In March 1945, the camp housed American, British, and Dutch civilians who sensed they were being mustered for the last time before their Japanese guards massacred them. A dawn reveille formation was interrupted by Rangers who shot as they charged, wiping out the Japanese guard force before the Japanese could kill the inmates. That was one of the most spectacular and successful recovery operations in military history.

One of the original Special Forces missions was, and still is, escape and evasion (E & E)—the procedure concerned with the recovery of downed airmen. Before flying into enemy rear areas, U.S. airmen are briefed on E & E areas where they can expect to contact U.S. Special Forces. Mutual recognition signals are agreed on before operations begin so the Special Forces can be sure the men they pick up are truly Americans, and the downed pilots can be sure that their contacts are, indeed, American Special Forces. The two services have never agreed on just who should expose themselves first, but somehow the job gets done. All of the major unconventional warfare field-training exercises have an E & E phase. U.S. pilots are dumped off the back of a truck, somewhere in aggressor-controlled territory, and have to make their way cross-country to designated E & E contact sites. In the past, the Air Force has played the game by some tough, self-imposed rules. A pilot landing from a training flight at a U.S. base will be met and have everything he is wearing inventoried. When he is injected in the field-training exercise as a downed pilot, he is allowed to wear exactly that and nothing else. If the pilot happens to be wearing low-quarter shoes and silk socks, that is what he wears into an exercise in the chill of a Bavarian autumn with twenty-odd miles of cross-country travel before him.

The recognition procedure until recently included taking the fingerprints of downed pilots, encoding them and sending them back to the Special Forces Operational Base for identification at the Central Fingerprint File in Washington. There was a certain amount of justifiable resentment at this procedure that required sending a lengthy message from the field to the base for the short reply, "Yes, that is Capt. John Doe." Most Special Forces men believed that they should tell the base they had a Capt. John Doe, and let the base send *them* the fingerprint-encoded data. The Air Force, understandably, didn't want to give a bunch of ragged guerrillas the life-and-death decision over their pilots. The controversy has been settled satisfactorily to both services.

In the Vietnam War, there were numerous documented attempts to recover U.S. prisoners of war, reportedly forty-five between 1966 and 1970. No single operation is more difficult to accomplish successfully, due to the difficulty of insuring that POWs are actually present in the target, and if present, that they are not dispatched by enemy guards before they can be liberated. It is no surprise that only one American was successfully rescued in the forty-five attempts, and that he died shortly after rescue from wounds inflicted on him by his guards.

Particularly in 1966 and 1967, when Col. Francis Kelly commanded the 5th Special Forces Group, the rescue of prisoners of war was a major objective. Under the aegis of the MACV Joint Personnel Recovery Center in Saigon, repeated attempts to recover POWs were mounted, in the U Minh Forest of IV Corps, War Zones C and D in III Corps, and in the An Loa Valley of II Corps. Several enemy prison camps were overrun, but the VC followed a policy of constantly moving the POWs, and no attempt was successful. Undoubtedly, it was just as well, as the VC had standing orders to kill their prisoners if there was any chance at all of their regaining their freedom.* Still it was morale-raising for the Americans who were not captive to know that every effort was being made to recover

---

*Lt. Nick Rowe in his book *Five Years to Freedom* made it plain that as much as he yearned to get away, he feared attempts to liberate him would result in his instant death, p. 425.

captured Americans, however hazardous to everyone's life.

The most meticulously planned, well-rehearsed, and heavily supported POW rescue attempt in the history of this nation was that made on Son Tay prison camp on 21 November 1970. Son Tay is located twenty-five miles west of Hanoi and was believed to hold seventy Americans. A Special Forces rescue force of fifty-nine officers and noncommissioned officers, together with strong support of Air Force helicopters, gunships, and C-130 aircraft, rehearsed the rescue over 100 times in a secret camp in Florida. All rescuers were volunteers, handpicked for the mission, led by Col. "Bull" Simons, himself selected by Brig. Gen. Don Blackburn, head of the unconventional warfare branch of the Joint Chiefs of Staff, SACSA. The operation, directly under the JCS, was kept completely secret from all but a handful of need-to-know officers and officials. The operation took place at night, flying in by helicopter from Thailand, refueled by accompanying tankers, and escorted by A-1 fighter aircraft. The raiders landed in Son Tay, shot up the guards, but discovered that there were no prisoners there. They piled back in their helicopters and made it safely back to Thailand, the Special Forces men performing almost perfectly. Even then, there were mistakes, beyond the absence of prisoners. The communications link between the raiding force and the overall commander of the operation in Danang was faulty. One of the choppers landed outside a compound 400 meters from Son Tay by mistake and shot up a company or so of foreigners, too tall to be Vietnamese (Chinese/Soviets?). It was later determined that the prisoners had been moved over four months previously, due to the threat of a flood drowning the camp.

One recovery mission that *was* successful occurred in the Christmas season of 1966, in III Corps, Vietnam. An American U-2 reconnaissance plane was downed in the thick jungles along the Cambodian border. The pilot ejected safely and was recovered, but the downed U-2 contained a secret "black box." Since it would be very revealing if it fell into the hands of the enemy, the Air Force wanted that box back. The exact location of the downed aircraft was not known, but a cone-shaped area was delineated, based on the known recovery point of the downed pilot and the direction of flight of the aircraft when it exploded. Aerial reconnaissance and photography failed to locate the aircraft—it would have to be done on the ground if it were to be done at all.

General Westmoreland turned to the 5th Special Forces Group in Nha Trang, then commanded by Col. Francis Kelly. Kelly was not one to ignore the requests of his commanding general, however impossible the task seemed, and he in turn went to Lt. Col. Tom Huddleston, the commanding officer of A Company in Bien Hoa, III Corps. Tom Huddleston turned to his Mike Force, the Third Mobile Strike Force, commanded by Capt. James G. ("Bo") Gritz. The Third Mike Force at Bien Hoa, then consisting of three companies of 150 men each and three reconnaissance platoons of 35 men each, was headed by a 12-man A Team in command of the Mike Force. For this recovery operation, Gritz took one company and a recon platoon, with the other units in standby-reserve. The jungle of War Zone C was not the primarily double- and triple-canopied formidable obstacle like that in II Corps and much of I Corps. There were numerous bamboo clumps and many clearings with ten-foot-high elephant grass, but the forests were small with relatively thin trees some twenty-five to fifty feet high. Though the taller trees did form a double canopy in the deeper reaches of the zone, the visibility was quite good, enabling men to see twenty-five or thirty meters. There were literally dozens of trails going in all directions and numerous abandoned foxholes, many with overhead cover. An oddly alien presence was the thousands of propaganda leaflets scattered everywhere, no doubt providing the VC inhabitants some amusement as well as more elementary utility as toilet paper.

Gritz and his men studied the map the Air Force provided, together with photographs of the U-2 and its vital black box. After insertion by helicopter, they tracked back and forth for three days, covering an ever greater width as they plunged deep into enemy territory. The trails were used by couriers and small parties of VC, traveling in what they believed to be impunity in their own territory. Inevitably, the Mike Force made contact with those little groups and dispatched them in one way or another. Holes in the jungle allowed helicopter-evacuation for whatever friendly casualties ensued. They did not attempt secrecy as they were a big enough force, equipped with full automatic firepower, to handle almost any force they met. If they met a force they couldn't handle, they could run, call for air support, and be evacuated by the ubiquitous helicopters.

Incredibly, the third day they found the downed U-2. To their profound disappointment, the black box was missing. Gritz concluded that the VC had correctly identified its importance and removed it. He further believed that such a find would be known to the VC over a wide area of the war zone, so he proceeded to look for prisoners. After several tries, they finally got a live POW, somewhat battered from being subdued. They managed to persuade him to guide them to the force holding the black box. He saw the wisdom of guiding them into the camp. The entire force went through the designated base camp with M-16s blazing. The VC inhabitants ran or hid in tunnels, leaving the camp to the Mike Force troopers. A hasty search turned up the black box, and they quickly backtracked toward home, stopping briefly to helicopter-evacuate the black box, their wounded strikers, and the wounded VC guide. It was Christmas Day of 1966, and the U.S. Air Force got the Christmas present it wanted so badly. Gritz and his force got to walk out several more days, fighting off infuriated VC attempts to destroy them. By a combination of courage, persistence, military skills, and luck, the recovery operation succeeded. If, however, the black box had been a U.S. POW, it is likely that he would not have survived his recovery.

One final recovery operation serves once again to underline the difficulty of such missions. It is, of course, the attempt to release the Iranian hostages in late April 1980, code-named "Operation Blue Light." Like the Son Tay raid, it was conceived and ordered at the highest levels. It was a joint operation of U.S. Special Forces, Marine helicopter crews, and Air Force C-130 aircraft and crews. It, too, was planned in great detail, was thoroughly rehearsed in the deserts of the west, and was handled with the highest degree of secrecy possible. Blue Light preparations began a few days after the seizure of the hostages in November. The Special Forces element, which had been formed in 1977, shortly after the German and Israeli rescues at Mogadishu and Entebbe, was sequestered in its own secure compound at Fort Bragg. The commander of the Blue Light element was Col. "Charging Charlie" Beckwith, a veteran infantry and SF officer who, although widely known to the troops of SF, was unknown to the general public. Although there have been press reports that the Blue Light element referred to itself as "Charlie's Angels," that is entirely uncharacteristic of that band of volunteers and, moreover, is not true.

The operation called for ninety Special Forces and ninety Air Force helicopter crewmen to fly from Egypt to a desert landing strip called "Desert One," some 250 miles southeast of Teheran. There they would rendezvous with eight Sikorsky RH-53 helicopters, flown in darkness from the U.S.S. *Nimitz* somewhere in the Arabian Sea, said to be 530 miles from Desert One. All aircraft would fly low to escape radar detection. There in the desert the helicopter crew that practiced with the Blue Lights would take over the choppers, load the SF, and fly to an undisclosed landing site outside Teheran. Details of the plan have never been released, but presumably the Blue Light force would make its way to the U.S. compound, release the hostages, and call in the helicopters to lift them all out. The retrograde movement would probably have been a reversal of the approach, with rendezvous with the C-130s at some point and withdrawal out of Iran's airspace.

As is well known, the operation never moved past Desert One. The helicopters were the weak point in the plan. One broke down en route to Desert One and was abandoned and destroyed. A second chopper lost its gyroscope while flying through a sandstorm. Its pilot was afraid to rise above the sand for fear of appearing on Iranian radar, so it returned to the *Nimitz*. Once on the ground at Desert One, the Air Force told Beckwith that only five of the big birds were operable. That provided a lift capacity of 275 passengers, and the operation required *at least* 232 raiders and hostages. The loss of one more chopper would entail leaving behind at least 43 passengers and the Marine aircrew. Beckwith pondered, and in what was probably the toughest decision of his career, recommended withdrawal. That was approved by the White House, with great disappointment. The operation could have remained secret at that point, but it was not to be. An Iranian bus loaded with passengers going from Teheran to Tabas drove right up to the gaggle of American planes, forcing the troops to stop it and unload the driver and passengers. About the same time, a tank truck drove by, was shot and stopped, causing the driver to flee in a small pickup that had followed his truck.

The order was given to reload the planes, and preparations were made to depart. The pilot of one of the Sea Stallions lifted his plane about twenty feet into the air to go around a C-130 transport to a tanker plane on the other side. As he banked in the darkness, a rotor slashed the transport just behind the crew compartment. The C-130 burst into flames, killing the five crewmen. Four Marines also died, with the pilot of a Sea Stallion badly burned. Beckwith ordered the other four helicopters abandoned, and the C-130s took off, leaving eight American bodies behind. The dangers of spreading fire and explosions motivated Beckwith's decision to leave behind four operable heavy-lift helicopters.

Another American recovery operation failed, and the world media trumpeted, hooted, and scorned. President Carter went on national television and said: "It was my decision to attempt the rescue operation. It was my decision to cancel it when problems developed. The responsibility is fully my own."

Special Forces really should not be used for recovery operations. Too much money, time, and effort goes into training each individual SF soldier and the A teams to which most of them belong. To take volunteer skilled radiomen, demolitions experts, engineers, and medics to perform a mission any well-trained weapons man could successfully do is a waste and misuse of valuable men. The two Ranger battalions, at the least, should perform those raid missions. They are filled with young, physically tough, skilled, and motivated soldiers who are perfect for raids. Of course, the differences swing the balance to SF. The SF are mature, combat-experienced, and fiercely loyal to one another. Most of them are career soldiers who reenlist time after time, providing a great deal of stability. Commanders of recovery raids like to use the best men available, and as they are invariably SF officers themselves, they turn to those they know best—but they really should not.

14. SPECIAL OPERATIONS AND UNCONVENTIONAL WARFARE (UW)

Probably no aspect of the Vietnam War is more confusing than the relationship between the various Special Forces–manned units *not* in the CIDG program. The CIA used Special Forces detachments in many parts of Vietnam for a variety of purposes. For example, the elite airborne ARVN Ranger Battalions were trained by SF detachments, usually on temporary duty from Okinawa. The South Vietnamese Special Forces were trained by SF detachments. The CIA also used some fifty SF soldiers to train and supervise its paramilitary Provincial Reconnaissance Units (PRU) program. One of the largest users of SF soldiers outside of the CIDG program was the Special Operations Group (SOG). Although it used SF soldiers, it had no official relationship to the 5th Special Forces Group.

As the 5th Special Forces Group evolved and enlarged, it had special needs, mostly for reconnaissance work, that it fulfilled out of its own resources. Project names, such as "Sigma," "Omega," and "Delta," were given those units. It also created Mobile Guerrilla Forces which all carried project names of "Black Jack" followed by a number. The 5th SFG created and ran a school of reconnaissance to train the allied forces under COMUSMACV, called the RECONDO School. It is very easy to mistakenly place "Project Delta" under SOG, as has often been the case, but the point is that there were two principal chains of command for Special Operations, the 5th Special Forces Group under MACV, and SOG under the JCS with MACV supervision.

The SOG was the oldest of the special projects. It operated under the cover name of "Study and Observation Group," and was a combined force—that is, it had Army, Navy, and Air Force elements, and consisted of both Vietnamese and Americans. It was a highly classified operation for which there is no single unclassified history. Although the operation was large and stretched over a period of ten years of U.S. participation, the constraints and limitations that were imposed for political reasons reduced its effectiveness to that of relatively minor harassment of North Vietnam. From the start of U.S. involvement in South Vietnam, the American leaders stressed that the purpose of U.S. participation was to insure a free South Vietnam with the freedom to determine its own future. There was never a U.S. policy with the objective of overthrowing the North Vietnamese government. The subversion of North Vietnam was never our policy. The goal was to place pressure on the government of North Vietnam to cause it to cease its subversion of South Vietnam.

The beginning of SOG was the Vietnamese Army's 1st Observation Group, organized in February 1956, with an authorized strength of 300 men. It was a Special Forces-type of unit with the mission of operating in South Vietnam. Many of the original members were from North Vietnam. They were trained for guerrilla operations at the group's home base at Nha Trang. They were to prepare guerrilla stay-behind units just south of the seventeenth parallel for the eventuality of an invasion by North Vietnam. The unit was supported by the U.S. Military Assistance Program (MAP), and had CIA training and radios (RS-1s). It was organized into twenty fifteen-man teams. It was not in regular Republic Vietnam Armed Forces (RVNAF) command channels, but was classified and segregated with a command line direct to President Diem. All operations of the group were directed or approved by the president.

As a result of the deterioration of the South Vietnamese position in the spring of 1961, President Kennedy approved the dispatch of 400 U.S. Special Forces men to act as trainers and advisors to the ARVN, but specifically to Nha Trang to train the embryo Vietnamese Special Forces. At the same time 100 other American military advisors were also approved. The president also directed that a campaign of clandestine warfare be waged in North Vietnam, to be conducted by South Vietnamese agents directed and trained by the CIA and American Special Forces. Those agents were to form networks of resistance, establish bases in North Vietnam, and conduct light harassment. Other South Vietnamese Ranger units were to be trained to conduct ranger raids and other military actions in North Vietnam. Naturally, the ARVN 1st Observation Group was given the primary clandestine mission.

In October 1961, the president approved additional missions for the 1st Observation Group against North Vietnamese operations in the Laotian panhandle. The use of U.S. advisors on the ground was authorized on an "as necessary" basis.

Those actions were the implementing directives of recommendations from an interdepartmental task force comprising representatives from the Department of State, the Department of Defense, the CIA, the International Cooperation Administration, the U.S. Information Agency, and the White House Office. The recommendations for covert action were part of a larger program which included other military actions, as well as economic and psychological actions. On 11 May 1961, those recommendations were approved by National Security Action Memorandum Number 52, which called for explicit unconventional warfare actions in these words:

> Expand present operations of the First Observation Battalion in guerrilla areas of South Vietnam, under joint MAAG-CIA sponsorship and direction. This should be in full operational collaboration with the Vietnamese, using Vietnamese civilians recruited with CIA aid.
> In Laos, infiltrate teams under light civilian cover to Southeast Laos to locate and attack Vietnamese Communist bases and lines of communications. These teams should be supported by assault units of 100 to 150 Vietnamese for use on targets beyond capability of teams. Training of teams could be a combined operation by CIA and U.S. Army Special Forces.*

Under CIA auspices, the 1st Observation Group was augmented by a Vietnamese Air Force Transport Squadron to provide a means for infiltration by air. The U.S. Army Special Forces trained the Vietnamese in ground operations, and a detachment of Navy SEAL frogmen taught them how to infiltrate by sea. The CIA also set up an alleged Vietnamese private air transport company (VIAT) and hired experienced pilots from Taiwan. The purpose of VIAT was to provide a plausible denial that the Vietnamese or U.S. governments were involved

---

*Neil Sheehan, *The Pentagon Papers as Published by the New York Times* (New York: Bantam Books, Inc., 1971), p. 131.

in operations over North Vietnam.

CIA operations against North Vietnam were disappointingly unsuccessful. An unknown number of teams of Vietnamese agents were dropped into North Vietnam, and some were inserted from the sea. In almost every case, they were captured or failed to report by radio. The North Vietnamese interrogated the captured agents and complained to the cochairmen of the 1954 Geneva Conference, from Great Britain and the Soviet Union. The Chief of Station, CIA, Vietnam, became convinced that the infiltration of agents into North Vietnam was futile and began to redirect the program to one based primarily on propaganda, using radio broadcasts, leaflet drops, and deception actions to convince the people of North Vietnam that peaceful coexistence, political collaboration, and economic development between North and South was a better policy than the North's armed subversion and violence in the South.

In December 1963, the program was switched from CIA control to military control ("Operation Switchback"), as part of a worldwide replacement of CIA leadership of clandestine paramilitary operations. CIA was asked to continue to contribute to this program in the political and propaganda fields, and several CIA officers were attached to the military program for that purpose.

SOG was now established in Saigon as a Joint Unconventional Warfare Task Force for North Vietnam and Laos. It was commanded by Army colonels and included representatives from all U.S. services, and a few liaison personnel from the CIA (the SOG deputy commander was designated to be from CIA, but a CIA man was never provided for that position). Although SOG was established and manned by MACV, it was actually virtually independent of MACV, except through one staff officer (the J-5, Plans) who had "cognizance" of SOG operations, as MACV did not have a charter to operate in Laos and North Vietnam. The actual supervisor of SOG was the Special Assistant for Counterinsurgency and Special Activities (SACSA) in the Joint Chiefs of Staff in the Pentagon. From the first, the Pentagon exercised the closest control over SOG's operations and followed with great interest its reports, available outside of SACSA on a "need-to-know" basis only. CINCPAC was also on the line monitoring SOG's activities, but had authority only to veto proposed SOG operations; approval remained with SACSA. Habitually, specific operations were preplanned and submitted to SACSA via MACV and CINCPAC for approval. If no objections were received within a short designated time period, approval was assumed.

Initially, SOG had a U.S. strength of about 150, half of them officers, but it grew almost continuously as its operations expanded and as further operations, such as communications and psychological operations, were incorporated. Most of the troop strength was Special Forces noncommissioned officers, carried on the rolls of the 5th Special Forces Group, but actually assigned full time at SOG bases with minimal contact with the group.

Prior to the creation of SOG, the CIA had been unsuccessful in the operations of the agent teams dropped into North Vietnam. Those teams that were not captured shortly after infiltration were subsequently apprehended attempting to leave. The CIA legacy to SOG was five "in-place" teams in North Vietnam. SOG attempted to infiltrate other agent teams, but with little more success. They added one team to those in place, but had severe resupply problems due to the monsoon weather. Probably all six teams were under the control of the North Vietnamese. The teams were given the initial mission of escape and evasion, harassment, destruction, and limited intelligence activities. After October 1965, the mission was redirected to become psychological operations, escape and evasion, and limited interdiction. No U.S. personnel accompanied any of the teams.

Considering the fact that CIA was forced to give up this program to the military, had not had laudable success at infiltration of teams into North Vietnam, and had failed to meet its personnel responsibilities to SOG, it is doubtful that they provided much intelligence on North Vietnam to SOG. CIA may have been handicapped in its efforts by:

- A "hurry-up" attitude in Washington to put pressure on North Vietnam, preventing the necessary painstaking care in preparation of the teams.
- The attitude of CIA leadership reared in the OSS in World War II where they almost always worked in occupied territory with plenty of known resistance and contacts, friendly people in comparative abundance, and

other favorable factors, including an abundant availability of natives of the occupied areas for OSS missions. A truly denied area, such as North Vietnam, was new to the CIA.

The "no-resistance potential" was a comfortable dodge, if not a cop-out. There was no hurry to send in teams, as it turned out, as it was a long war. CIA should have started more carefully developing a resistance potential through the use of single agents, propaganda, and research, followed by careful preparations for unconventional warfare. North Vietnam might have been an entirely different story if they had.

Another SOG airborne operation, code-named "Leaping Lena," consisted of dropping six-man teams of Vietnamese by parachute to reconnoiter the Ho Chi Minh Trail in Vietnam. Those efforts were largely unsuccessful, as the North Vietnamese showed a real aptitude for detecting and mopping them up. The SOG Vietnamese also showed a real reluctance to parachute into enemy territory, so it was determined that American military presence would be added to induce the needed backbone and success.

An SOG mission code-named "Shining Brass" was cross-border operations against North Vietnamese installations and movement in Laos. It was carried out by twelve-man teams, including three Americans and usually nine Montagnard civilians under the employ of SOG. The command and control center was in Danang at Marble Mountain, and forward operating bases (FOBs) were usually located in Special Forces CIDG camps along the border, such as Kham Duc, Khe Sanh, and Kontum. The basic mission during the early days of "Shining Brass" was the location of targets for aerial bombing; yet at times when they had little choice, those teams would fight, or destroy enemy supplies found undefended. In later months, there were three battalions of American-led Vietnamese used as a reaction force, or to carry out larger combat missions in Laos. The authorized areas for those operations were strips of Laos that stretched twenty kilometers deep into the country. Only certain pieces of Laos were authorized, and those strips were not necessarily contiguous. Initially, the SOG commander was not allowed to lift his reconnaissance teams in by helicopter, although authorized to extricate them if necessary. As

SFC Fred W. Zabitosky (U.S. Army photo)

the Laotian border consisted of some of the most rugged terrain in Southeast Asia, daily movement of reconnaissance teams was counted in meters, not kilometers. Due to the difficulty of movement, helicopter infiltration was ultimately authorized and became the norm. The reconnaissance teams were able to direct air strikes on known targets through a rather elaborate procedure which included getting the permission on a target-by-target basis from the U.S. ambassador to Laos.

This was but one example of the political nonsense that plagued the successful conduct of the Vietnam War. Ambassador "Field Marshal" Sullivan, and his successors, had complete control over U.S. military operations in Laos. He exercised it as if he were a commander running his own war under CIA jurisdiction. Often when intelligence would develop leads suggesting operations into areas beyond the twenty-kilometer limit, requests for authority to insert teams would be denied on the grounds that CIA had teams in that area. When asked for intelligence from the CIA teams in periodic SOG/CIA meetings, SOG was given nothing. There never was established a central authority over military operations and CIA in Southeast Asia, as a theater. The overall coordination from the Pentagon was equally lacking as a control over CIA operations.

In later years, the reconnaissance teams were expanded to approximately twenty teams. Until 1970, six A detachments from Okinawa were placed on temporary duty (TDY) with SOG for six months at a time to perform the hazardous reconnaissance operations. Despite the dangers, there was never a lack of volunteers in the 1st Special Forces Group. Also surprisingly, there were very few fatalities and relatively few wounds among the recon men. From 1965 to April 1972, there were only 103 U.S. Special Forces killed on 2,675 cross-border operations.*

Not to *underestimate* the dangers of these missions, let us look at one of the hairier ones, the one on which Sgt. Fred Zabitosky won the Medal of Honor. Zabitosky is a well-built six-footer with black hair and a slightly nervous manner. He probably does not like being put in the position of a national hero, but bears it with dignity, although he tends to be an introvert. Zabitosky had behind him thirteen cross-border recons in both Laos and Cambodia, and had served two previous tours in South Vietnam. On 19 February 1968, he was acting in command of a nine-man recon team inserted into one of the more active recon zones west of CIDG camp Dak To and east of Attopeu, Laos. The terrain in that area alternated between triple-canopy jungle, ten-foot-high elephant grass, and vicious bamboo thickets. There were enough open spaces for landing zones (LZs) to practice the usual deception of helicopter infiltrations. A train of three or four transport helicopters ("slicks") accompanied by several gunships entered the recon zone flying in trail. The lead "slick" touched down momentarily, then tagged on to the tail of the column. Each "slick" in turn simulated

*U.S. Department of Defense, *Report on Selected Air and Ground Operations in Cambodia and Laos*, Sept. 10, 1973 (to Congress).

Camp Kham Duc on Laotian border, a joint CIDG/SOG camp, 1967, I CTZ

landing and rejoined the flight. At one of the simulated LZs, the recon team jumped out. The enemy suspected, or knew, that infiltration had taken place, but he couldn't be sure where. Even so, the LZs were dangerous places, frequently mined and/or booby-trapped, and sometimes covered by human surveillance.

Zabitosky was by far the most experienced American on the recon team, though the Nungs included two men who fought for the French. The team made contact with a large North Vietnamese Army (NVA) force immediately after landing and was engaged in a massive firefight. Zabitosky called for the two A-1E Skyraiders on standby nearby to bomb and strafe his white smoke. He emplaced a claymore electrically activated mine with attached white phosphorous grenades and detonated it into the enemy ranks when the charging NVA came within range. The Skyraiders dropped napalm bombs on the first wave and wiped it out. Zabitosky emplaced a second claymore and brought the second wave under fire with his CAR-15 automatic rifle. The second mine burst into the NVA and brought the Skyraiders back in with high-explosive bombs. Zabitosky ran to the nearby LZ and called for extraction choppers, but was told that none were available at that time, due to similar trouble at other LZs.

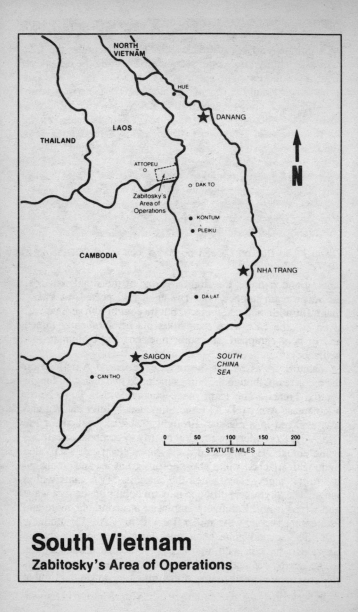

South Vietnam
Zabitosky's Area of Operations

A company of NVA attacked the team defending the LZ. Zabitosky coolly circled the perimeter, directing the defensive fires. Two A-1Es stationed overhead attacked the NVA and turned back twenty-two separate attacks. The nine-man team was still intact, credited with killing 109 NVA on the LZ alone, when evac helicopters come in. He sent half the team off on the first chopper, keeping an American and three Nungs with him. Zabitosky and his team jumped on the second "slick," which lifted off the ground and was seventy-five feet in the air when hit by an enemy rocket grenade. Zabitosky was thrown out of the door and regained consciousness on the ground twenty feet from the crashed and burning chopper. He pulled out the pilot who was only dazed, then ran back and was pulling the copilot out when the fuel cells exploded, throwing them both clear of the burning wreck. Though burned and with crushed vertebrae and ribs, Zabitosky put the husky copilot over his shoulder and made toward another helicopter that landed to aid them, picking up the dazed pilot en route. They were all successfully evacuated, but the copilot subsequently died of his wounds. That was not exactly a typical mission, but who can say the recons were not dangerous? Over the years, SOG members earned a total of six Medals of Honor.

Permanent FOBs were later established at Danang, Kontum, and Ban Me Thout and renamed Command and Control North (CCN), Central, and South, respectively. Eventually, there were approximately 3,500 persons devoted to the ground mission in Laos. They were successful in obtaining an excellent intelligence picture of North Vietnamese operations in Laos in those areas they were permitted to reconnoiter. They also caused the North Vietnamese to secure its line of communications by deploying thousands of troops in an anti-infiltration mode. Over the years, the North Vietnamese became very proficient in detecting and attacking those infiltrating teams, making such a role increasingly perilous.

SOG had many other brave men conducting air and marine operations, as well as psychological operations, whose feats are deserving of much wider knowledge. However, the ground operations in Laos and Cambodia were the star of the show and a Special Forces operation from start to finish.

In May 1964, the JCS authorized the U.S. Mission in Saigon

to undertake the long-range reconnaissance mission in South Vietnam, code-named "Leaping Lena." The next month the mission was transferred to the Military Assistance Command and the Special Forces under Operation Switchback provisions. "Leaping Lena" was then to be implemented by a force called "Project Delta," organized into a reconnaissance element and a reaction force. At full strength, Delta consisted of over 1,300 men, a powerful long-range reconnaissance and intelligence-gathering force that was the first of the special operations that came to be among the most effective combat operations of the Vietnam War. Project Delta had a reconnaissance element consisting of sixteen reconnaissance teams, each composed of two U.S. and four indigenous personnel. There were also eight road patrol teams consisting of four indigenous personnel each, the so-called Roadrunners. They dressed and were armed to pass as VC, and would follow trails used by the VC to observe and talk with the enemy. The support element of Delta was the ARVN 91st Airborne Ranger Battalion of about 850 men, consisting of six companies. The missions of Delta were country-wide and were approved by the Vietnamese Joint General Staff in conjunction with COMUSMACV. The missions were generally intelligence gathering, though they did perform acts of sabotage and combat. They were originally conceived to enter the reconnaissance by parachute, but later all of their operations were inserted by helicopter. They moved wherever required in South Vietnam, and were capable of supporting and defending themselves. Delta usually based on a CIDG camp, bivouacking outside the defenses and adding strength to the camp's positions. Upon the arrival of the American units, Project Delta was out on missions almost continuously, as the demands for its services outstripped its capabilities.

For that reason, in 1966 two more reconnaissance projects, "Project Omega" and "Project Sigma," were organized to supplement Delta. They were similar in organization to Delta, but were smaller, consisting of just over 1,000 men. The reaction forces were Mike Force battalions of three companies of 150 CIDG each, led by 25 SF officers and men. Initially, there were no Vietnamese Special Forces in Sigma and Omega, though later they were admitted. Omega operated in the II Corps area under I Field Force, Vietnam, and Sigma operated in the III

Corps area under II Field Force, Vietnam. They operated in what had previously been exclusively enemy territory, adding a psychological burden on the enemy when he began taking casualties from air strikes guided in by the "Greeks" deep in War Zones C or D. In their first nine months of operations, Omega and Sigma inflicted 191 enemy killed, by USSF body count. They were in the field 60 percent of that time.

U.S. Army "search and destroy" operations in Vietnam were invariably conducted with extensive use of helicopters, engineer construction of fire bases, and artillery and gunship fire support. It was not difficult for the VC and NVA to determine when and where those operations were being conducted, and to simply stay outside the range fans of the artillery on the fire support bases. There were vast areas of South Vietnam that were so remote and unpopulated that the U.S. Army never operated there. Those areas became the targets for mobile guerrilla operations using Mobile Strike Companies and platoons, and U.S. Army SF commanders.

Mobile guerrilla forces were created by the 5th Special Forces Group in late 1966 to harass and interdict the enemy in his own backyard in South Vietnam. They were to do so using the enemy's own guerrilla tactics, principally stealth and surprise. The guerrilla forces were to infiltrate by stealth, interdict enemy lines of communications, conduct surveillance of enemy base camps and way stations, and gather intelligence. When possible, they would destroy food and ammunition caches, leave booby traps and delayed-action explosives, and generally spread chaos and despair. As it was envisioned that the operations would continue for weeks at a time, and as it would not be possible to live off the land entirely, a method of resupply was devised. At first or last light an A-1E fighterbomber would proceed to the resupply point, not necessarily a DZ or LZ. The guerrilla band would signal the desired impact area, and the A-1E would "bomb" napalm containers filled with food, uniforms, and ammo. It would then go to another point safely away from the guerrillas and drop high-explosive bombs. In the jungle, uniforms last about a week and are a necessary resupply item. The guerrillas can carry food enough for five days on their persons, so resupply took place about every five days, weather permitting. The pilots that flew those resupply missions were from the 1st Air Commando Squadron in Pleiku, and among the best in the Air Force.

The mobile guerrilla forces differed from the mobile strike forces in several ways. Organizationally, they had a full U.S. Special Forces A Team in command. The force consisted of a Mike Force company of 150 men, less the weapons platoon, and had an organic reconnaissance platoon, bringing the overall strength to about 184 indigenous and 12 U.S. As an unconventional warfare unit, they followed UW procedures. Each mission was preceded by a detailed area assessment and highly detailed planning. The A detachment would present a detailed "briefback" which summarized their analysis and planning, telling their commanders of their intended route of march and actions, their emergency procedures, their resupply needs, their analysis of enemy deployments in their area of operations, their communications procedures, and all other aspects of their mission that could be anticipated. The "brief-back" provided the commanders an opportunity to question the team and provide for any possible omissions or oversights, while giving the commanders a good sense of the team's intentions and contingency plans. Dozens of Black Jack mobile guerrilla operations were carried out in all four corps, and all were successful, due to the detailed analysis and planning. In almost every case, each Black Jack operation attracted so much enemy reaction that they had to be extracted before they reached their planned exit point. In no case did a Black Jack operation take heavy casualties or fail to interdict and harass the enemy's lines of communication as planned. The success of those missions definitively proved that mobile guerrilla forces can and should be used against a guerrilla enemy in counterinsurgency operations.

Black Jack 22, during December 1966 and January 1967, conducted one of the longest mobile guerrilla operations on record—34 days. The operation was commanded by Capt. Robert Orms, newly arrived in Vietnam, with Lt. Gilbert K. Jenkins, a veteran SF officer, second in command. The mobile guerrilla force consisted of 12 U.S. Special Forces and 173 Rhade, including a reconnaissance platoon, comprising the 2nd Mobile Guerrilla Force from Ban Me Thout. Detachment B-23 in Ban Me Thout was commanded by Lt. Col. Robert Gillette, nearing the end of his Vietnam tour.

The force was trucked out of Ban Me Thout south seventy kilometers to the An Loc CIDG camp, some 6,000 feet high in a mountain valley. The operation was planned for sixty days to penetrate the area east and north of An Loc, terminating at an abandoned CIDG camp site at Buon Mi Ga. That area had never been penetrated by government troops, though it was believed to be a line of communication between Cambodia and Nha Trang. The force took to their feet on 10 December, moving through a tortuous valley due east. It took them five days to cover eighteen kilometers, when they debouched into a beautiful valley covered with soft green grass, with scattered lakes teeming with fish. Waterfalls dropped from the surrounding cliffs and the valley was full of wildlife—deer, monkeys, and thousands of birds. There was no sign of human life of any kind and no sign the valley had ever been inhabited. They took an airdrop of twenty-two bundles, then moved on to the north. The mountains were rugged, and the only trails were game trails. They were afflicted by blood bees, reportedly twice the size of mosquitos, but bloodsuckers, not biters. They made slow progress and took a second air supply on 20 December. On 23 December, they received an unasked for and unexpected resupply drop containing champagne, fried chicken, fruitcake, and Christmas mail. Naturally, they stopped and celebrated Christmas then and there.

On 24 December, they came upon an abandoned VC village, complete with a punji stake factory. Discovering a pen of pigs, they delivered the coup de grace with a silenced Sten gun and had barbecued pork for Christmas dinner. Moving on north up the Buon Mi Ga Valley, now following a man-made trail, they discovered the first of the VC rice caches. The next day they found another cache/way station with three tons of rice, and in the next few days found sixteen more, each with two tons of rice. The temperature went as low as forty degrees at night, and the force was suffering from colds and multiple leech bites. On 9 January, they found a battalion-sized camp/way station, complete with abandoned barracks and classrooms. Nearby was another company-sized way station. They were obviously invading VC territory.

The same day they were brought under attack by a sixty-man VC company, which killed Sergeant Waymire and wounded

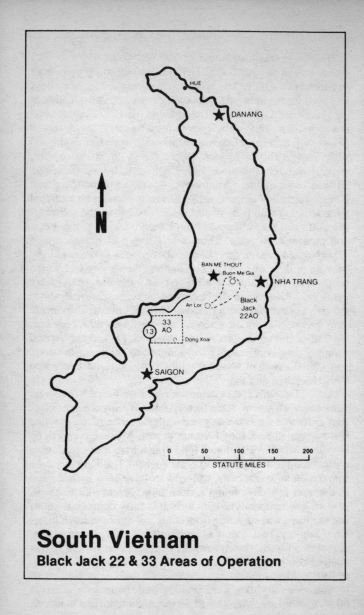

South Vietnam
Black Jack 22 & 33 Areas of Operation

A Co. Project Sigma: Roadrunners in VC disguises, 1967

Captain Orms and several strikers. They were medivacked, losing all possibility of secrecy. Actually, they found out later through captured VC documents that they had been under surveillance since 29 December. VC documents also revealed that two VC Main Force battalions were planning to ambush them at the abandoned airstrip at Buon Mi Ga. Black Jack 22 was ordered to an LZ for evacuation by Colonel Gillette, while the two battalions were attacked from the air on the airstrip. Black Jack 22 had one further ordeal. They were ordered to Nha Trang, 5th Special Forces Group headquarters, for a step-by-step and minute-by-minute debrief by Brig. Gen. S. L. A. Marshall, which lasted thirty days.

Another notable mobile guerrilla operation was the marriage of Project Sigma, commanded by Lt. Col. Clarence T. Hewgley, and a mobile guerrilla force from III Corps, commanded by Capt. "Bo" Gritz. The operation took place between 27 April and 24 May 1967, in War Zone D, north of CIDG camp Dong Xoai, about eighty kilometers north of Saigon. All the reconnaissance teams and all the Roadrunner teams were used repeatedly, most of them making contact with relatively small units of VC from the 9th VC Division. The mobile guerrilla force wended its way through War Zone D, killing couriers, destroying food caches, and leaving delay-fused demolitons and booby traps behind. Near its destined exit point, it found an estimated enemy regiment waiting for it, and a grand firefight ensued. TAC air was called in, a Mike Force company reinforced "Bo" Gritz, and an estimated 300 of the enemy were killed. Captured documents verified the presence of War Zone D of two regiments and the division headquarters of the 9th VC Division. There were other successful mobile guerrilla operations, but none so successful as Black Jack 33, under Hewgley and Gritz.

Special operations in Vietnam were placed in the hands of commanders who knew and understood their jobs. In the main, they were professionally handled and performed by the American volunteers who comprised the leadership of all special operations. The Vietnamese suffered a major lack of leadership at all levels, particularly noticeable at the junior officer/reconnaissance patrol leader level. The special operations were devised by Americans, supplied and paid for by Americans, and most of the special operations were led by Americans. The officers and men of SOG and the 5th SFG's extensive special operations capability can be proud of performing hazardous and difficult tasks with a minimum of recognition and honor, and no public cognizance. It is hoped that the above will assist in giving them credit long past due.

15. CIVIC ACTION AND PSY OPS, VIETNAM

At the other end of the spectrum of counterinsurgency from the guerrilla-killing activities of the special operations and Mike Forces, there were the equally important, if less glamorous, accomplishments of the Civic Action and Psychological Operations operators. Their activities, often denigrated by the tough, hard-line soldiers, were extensive and productive. They understood, as Larteguy puts it in his *Centurions*, that war "nowadays is a mixture of everything, a regular witches' brew . . . of politics and sentiment, the human soul . . . religion and the best way of cultivating rice, yes, everything, including even the breeding of black pigs." A team leader at Camp Bu Prang understood this, too, when he scrounged a white water buffalo. The sacred snake of the mountain had been killed and eaten by a Cambodian Mike Force, and the Montagnards of the village of Bu Krak had to have a big sacrifice to pacify the offended spirits. Hence the white carabao.

At its worst, Psy Ops is measured in millions of leaflets and thousands of hours of radio broadcast time; Civic Action is a give-away program and sick call. At its best, it can be of overwhelming importance, but only if it is integrated into the overall program and administered with an understanding of the needs and motivations of the people. Put out without a modicum of real sympathy and commitment, it becomes empty propaganda and phony charity, breeding indifference and apathy. Provided without continuity, it is counterproductive and plays into the hands of the insurgents who reiterate: "You see, it is just as we told you. The government tells you lies and cares nothing for your welfare."

Civic Action and Psy Ops conducted in the A camps tended to stay on the track because those who were carrying out the programs were in continuous, close contact with the target audience. Further, they lacked the big money and resources to launch a major give-away program. If the local people did not want the new school badly enough to build it, the busy SF

NCOs damned well would not build it for them.

At the lowest and simplest level, as it had been in Laos and Buon Enao, the first move in any new CIDG camp was to set up a primitive dispensary and start treating the troops, their families, and the local villagers. They worked under a tree at first, then in a tent, and finally in a whole new building, usually the best in camp.

For the long haul, simply providing medical care with U.S. medics is humanitarian, but shortsighted. The long-range goal was to create an indigenous capability, and that was done in countless locations. When you went to any Special Forces CIDG camp in Vietnam, you found a dispensary, complete with a primitive clinic, waiting room, ten-bed hospital, operating and treatment rooms, laboratory, and pharmacy. A young SF sergeant would show you around, but the nurses and medics doing the treatments would be local Vietnamese who learned their skills on the job.

Far more advanced and sophisticated were the CIDG hospitals organized in each of the four Special Forces company locations. There facilities existed for surgery, X ray, physical therapy, post-operative care, and all the other amenities of modern hospitals. But there too the real legacy left by SF was not so much the healed wounds and cured diseases as it was the trained Vietnamese personnel.

Another activity, more like the Peace Corps than the sensational John Wayne image, was in the field of agriculture and animal husbandry. Although there were no slots for agricultural experts within the Special Forces group (there were in SA-FASIA on Okinawa), and that type of expertise is considered to be the province of AID rather than SF, the wide range of talents found in Special Forces always included a few frustrated farmers and ranchers. Further, the system and the men in it were flexible enough to accommodate and support their ideas.

Many an early agricultural project was the brainchild of a single NCO looking for some way to improve the local condition of life in the area near his isolated A Camp. Such was the case with M. Sgt. Dennis Kidd's experimental farm at Minh Tanh in 1965. So successful was that project, devised and set up almost entirely by Kidd himself, that the VC in a rare case of selective terror directed against one American, ambushed and killed him. But they could not kill his idea.

More formalized than the individual efforts of the type that Kidd and others initiated were projects like the experimental and training farm run by the SF C Detachment in Pleiku. There student farmers from CIDG camps in the II Corps highland area were taught such peaceful skills as crop raising, pigpen construction, the inoculation of swine, and blacksmithing. That farm was run by such dedicated and knowledgeable men as M. Sgt. Paul Johnson and Sfc. John Roberts. It raised cattle, pigs, chickens, sheep, goats, rabbits, geese, guinea pigs, and pigeons, plus carp in fish ponds. The permanent party of Montagnards were refugees. The student farmers grew peanuts, okra, eggplant, corn, sweet potatoes, and sugarcane. After a course at the school, the graduates took their ideas home along with packages of seed, some livestock, and some tools. The local SF/CIDG camps provided a little support to get the projects going.

The range of activities under the heading of civic actions and political warfare was almost endless. It included construction of dependent housing, presentation of entertainment by culture and drama teams, medical patrols, newspapers published in the Montagnard dialect, inoculation against disease, bridge building, rehabilitation of village marketplaces, training for nurse's aides, dissemination of leaflets, and even the aerial movement of elephants.

That latter admittedly unusual operation was dubbed Operation "Bahroom," in recognition of the noisy intestinal gas reaction caused by elephant tranquilizers. Word of the operation reached England and caused protest from animal lovers who understood that an elephant was to be dropped by parachute. Actually, there were two elephants—Bonnie and Clyde—but their movement to the CIDG camp at Tra Bong in I Corps was not by parachute, but by Air Force C-130 aircraft, and finally by a Marine Corps CH-53 helicopter. The Marine Corps, never shy about publicity and fearful that the April Fool's Day operation might not be credited, provided two helicopters to members of the press. The entire considerable Montagnard population of the vicinity of Tra Bong attended, and apparently curiosity overcame the usual VC caution, as a CIDG ambush patrol picked off three enemy rubberneckers. "Bahroom" was unquestionably a grandstand play, but the Montagnard sawmill where Bonnie and Clyde went to work and a host of other locally developed projects were not.

The Civic Action NCO at Tra Bong for three years, Sergeant, First Class Campbell, was a great collector of Montagnard artifacts. He encouraged the local handicraft industry by purchasing various kinds of baskets from his Yards when they visited the camp. He also established liaison with one particular Yard who came in once a month bearing a single silver "Piastre de Commerce" minted in 1886. Apparently the Yard had a trove of those coins stashed away and satisfied his needs by selling them one at a time to the SF sergeant. Allegedly, each Vietnam-minted piaster sold in U.S. coin shops for approximately a thousand dollars, allowing Sergeant Campbell to educate his son in college with enough left over for a graduation automobile. The author has carried an 1887 piaster, unfortunately worth about eight dollars in silver content, given him by Sergeant Campbell, since 1967 as a good-luck piece. One wonders if somewhere outside Tra Bong that Montagnard is still sitting on a pile of those valuable piasters.

There is no intent to intimate that only Special Forces in Vietnam carried out civic action and psychological operations, for there was a great deal of the same sort of thing done by troops everywhere. However, it is important to note that in the SF/CIDG program that activity was intimately tied in with an overall concept that in turn was based on the local people. It was not simply a give-away program or a humanitarian, do-gooder effort. It was associated with a capability to provide security and had definite goals. Too much so-called civic action has no purpose beyond seeking friendship, but as any welfare worker knows, charity does not buy friends.

The 5th Special Forces Group believed that civic actions and psychological operations were so important that in 1966, a major reorganization was effected to accommodate that belief. The S-5 Section was relieved of responsibility for psychological operations and was renamed the Revolutionary Developments Section. Psychological Operations were placed under the S-3 (Plans and Operations) Section to conform with the Vietnamese political warfare section, and given responsibility for education, information, troop benefits, dependent care, and the other matters that affected the morale and welfare of the civilian irregular troops. The first priority was given to the strikers, the next to the dependents and general population, and the third to the enemy. The care and assistance of the CIDG soldier and his family were given increased emphasis. In addition, the A detachments were augmented by a Psychological Operations officer and a Psychological Operations noncommissioned officer. They also had responsibility for the Civic Action program, answering both to the S-3 and Revolutionary Development Sections. The reorganization was both to enhance those operations and to involve the Vietnamese Special Forces more fully in preparation for the visualized "Vietnamization" of the CIDG program.

The whole concept of Special Forces operations from the earliest guerrilla days had always been to get the indigenous people to do the job. It was only natural that that doctrine was carried on into the noncombat effort as well. The name of the game was self-help and training, not give-away. The give-away aspect was limited to the donation of thousands of kits—farmer tool kits, midwife kits, barber kits, blacksmith kits, carpenter kits, health kits, and school kits. The work was homegrown. Vietnamization, billed as a new and startling idea in 1969, had been the basis for the CIDG program from 1962 on.

On 24 September 1970, the Chief of Staff of the Armed Forces of the Republic of Vietnam awarded the 5th Special Forces Group the rather unusual "Civic Action Medal," citing among other accomplishments the setting up of 49,902 economic aid projects, 34,334 educational projects, 35,468 welfare projects, and 10,959 medical projects; furnishing 14,934 transportation facilities; supporting nearly half a million refugees; digging 6,436 wells and repairing 1,949 kilometers of road; establishing 129 churches, 272 markets, 110 hospitals, and 398 dispensaries; and building 1,003 classrooms and 670 bridges. Special Forces old-timers know that it was not Americans who accomplished those feats, but they know, too, that the Civic Action streamer on the colors of the 5th Special Forces Group was well earned and means more than many of the more traditional battle honors.

16. SPECIAL SUPPORT AND SPECIAL PROBLEMS

As noted earlier, the Central Intelligence Agency conceived the initial CIDG program, started it, and ran it during the early days. With relatively few Americans in-country, and fewer still in the remote highlands, the quiet and inconspicuous Village Defense Program was allowed to freewheel with little or no interference. Only a handful of CIA officers controlled the ever-growing program, including the provision of arms, equipment, supplies, and money to pay the CIDG full-time strikers. Under the simple CIA regulations, accountability was virtually non-existent, for once equipment or money was distributed, it was just written off—there were no property books as such. CIA money was used to purchase services and material that would have been quite impossible if the funds were subjected to official audits or fiscal accountability.

When MACV took over the CIDG program in 1963, the CIA was pretty much phased out (of the program, not Vietnam) and left the program with the greatest legacy possible—the CIA funding and support system remained in effect. Whoever was the genius who arranged that transaction should get a high-ranking medal, for he saved the U.S. government hundreds of millions of dollars over the next nine years. That unique funding program was named "Parasol-Switchback," and funds for the CIDG program were delivered directly to Special Forces in Vietnam. Of course, to protect the commanders, logisticians, and payroll officers, there was a system of records and accounting internal to Special Forces which pretty much followed standard Army procedures, but the provisions of the U.S. Military Assistance Program for Vietnam were not applicable, and offshore procurement without abiding by the U.S. balance-of-payment control regulations was possible. This meant that control of materials, supplies, and, above all, funds (to include CIDG pay for the strikers) remained in the hands of the U.S. Special Forces until the time they were issued to the ultimate

174

users. It also meant that goods and services could be purchased by all levels of the command from local sources. Much of the CIDG food was purchased locally, which helped the economy of the areas in which the CIDG was located. All requisition and other supply procedures were greatly simplified. If an A camp needed something on an emergency basis, it had simply to get on the radio and put in an emergency request; the supplies would be airlifted to them within hours, direct from the Logistical Support Center in Nha Trang. Repair facilities were concentrated at Nha Trang, with a simple exchange procedure for damaged or unworkable equipment. There was a fairly large staff of Filipino civilians hired to repair all the thousands of line items used by the CIDG program. Virtually none of the above would have been possible following standard MAP or U.S. Army supply and funding procedures.

In the summer of 1964, when Gen. Doan Can Quang took over as the new commanding general of the Vietnamese Special Forces, he complained of this situation to Col. John Spears, the new commanding officer of the U.S. Special Forces, his "advisor." He pointed out the inconsistency of his ostensible command position and the hard fact that "he who pays commands." Spears handled the statement with his usual rough and hearty diplomacy, but to himself he said: "You're damned right!"

CIA's special funding and support system was not tied to the Army's complex and ponderous logistical system, except where it suited. If a local U.S. Army ammo dump had the necessary mortar shells, SF would draw from them and later transfer the money to pay for it, but since the CIDG program was armed with obsolete U.S. weapons, most modern ammo would not be suitable. For the diminutive CIDG, U.S. Army boots and uniforms were too big, too fancy, and too expensive, so Special Forces called on its own Counterinsurgency Support Office (CISO) on Okinawa, a small but immensely effective special logistical support mechanism. CISO's only military man was an Army colonel, the other dozen or so being long-time DA civilians. For boots, uniforms, ponchos, and other CIDG items, CISO would simply let a contract in Japan, Korea, Taiwan, or even Saigon, and cheap Oriental labor would provide what was needed fast and at a fraction of the cost of a comparable U.S.-supplied item.

When SF and CIDG found they needed rucksacks for troops on extended operations and patrols, a captured VC model was sent to CISO. Within a couple of months, 5,000 rucksacks were on hand at a cost of $2.80 a copy. Over the years almost 350,000 of these simple packs were used by the CIDG in Vietnam at a cost of some $5 million less than for a like number of the standard Army model.

The story of the patrol ration is another classic example of the simple flexibility of the CIA/CISO system versus normal development and procurement. A light, compact field ration was sorely needed for CIDG, and again the standard U.S. Army canned C rations were too big, too heavy, unsuited to the Asiatic taste, and too expensive for the CIDG budget. The 5th Special Forces was pressuring CISO for help because the strikers were getting tired of ten-day patrols with a sockful of rice, a few cans of sardines, and some *nuoc mam** sauce. Conrad "Ben" Baker, the civilian deputy of CISO, wrote the Army's Combat Development Command for help. The response took two months and rested on bureaucratic charter—"indigenous feeding is not within the purview of this command." Next he wrote the Quartermaster Laboratory in Natick, Massachusetts, only to be told that such a development would cost $5 million and would take five years. Ben doubted the war would be over in five years, but he knew the CIDG budget couldn't stand the $5-million price tag, and besides the guys in the 5th SF were getting damned impatient. In desperation, he bought $200 worth of rice, shrimp, raisins, pepper, squid, and other odds and ends—even some whale meat—and went to work in his own kitchen. After working out the problems, he found a local Ryukuan named Yogi Skokai to package and produce his invention.

The result was the PIR (Patrol Indigenous Ration). As Ben Baker said, "They may not be mother's home-cooking," but they were light, cheap, easy to prepare, and highly successful. The dehydrated rice and the meat or fish came in a plastic container into which some water was poured. In a short time,

*A delicious and nutritious sauce of rotted fish and red peppers, rich in protein, richer yet in odor.

the contents reconstituted. The ration in one sack was big enough to last all day, and the strikers would tie it on the back of their belts in the morning and snack out of it when hungry. Over a period of six years, CISO and Yogi Skokai made and shipped about 20-million-days supply of PIRs, at a cost to the United States of $23 million. It would have cost $22 million more to feed U.S. C rations, which were too heavy anyway. The U.S. Army's lightweight patrol ration would have cost $73 million more.

In addition, Special Forces dealt through civilian contractors to have various buildings built, such as the very extensive Logistic Support complex at Nha Trang, where all classes of supply for 40,000 men for sixty days were stored. The dedicated Filipino civilians who performed all the repair and maintenance were employees of the Eastern Construction Company, Inc., and fully paid their cost in salvaged carbines, radios, and vehicles that were saved for future use.

Without the special funding system of the CIA, there simply could not have been a CIDG program. Legislation prohibits the expenditure of MAP money to pay indigenous troops or to buy such items as the uniforms, boots, and webbing. Gold flow restrictions forbid the purchase of large quantities of non-U.S. goods, but CIDG soldiers were paid, fed, clothed, equipped, housed, and even buried with inexpensive locally procured materials.

Best of all, the system gave speed of response and great flexibility. If a SF/CIDG patrol came back out of the jungle with 100 starving Montagnard refugees from VC slave labor camps, bags of rice and the beginnings of materials to build a village could be delivered on site in less than twenty-four hours. The dedicated Army, later Air Force, Caribou pilots and crews were largely responsible for rapid response. Many a time they flew at night, in the mountains, and in bad weather to resupply an embattled CIDG camp by parachute drop or low-level extraction. Outside of the system, provisions to build a village had to go through the Government of Vietnam or U.S. AID channels and might take many weeks, or could be disapproved by an official in an air-conditioned office who didn't like Montagnards.

Naturally, the system had its flaws and its problems. It

placed great responsibility on the shoulders of the lowest-ranking SF operators, who in addition to advising and leading a "jackleg" battalion of irregulars, were saddled with highly complex financial and logistical responsibilities. A twenty-five-year-old SF captain detachment commander was expected to lead his fourteen-man detachment, advise a veteran and frequently hardheaded Vietnamese Special Forces detachment, train a 400- to 500-man battalion of illiterate Montagnards, be responsible for approximately half a million dollars of equipment and ammunition, pay a monthly payroll of approximately $15,000, supervise intelligence funds, obtain approximately $50,000 worth of supplies each month, conduct operations that kept one-third of his force in the field at all times, and conduct psychological operations, intelligence operations, and civic action projects, while being capable of briefing General Westmoreland who might drop into any CIDG camp with no notice. It asked a great deal of the fine young men who lived far from friendly forces, literally surrounded by the enemy and under intense physical, mental, and moral pressure. It also meant that in the SF/CIDG program Special Forces officers and NCOs became aware of problems of graft and corruption that never touched the U.S. advisors with other Vietnamese ARVN units. Because SF officers controlled pay, rations, and supplies, they noted and reported the problems and worked to correct them. MACV, in its isolation, deduced that only SF had graft and corruption, and chalked it up to "typical inefficiency of an irregular operation run by those snake-eaters."

It is doubtful that the expenditures versus accomplishment of the Vietnam War can ever be adequately calculated, for war is by nature an incredibly inefficient and wasteful business. It is too bad, because if it could be done, there is little doubt that it would show that the United States got a better return on the CIDG dollar than it did on any other. It is the fond, and perhaps vain, hope of the few men who know and understand the unique nature of the CIDG funding system that it might serve as a model for providing support to any future U.S. operation struggling with the complex problems of counterinsurgency.

No story of the Special Forces in Vietnam would be complete without some comments regarding the companion Vietnamese organization, the Vietnamese Special Forces (VNSF),

*Brigadier General Quang, CG ARVN
Special Forces at dedication of memorial to LLDB dead, Nha
Trang, 1966*

or more accurately the *Luc Luong Dac Biet* (LLDB). Feeling
within SF runs very high on this subject, and one can easily
find many SF veterans of Vietnam who roundly condemn the
LLDB and can tell stories by the hour of laziness, cowardice,
and corruption. The LLDB was certainly a mixed blessing and
in some cases a serious problem, but to write off the whole
outfit would be grossly unfair to a great many dedicated, courageous soldiers who fought that war for a long, long time. In
the many talks of disagreement and even open warfare between
the USSF and the LLDB, the two sides of the story differ
markedly, though often only one side was heard. There were
cases of laziness, cowardice, and corruption on the part of
USSF too, but one doesn't hear these too often. The USSF
supervisory chain of command had exceptionally high mobility
with its attached helicopters, while the LLDB were almost
totally dependent on their American advisors for transportation
to supervise their field detachments. Close supervision can do
a great deal in detecting and correcting lack of effort or wrong-
doing, and very few USSF field team leaders and members
survived their transgressions for any significant period of time.

One must recognize, too, that in the rapid expansion of Special Forces, a great many young American officers and soldiers came into the program who had absolutely no ability or desire to get along with Asiatics, and hence created friction and misunderstanding. That fault was unfortunately not always limited to the inexperienced and the young. The problem of the LLDB, however, was larger than a personal one—it was historical and conceptual, and needs some explanation.

As we have seen, the Vietnamese Special Forces were organized in 1956, under the name of the 1st Observation Battalion. Not an official part of the Vietnamese Armed Forces, they operated directly under the Presidential Survey Office (PSO), enjoying a very special status. During the turbulent days just before the overthrow of President Diem, they were the object of considerable unfavorable publicity as a band of Brother Nhu's bullyboys who beat up monks and burned pagodas. Colonel Tung, the commander, was among those murdered at the time of the coup; it was not surprising that he was high on the blacklist of those who eliminated Diem and Nhu.

That was scarcely a promising heritage for an organization that was to work with U.S. Special Forces and the rural population in an effort to win the hearts and minds of the people. If you have difficulty understanding why the LLDB was ever brought into the CIDG program in the first place, it should be recalled that the CIA was involved both in the training of the LLDB and the founding of the CIDG program, using USSF detachments in both cases. There is a long history of the CIA using USSF teams to make up for its perennial shortage of manpower. Many of the CIA field operators were (and are) ex-USSF, so it is not unnatural that they turn to the Army outfit they know best. Further, the marriage of USSF and the Vietnamese Special Forces has a certain superficial logic.

After the death of Diem, Nhu, and Tung, the VNSF became officially a part of the Vietnamese Armed Forces, and the new LLDB officially dated its birthday from 1963. Ended were the palace guard missions, but suspicion and lack of rapport within the Vietnamese Army would not be erased so easily. That problem was to hound the LLDB in the years to come and seriously hamper its efforts to obtain the high-quality people it so badly needed.

More serious than that internal problem were the organizational, conceptual, and command complications that arose from the mere presence of *any* Vietnamese unit placed between the USSF, and the CIDG and the people. The incredibly unwieldy system created meant that technically the USSF were advisors to the VNSF, who in turn commanded the CIDG troops and the camps. In actual practice, the SF troops made it work, but it worked in spite of the system, not because of it, and it worked because the USSF advisors controlled the purse strings and everything else important.

In the regular MACV advisory system, a twenty-five-year-old American captain, on his first overseas tour and undergoing his first exposure to combat, was expected to advise a thirty-five-year-old Vietnamese *Dai Uy* (captain) who had fought the Viet Minh and VC for years. His only leverage was to be his personality and superior logic—a little difficult to put across without a knowledge of the local language. In the SF advisory effort there were some old veterans, and usually language-trained men, but if that did not work they still controlled the pay, the rations, the weapons and ammo, the transportation, the air support, the intelligence fund—in short, everything important.

The problems that arose from that double-layered system were often serious and sometimes fatal. Particularly in the highland areas, the interposition of flatland Vietnamese between the Americans and the Montagnards often resulted in friction which sometimes escalated to fights and shoot-outs. In September of 1964, the bad feelings between Montagnards and the Vietnamese resulted in armed uprisings in five CIDG camps in the II Corps Tactical Zone: Buon Brieng, Ban Don, Bu Prang, Buon Sar Pa, and Buon Mi Ga. Some twenty-six Vietnamese Special Forces soldiers were killed, others were held captive, together with several hundred Vietnamese civilians. The situation was ripe for a bloodbath, and seventeen other Vietnamese Popular Force soldiers and two Vietnamese civilians were also killed. Due to the intervention of U.S. Special Forces advisors, the situation was brought under control with some governmental concessions to Montagnard nationalism. Intelligent, courageous action by such SF men as Capt. Vernon Gillespie at Buon Brieng saved the lives of many more Vietnamese and stopped the spread of the rebellion. For the record, it should be added that in the eyes of SF, the widely publicized activities of "Fritz" Freund, a "leg" colonel from the MACV advisory team, were not what saved the day. As usual, not everyone agrees, and Freund emerged a hero, parlaying the affair into a brigadier general's star, finally retiring as a major general.

Fortunately for the program, not all the VNSF were so shortsighted. Many understood the Montagnard problem and dealt with it intelligently. In a few cases, Montagnards were commissioned as officers in the LLDB, and were highly effective leaders. A Montagnard LLDB captain camp commander at Cheo Reo Camp in II Corps kept a notebook with the names of the complete VC infrastructure in an area of operations, crossing them out one by one as they were killed or captured. General Quang, who commanded the LLDB from 1965 to 1969, understood the problem as well as anyone in Vietnam, as did his deputy, Col. Ho Tieu. Correcting a situation that had built up over centuries, however, was something else again.

Another aspect of the LLDB presence caused a broader, though less dramatic, problem. The concept of the CIDG program was to move into an area, help the local people develop a capability to provide their own security and improve their condition of life, creating ultimately a situation stable enough to permit Special Forces (both U.S. and Vietnamese) to leave. If that departure were to take place, that which was left behind must have its own homegrown leadership. As long as LLDB officers were on site, *they* were in charge, severely limiting the effective training of local leaders. As a matter of policy, CIDG leaders above the company level were forbidden, though most every camp had a leader acknowledged by the CIDG, if not by the LLDB. The regular army LLDB officer or NCO, with his family living in Da Nang, Saigon, or Dalat, often had little feeling for the scruffy peasant hamlet of Phan Hoa. What was needed was local leadership—men whose family, roots, and rice fields were all there and who had real long-range stakes in the future of their communities. It would be unjust to blame that situation on the LLDB, who are unable to defend themselves and who for the most part functioned as well as they could. It was a basic error of concept and once the program was under way, became nearly impossible to change.

There were other conflicts, frictions, and misunderstandings for Special Forces in Vietnam. That was scarcely unique to Special Forces or even to the military services. Veterans of the Washington scene are only too well aware of the massive efforts devoted to infighting between government agencies, institutions, and departments. Generally speaking, this competition and rivalry dies away as one gets out in the field and further away from the high-level planning and budget fights. Doctrinal squabbles over service roles and missions seem rather foolish when the bullets fly. The Air Force pressured the Army into giving up its twin-engined Caribou transport aircraft that were so vital to supplying the over 100 CIDG installations in South Vietnam. The Air Force then took over those aircraft and performed as well as, if not better than, the Army airmen who had supported Special Forces so well. For the 5th Mike Force parachute drop onto Bunard, the Air Force fleet of eight C-123 aircraft could not have performed more perfectly. They were lined up at midnight in perfect alignment, with the aircraft inspected and ready to go. The troops filed on board about 0200 hours in the morning. Every clamshell door closed together, every left engine started simultaneously, followed by every right engine. All turned to the left together and taxied to the end of the runway in exact spacing. Then one by one at five-second intervals, they took off. They flew several hundred miles to the drop zone ninety miles north of Saigon and arrived within sixty seconds of the planned time, where they proceeded to drop the troops at a precise 700 feet above the ground, flying in trail. It has never been done better. The Air Force FACS (Forward Air Controllers), with their little Bird Dog propeller aircraft, lived in many Special Forces camps and performed essential and flawless aerial reconnaissance over many camp sectors of operations. As noted, the Air Commandos were the blood brothers of Special Forces and will always be blessed in the memories of Vietnam veterans (indeed I myself would not be here today but for the intervention of the 1st Air Commandos).

Generally speaking, at the action level, people in Vietnam

got along pretty well across the board—Special Forces and conventional troops, ground forces and air forces, military and civilian, all the jumble of alphabet soup (such as CIA, USOM, MACV, CIDG, USIS, CORDS, and USAF). Gerry Hickey, a civilian anthropologist from the Rand Corporation, fought side by side with Roger Donlon at the battle of Nam Dong. Conventional unit artillerymen lived and fought in CIDG camps. Navy Seabee construction teams and Army engineers lived in and built many new CIDG camps throughout the country. CIA field operators worked hand in glove with local SF Teams (in many cases, they were ex-SF anyway). AID loaned SF seed, corn, or cement for civic actions, SF loaned AID representatives weapons for self-defense. The instances of cooperation and mutual support are endless—and seldom mentioned.

It would be foolish to say that all was sweetness and light, or that there was no friction. Special Forces had its share, or more, for they came into the game with some ready-made rivalries dating from "before the war." The old charge of "lack of discipline" cropped up, particularly in the early days. Special Forces troopers would occasionally roll in to the relative security of some large Vietnamese town from one of their boondock camps. Dressed in their nonregulation tiger suits and muddy boots, they would proceed to whoop it up, blowing off steam with the assistance of liquid relaxing agents. If a fight didn't break out before dawn with some of the local MAAG types, it was pure luck. It was naturally frustrating to the local U.S. MAAG colonel that he had no jurisdiction over those hell-raisers, but in 1962 and 1963, CIA bowed to no one.

Col. George Morton, first commander of U.S. Army Special Forces Provisional (Vietnam), had no compunctions about going to bat for his troops and telling MAAG to keep hands off. That scarcely led to feelings of warm friendship, and the accusation was made, not without some justification, that SF was "not on the team." Col. John Spears and Col. Bill McKean, both highly respected infantrymen who commanded SF between '64 and '66, worked long and hard to kill that criticism. Besides, by mid-1964, the CIA had backed out of the CIDG program, and SF was under the MACV chain of command.

In 1965, the advent of the large American conventional combat units introduced a new set of pluses and minuses. The pluses resulted from the greatly increased and highly mobile combat strengths of big American units with their heavy firepower and almost unlimited resources. Many a time the presence of the Americans saved CIDG camps from almost certain overrun. General Westmoreland regularly identified the CIDG camps that his intelligence people told him were most vulnerable to attack and defeat, and he charged the U.S. commanders in each Corps Tactical Zone to see that did not happen. They, in turn, positioned combat units for rapid reaction, intensified reconnaissance around the threatened camps, reinforced the camps with engineers and fortification materiel, and generally took the camps under their protection. Without such support, the camps at Khe Sanh, Dak Pek, Dak To, Duc Co, Loc Ninh, and all the camps in War Zone C were very much at risk and might very well have been crushed.

The uniquely American policy of never operating outside the fan of supporting artillery caused many misunderstandings between the Americans and the SF. Numerous times division commanders would tell young captains advising supporting CIDG companies: "Son, you just take your Mike Force out on my left flank and find yourself an enemy force. When you yell for help, I'll take them off your back!" Young captains tend to believe generals, so they would enthusiastically undertake their armed reconnaissance and would end up surrounded, jubilantly radioing the general, "I've got them! They are all around me!" Invariably, they would be extracted by helicopter, and nothing further would come of the Mike Force's high-risk actions. American commanders just did not send their forces tooting off into unknown situations without artillery support, and the SF learned that over the years, to their sorrow.

The exceptions to that rule sometimes resulted in dramatic successes. Late in 1966, two CIDG companies from Camp Hiep Hoa on the Vam Co River were operating on Charlie's west bank of the river and succeeded in catching a VC battalion between two east-west lines of troops anchored on the river, but with the western end open for the VCs to escape. Their radio calls for support attracted a skinny little bantycock, Brigadier General Shaw, the Assistant Division Commander of the 25th Division. He flew over to ascertain the situation and, without hesitation, called for a battalion of that division to be inserted at the west end as a "catcher's mitt." Indeed, he subordinated the command of that battalion to the senior SF officer on the ground, a captain. The daylight operation that ensued resulted in the destruction of the majority of that VC battalion, with a spectacular number of enemy killed and captured. That quiet little professional general now lives in the minds of at least some of us as a man who knew how and when to fight and one who would fight when appropriate—they aren't all that common.

Other problems with the Americans came from their tendency to equate the light little CIDG companies with their own heavy infantry. They also mistakenly thought of them as subordinates rather than allies, and frequently took command of situations that were well in hand of the SF leaders. In early 1967, the company commander of A Company in III Corps, Lt. Col. John Hayes, had two Mike Force companies patrolling in War Zone C. They bumped into a VC hospital which the VC defended fiercely until it could be evacuated, and the lead Mike Force company was badly mauled. John joined the operation after they blasted a one-chopper LZ in the jungle and called for a replacement Mike Force company to fly in and evacuate the combat-ineffective company. Twenty HU-1D helicopters from a helicopter unit that usually supported the Big Red One Division, one by one deposited the replacements, loaded casualties and evacuees, and took off. John was on the ground guiding each chopper in with hand signals, and everything was going about as well as it could. The chopper movement attracted an assistant division commander of the 1st Division, known for his macho and profanity, who radioed to John on the ground, "Let go, dumb-shit. I'm in charge now." Under the guidance of the airborne general, the last two choppers, numbers nineteen and twenty, crashed upon landing and created a major evacuation problem themselves.

In 1965, the situation in II Corps was badly deteriorated. The highway from coastal Qui Nhon to Pleiku was cut, Pleiku was near starvation, and there was a critical shortage of troops throughout the corps. The top brass in II Corps ordered SF to move several companies of Rhade Montagnard CIDG from Darlac Province to An Khe to open the highway. Special Forces officers protested the order on the grounds that road-clearing against VC and NVA regulars was no mission for CIDG, that the troops had been recruited to defend their own tribal areas and families, and worst of all that you just couldn't move Rhade into the middle of Bahnar country. SF was told in no uncertain terms to stop clouding the issue with a "bunch of anthropological crap," that there was a war on, and to "get on the team." The Rhade were moved, taking heavy casualties. Many deserted and returned to Darlac, reinforcing Vietnamese arguments about the "worthless savages (moi)," and fueling the MACV complaint about never being able to count on "that undisciplined Special Forces rabble." Back in Darlac, the SF recruited the Rhade remnants back into the CIDG.

To many officers in the air-conditioned headquarters of Saigon, the entire CIDG concept was wrong. Its very name "civilian irregular" was unmilitary, and the whole operation, including that loose CIA money, badly needed discipline and regularizing. Fiascos, such as the Montagnard revolts of 1964 and 1965, only reinforced that belief. Overlooking the centuries-old sociological problem, the military "solution" was to "put all those damned people in the Army where they can be controlled."

Col. Jasper "Jap" Wilson, senior advisor of I, II, and finally III Corps, hated all airborne and the SF worst of all. He made no bones that he would rather have none in his area, and then went back to the States and blasted his anti-SF message from the podiums of the Army's service colleges.

The Chief of Staff of the Army, Gen. Harold K. Johnson, was incensed over the SF dominance in the press coverage. He always opposed specialty troops of all kinds, and held to the line that counterinsurgency was the Army's business, not the exclusive province of SF. Special Forces couldn't have agreed with him more and would have been happy to have the reporters off their backs, to say nothing of sharing the heavy counterinsurgency burden.

Another source of friction in the early days was a big pay differential that existed up until the end of 1964. The MAAG advisors were in Vietnam on one-year tours, which the Army calls Permanent Change of Station (PCS). SF teams, as they were in Laos, were on six-month TDY tours and thus drew extra "per diem" money. The system had many advantages besides the obvious financial boost to SF troopers. It was a major incentive to repetitive tours in Vietnam and thus guaranteed a heavy leavening of Laos and Vietnam veterans on all teams. Further, it permitted the 1st Special Forces Group on Okinawa, and the 5th and 7th Special Forces Groups at Fort Bragg, to select and train entire teams that would then deploy and serve together in Vietnam. The importance of team integrity was something that the old-timers learned back in the OSS days, when putting together of Jedburgh Teams was referred to as "engagement" and "marriage." But the voices of those who wanted SF to be just like everybody else won out. By early 1965, SF was on PCS, and the old USASFP(V) was replaced by the 5th Special Forces Group.

It would be wrong to exaggerate the friction, to imply that it was all unreasonable, or that SF was blameless. The fact is that it did exist, it hurt, and should not be discounted in understanding that when the CIDG program was Vietnamized and Special Forces went home, there were few voices of regret.

17. INTELLIGENCE

Contrary to popular opinion, the field of intelligence is not a particularly strong point with Special Forces, though both guerrilla and counterinsurgency operations can be no more successful than the intelligence on which they depend. It is necessary to explain that the military use of the term *intelligence* is not that of Webster's Dictionary. Information becomes intelligence only after it is collated with other information, analyzed, interpreted, and disseminated. The sources of information vary widely, from patrol reports to satellite imagery, and the more sophisticated the source, the higher the classification on the information derived from that source. The more widely known classifications, such as "secret" or "top secret," are used if appropriate, but some sources are so sensitive that they are given additional "code word"* classifications. For example, if it were possible to fasten a tiny camera to a dragonfly trained to fly over Vietnam, the results of that imagery could be code-worded with some such label as "Alpha" and the dissemination of those photographs limited to only those with an Alpha clearance. Only people with a "need-to-know" the contents of the photographs would have access to them. If cleared for access to a code word category, it is forbidden to tell anyone else of the existence of that code word, to say nothing of the subject or the means of collection. Thus the Army is divided into two camps, the vast majority ignorant of code word intelligence, and the tiny minority with access to most of the nation's secrets.

By 1966, in Vietnam the 5th Special Forces Group had grown to a strength of about eighty CIDG camps spread the width and breadth of the country. Each camp had at least one man whose specialty was intelligence on virtually a full-time basis. The group headquarters had a sizable S-2 (Intelligence)

*This is *not* the term used by the military.

section at Nha Trang, kept very busy collating and reporting information from the field to J-2 MACV. The J-2 was suitably grateful, as something around 50 percent of *all* information reports that came into his hands came from the 5th Special Forces. In return, J-2 provided the 5th with maps, terrain studies, and readouts of infrared imagery, suitably sterilized as "hot spot" maps. Nobody in 5th Special Forces was particularly surprised or upset about that, as they never had gotten much from J-2—it was pretty much a one-way street. In addition, most of the intelligence people in the 5th were combat intelligence types, more accustomed to debriefing a reconnaissance patrol than interpreting an aerial photo. The 5th Group S-2 officer was usually some crackerjack young infantry major picked for his combat experience and sharpness rather than his knowledge and intelligence. The analytical capability of the S-2 section was minimal, and the CIDG camps didn't get any more help from the Group S-2 section than the group got from J-2. In fact, the Group S-2 section posted the results of each camp's reports as the basis for its Order of Battle of the enemy forces.

The status of each camp's intelligence holdings was pretty much a product of how good an intelligence sergeant it had, and of how active it was in operations outside the camp. It was pretty easy to tell which camps were active on operations by listening to their intelligence briefing. To a lesser extent, the number of contacts, KIAs, and captured weapons was also a direct measure of intelligence excellence or failure. Most of the camps patrolled blindly, covering the assigned area of operations in its entirety about once a month. An elite few of the camps knew exactly what they were looking for and approximately where to find it. The camp on Phu Quoc Island was an excellent example of a camp that knew its enemy. Working with the local police and Vietnamese military, Capt. Bob Maples, a veteran Special Forces ex-NCO, compiled the names and locations of all VC units on the island. He knew most of the names of the listed 385 VC members of those units. He systematically went after those units, using combined (all services) amphibious operations, and eliminated all but a handful in less than six months—a storybook operation. His immediate predecessor never left camp, and the only thing he knew about the enemy was that they mortared his camp several nights a week.

Some camps employed agents within their areas of operations, though most of the agents were simple woodchoppers, fishermen, or farmers who were depended upon for early warning against an impending VC attack. The advent of the NVA regular divisions in early 1965 pretty much negated the use of agents. The NVA depended on local VC agents to provide them the layout of the camps and to guide them to the camps for attacks. It was difficult to detect that sort of attack before it was right on you, and then it was too late.

In August 1966, when as the new deputy commander of the group in Nha Trang, I visited the S-2 section and asked to see the input from J-2 MACV, they showed me the maps, "hot spot" reports, and a few terrain studies, but that was it. A quick trip to J-2 MACV in Saigon supported the finding: the 5th Special Forces Group was not even on the distribution list for J-2 MACV intelligence products. Those products were virtually all "code word" documents and *no one* in the 5th Special Forces Group was cleared for code word, for the group did not have even one code word billet! It is highly doubtful that any of the relatively unsophisticated intelligence people in the group even knew that the code word category existed, though it's hard to believe that all of the previous commanders were also ignorant.

The solution to the 5th SF Group's intelligence dilemma appeared about a month later in the person of Lt. Col. Dick Ruble, a professional intelligence officer assigned to MACV. He had control of a large detachment of military intelligence professionals whom he wanted to distribute in a number of our border CIDG camps disguised as Special Forces, but *not* under the command of the Special Forces commander. I told him that the only way that could take place would be for him and his detachment to join the Special Forces group as bona fide members of 5th Special Forces Group, with his detachment distributed at every level from group headquarters to companies, B Detachments, and CIDG camps. He would be the Group S-2, and I would see that he was airborne-qualified at the earliest opportunity.

He finally agreed, and the detachment brought with it a number of code word clearances and billets, so that the senior officers of the group were allowed inside the "green doors" all over Vietnam, and the lights went on! MACV J-2 documents started to stream in once the billets were established and filled, the 110-man detachment became the vital nucleus for greatly strengthened S-2 sections at all levels of the group, and Dick got to put his agent nets out. Dick and his men labored deep into the night every day for six months, and got our group's intelligence regulations and practices in line with what the U.S. Army wanted. It was a shock for us to learn all the things of which we were ignorant and which we were doing incorrectly, simply out of necessity. The U.S. Army did not educate its combat arms officers that such regulations and practices even existed—not at any level of schooling, from basic branch course through the Army War College.

The Group S-2 and each company were augmented by an analysis branch and a counterintelligence branch. The rapidity of analysis dramatically improved the success of field operations as *intelligence* was provided the CIDG camps for almost the first time.

Counterintelligence was a particularly sensitive subject in CIDG camps. A primitive but effective method used among the highland tribes to ensure no VC were recruited into the strike forces of the camps was the "blood oath." That was simply making certain that every recruit was sponsored by two other members of a strike force, who swore a blood oath that the recruit was not a VC. Despite that, the U.S. Special Forces detachments always acted as though the strike forces were penetrated and contained VC agents. The Special Forces (U.S. and ARVN) lived in separate compounds inside the CIDG camps surrounded by fortifications and barbed wire, usually guarded by a detachment of Nungs under their command. Routinely, but secretly, the camp fortifications were wired for demolitions in the event that VC agents should capture a watchtower or machine gun position inside the camp—the firing point for those demolitions was invariably in the USSF inner compound. When operations were run outside the camp, the destination of the operation as a matter of Group policy was not revealed until the force was well out of camp and the operation could not be compromised. Of course, internal camp politics often negated that policy for practical reasons.

In addition to those rather simple safeguards, it was also necessary to establish agent networks for counterintelligence. Going by the book, *before* an agent operation is undertaken, it is necessary to write up a plan which describes the objective of the network, the operational details, and the specific agents that will be recruited. That plan is to be sent up the chain of command and examined at each level, to ensure that the new network will not disrupt the operations of any other intelligence operations under the cognizance of each level of command, and that the prospective agents are not already in the employ of some other U.S. (or ARVN, French, VC) intelligence service. Intelligence operations are closely examined at a highly centralized level in order that they may operate with minimum supervision—centralized approval and decentralized operations. Only after receiving top-level approval will the agents be recruited and trained, and the network placed in working order. Prior to the advent of Dick Ruble, Special Forces commanders merely did what they had to, to protect themselves, and the names of their agents were not known to *anyone* above the CIDG camps. After Ruble, all networks were recorded on written plans approved up the chain of command to MACV J-2 and above, and the agents were carded on central agent record cards forwarded to CIA. In the autumn of 1966, the entire nature of Special Forces intelligence operations changed drastically, though that fact was not widely known, due to the secret nature of the business. Once again, the CIA was in the Special Forces chain of command, though only for intelligence operations. Their role was almost entirely passive—that is, they monitored those Special Forces intelligence operations that the Saigon Chief of Station (CIA) had approved.

One such operation was a cross-border intelligence net operated by Special Forces Detachment B-57. It was a mixture of U.S. Army Military Intelligence personnel assigned to the 5th SFG, wearing Special Forces guise, and a few SF intelligence old-time NCOs, not really *of* the Special Forces. They were largely U.S. Army professional M.I. officers and men serving a one-time tour with Special Forces. B-57 was *not* SOG, as many believed, but was the direct result of Ruble's desire to establish agent networks in Special Forces camps along the Cambodian and Laotian borders. There was no participation by any member of the Republic of Vietnam government, and, in fact, the operations of B-57 were kept secret from all members of that government. The individual agents who carried out the actual operations were South Vietnamese civilians in the employ of B-57, with U.S. Army agent-handlers in Special Forces uniform. U.S. personnel did not otherwise take part in cross-border operations; they planned, directed, and managed them, and the information that resulted was handled strictly in U.S. Army intelligence channels.

That was the situation that prevailed in May 1969. Operations had gone up successfully until that time. The B-57 operation was deemed a success that provided vital intelligence, highly instrumental in saving American and South Vietnamese lives. In May, things began going wrong along the Cambodian border. Veteran agents disappeared and were killed, and some quit their jobs. The problem was investigated and narrowed down to the sectors managed by a South Vietnamese agent, one Thai Khah Chuyen, and by a long-time U.S. Special Forces sergeant. The sergeant and the suspected Vietnamese were ordered to Nha Trang where the Vietnamese was thoroughly interrogated. With the aid of the latest developments in interrogation that were legal (lie detectors and truth serum), it was established beyond doubt that Thai was a double agent in the employ of the North Vietnamese, and that he was the cause of the serious problems along the Cambodian border.

On 20 June 1969, Thai Khah Chuyen disappeared, never to be seen again. Between 20 June and 20 July, USARV (U.S. Army Vietnam) investigators made a detailed investigation that resulted in the arrest and confinement of seven members of the 5th SFG intelligence elements, to include the Group Commander. On 4 August, MACV released the news of the arrest and investigation, citing the alleged charge of murder and conspiracy to commit murder. The incident was given intensive coverage by the media, as USARV instigated an Article 32 pre-trial investigation that was open to the press.

The details are well known and much too lengthy to do justice to in a chapter, deserving a book by themselves. The investigation dragged on into September, with several well-known criminal lawyers traveling to Saigon on behalf of the defendants. The defendants gathered an impressive list of witnesses and data in their behalf, promising a circus if the case went to trial. Finally, at the end of September, from Washington, Secretary of the Army Stanley R. Resor announced that there would be no trial, as the CIA refused to testify. However, he made it plain that the U.S. Army does not and will not condone murder. This was something less than exoneration. The defendants were speedily shipped to the United States, where most of them left the Army, though two are still on active duty in Military Intelligence assignments, with appropriate promotions over the years. The entire affair was a "nowin" operation—for the defendants, Special Forces, the U.S. Army, and the United States itself. It was also unnecessary and probably due to several massive intelligence failures at levels ranging from 5th SFG to MACV to the Director of CIA.

The case is far more important than an example of intelligence failures. It was definitely a turning point in the history of Special Forces, to be followed by its decline and near extinction.

This case, the infamous "Green Beret Murder Case," has faded into history, as it should, but there are a few hard lessons to be learned by young Special Forces officers out there now, and in the years to come. When dealing in intelligence matters, don't fail to differentiate between those procedures you are taught to use when dealing with guerrillas and other groups of foreigners, and those that the U.S. Army requires for its own intelligence operations. If you don't know the U.S. Army regulations, as I didn't for many years, turn to a professional military intelligence man as a first step. Be aware of the fact that there are classified regulations for *every* aspect of intelligence operations—that is no field for improvisations. If you are not getting useful intelligence from your higher headquarters, again turn to the highest-ranking professional intelligence officer you can reach with your complaint. There is a world of intelligence available to those with the proper clearances. If the 5th SFG could operate in Vietnam for three years without the intelligence they vitally needed, it can happen again some day, and for no better reason. If you are ever involved with intelligence operations, the only time you can say "the buck stops here" is if you are the Director of CIA.

18. CIVIC ACTION AROUND THE WORLD

Civic Action differs from Civil Affairs in that it has nothing to do with combat operations; it is simply the use of men and resources of the armed forces to assist the governments and people of nations to improve on their conditions of life. The U.S. Army has a long tradition of Civic Action. One of the largest overall Civic Action programs followed the American occupation of the Philippine Islands in the early 1900s, when soldier labor and military resources were used by the U.S. occupation government to build schools, dispensaries, roads, and other civil infrastructure to better the way of life of the Filipinos, while incidentally improving the image of the U.S. Army. The Army today is still quite active in the United States in disaster assistance and relief, flood control, and the use of Army helicopters to evacuate sick and injured people in the vicinity of active Army bases.

Special Forces has participated in numerous Civic Actions all around the world. The area knowledge, languages, and cultural understanding, together with the maturity and responsibility of its members, enables the U.S. Army to send them off to remote areas for long periods of time without worrying about incidents that could damage international relations. Special Forces benefits from Civic Action missions in that it puts their detachments in the sort of situations they can anticipate if committed to combat; that is, serving in remote areas in foreign lands with the requirement to employ the local people in tasks that help themselves.

My first personal experience with Civic Action came in the early part of 1963, in Iran. I was the leader of a sixty-five man SF team consisting of four A Detachments and a B Detachment, all from my C Company of the 10th SFG in Bad Tolz. We were engaged in training 400 officers and NCOs of the Iranian Army in counterinsurgency at four sites in Western Iran. I was with the B and one A in Khermanshah, located on the Teheran-Baghdad road, high in the Zagros Mountains, when we were exposed one night to the severe shock of a major earthquake. We learned that the epicenter of the quake was to the east of Khermanshah and west of Hamadan, near a town named Kangavar.

Early the next morning, we loaded two dozen of our SF men into ¾-ton trucks together with medical supplies, simple construction tools, and radios, and dropped off a radio operator and radio with 1st Army (Iranian Royal Army) headquarters in Khermanshah. There were few villages and fewer roads in the rugged mountains trasversed by the Khermanshah-Hamadan road. In that country people do not live on individual farms and in farmhouses, rather congregating in villages from whence they till their fields and tend their flocks of sheep. The population of that area is Kurdish, oftentimes blue-eyed Aryans left over from one of the sweeps of history. On our travels through Kurdistan searching out field training sites, we often would pull off the main road to some mud-baked village perched on the side of a mountain. Young boys were posted on the roofs of each village to warn of visitors, so by the time we pulled into the village, all the village elders would be lined up, waiting to welcome us. Invariably, the welcome was warm and genuine, followed by a session sitting on the floor of the village chief's home, drinking tea and eating sweet cookies. We liked the Kurds and wanted to help them.

Kangavar early in the morning resembled a tiny bit of hell. The houses, having been constructed of rocks cemented together with mud, had all collapsed. As it was late at night when the quake struck, presumably everyone was asleep. Those who could pull themselves out of the wreckage of their houses had been busy all night trying to rescue others. There was no one on hand from the Iranian government except two young Constabulary Sarbaj, the Iranian rural police.

We quickly established a first-aid station and began treating the dozens of fractures, cuts, and concussions. The rest of us spread out through that village of several thousand people to assist in the rescue work. We radioed back to Khermanshah to request assistance from the 1st Iranian Army headquarters. We particularly needed ambulances, doctors, and medical supplies, as well as food and fuel. That town was without any useful resource except water, which was brought down from the mountains in shallow ditches thousands of feet in length. The people were miserable: injured, hungry, cold, without shelter, and with absolutely no modern medical facilities or supplies. I have never seen a more stricken place or a sorrier group of human beings. Poverty-stricken to begin with, they had lost all means of subsisting and surviving, and were beyond self-help.

Over the next two to three days, my two dozen soldiers must have seemed like angels of mercy as they treated the people's wounds, set fractures, dug out those buried in the ruins, organized the handful of Kurdish males capable of working, and began the business of restoring shelter to get the people under cover. Eventually, the Iranian Army and Constabulary responded. The U.S. MAAG in Teheran wired off to the U.S. European Command for medical assistance, and an entire Mobile Army Surgical Hospital was flown in from Europe. However, I have never forgotten either the tremendous importance of *immediate* relief for disaster victims, or what a handful of well-trained soldiers can perform when inserted into disaster areas soon after the fact.

In the days to come, we continued our assistance to the people of Kangavar. As all members of my five detachments could speak conversational Farsi, they were greeted with cries of *Salamon Aleikon* ("good-morning, afternoon, or evening") and *moteshakeram* ("thank you"). Invariably, the villagers shared their little cups of hot *cha* and whatever else they had. The word spread throughout Kurdistan, and the American soldiers with the funny green hats were welcomed, not just with courtesy, but with enthusiasm. Kurdistan today is undoubtedly the second (after Bavaria) best-prepared unconventional warfare area for Americans in the world.

In 1969, when I took command of 1st Special Forces Group on Okinawa, we immediately instituted the concept of Disaster Assistance and Relief Teams (DART) for use throughout eastern Asia. They consisted of a twelve-man A Detachment, augmented by two of the group doctors and four to six medical NCOs from the Medical Company of SAFASIA. We procured automatic inoculation "guns" for the rapid immunization of large numbers of people, and arranged to draw on the medical supplies in the warehouses of the 2nd Logistical Command on Okinawa.

Only a few months after the DARTs were organized, we deployed one of them to the Island of Luzon in the Philippines which had suffered a typhoon, causing flooding of large portions of central Luzon. With the Philippine Army, and supported by helicopters, USAID, and the American Navy, the DART team entered the flooded area and began rendering many forms of assistance. Food was in short supply, as the people were living on the tops of the one-story *nipa* huts spread throughout the area. On Luzon, the farmers lived on their land, making the mission of giving them assistance much more difficult. Small boats with outboard motors were flown in, and the members of the DART went from hut to hut, operating out of the little villages. The USAID cooked "AID Burgers," consisting of hamburger cooked inside a small loaf of bread, wrapped in foil. Thousands of immunizations were given, water was supplied, stranded people were transported, and some limited assistance in reconstruction from the damage of the typhoon was started with AID-supplied roofing tin. The DART was in communication with both Manila and 1st SFG on Okinawa, due to its organic long-range detachment radios. The DART got good training in operating as a team, in a foreign country, and working with the people. The United States got credit for its humanitarian rapid reaction to the suffering of one of its good friends.

There were several other similar disasters in the Philippines to which we sent DARTs to assist, but the Filipinos got the idea that they must organize their own military assets to help themselves in times of emergency, and our assistance became increasingly less necessary. Most foreign armies, even those equipped and trained by the United States, do not have a concept of using their armed forces to help their own people. Many foreign officers believe that such menial contact with the people is demeaning for their soldiers and themselves, and they are very reluctant to pitch in and help the people.

An exception to that rule must surely be the Republic of Indonesia. The armed forces in Indonesia are not provided with barracks; rather its members live in the local economy and report to military camps nearby every morning. Early morning throughout the islands of Indonesia sees thousands of young men walking and bicycling to their duty stations, wearing the uniforms of all the military services, the police, and coast guard. Thus the uniformed members of the regular Indonesian armed forces are a vital element in the economics of those towns abutting military installations. The commanders of the military installations are assigned the duty of Civic Actions with the communities in their area, and they are directed to use their manpower and other resources, such as trucks and bulldozers, to conduct regularly scheduled Civic Actions during duty time. Further, installation commanders are expected to raise a sizable fraction of the money needed to maintain their installations, and even pay their men. Unit commanders lucky enough to have such valuable assets as trucks, ships, and airplanes are expected to hire them out to local contractors to raise money for those purposes, and regularly do. Army trucks haul merchandise for pay, navy ships make commercial inter-island hauls, and the tiny air force does the same while supplementing the Civil Air Fleet.

Until 1965, and the overthrow of President Sukarno, the relations between Indonesia and the United States were minimal. After the removal of the pro-Communist government and the installation of Suharto, a U.S. Defense Liaison Mission was sent to Djakarta in 1967, and USAID began supplying them. Much AID-supplied material, at the request of the Indonesian government, was in support of rebuilding the economy of Indonesia. That economy was (and is) in critical shape, as all Soviet economic and military assistance ceased after 1965. Spare parts for Soviet equipment ceased after 1965. Spare parts for Soviet equipment dried up so that every day another Soviet ship or boat, airplane, truck, bus, or streetcar came to a halt and didn't start again. The streets of Djakarta are lined with men selling such salvaged parts as bolts and nuts, motor parts, electrical fittings, plumbing, and everything else imaginable to repair the obsolescent equipment of that economy.

In 1969, the 1st Special Forces Group was directed by the Commander in Chief, U.S. Army Pacific (CINCPAC), Gen. Ralph Haines, to make direct liaison with the U.S. Defense

Liaison Mission (DLM), Indonesia. My Operations Officer, the commander of the SAFASIA Civil Affairs Battalion, and I made the long flight to Djakarta to find out what was needed of 1st SFG. We determined that though the Indonesian government was strongly in favor of Civic Action programs, they lacked the know-how to plan them. Civic Action projects were conducted, but on an ad hoc basis with no planning objectives or goals, and in a highly decentralized manner. We proposed conducting a Civic Action course for officers of the Indonesian armed forces, to teach them how to survey their assigned areas of responsibility and then evolve Civic Action plans that would have finite and realistic goals and objectives. We also learned that much of the AID-provided equipment was unusable for the Indonesians, as they lacked the expertise to assemble and operate it. They had warehouses full of equipment, but did not have the ability to inventory and identify the equipment, much less employ it profitably.

We came up with an overall plan to assist the Indonesians in their equipment problems, which was approved by the ambassador. We sent a command and control liaison detachment, commanded by a major, to Djakarta, with instructions to coordinate with the DLM the operations of the small teams we sent to Indonesia to remedy their equipment problems. Several maintenance warrant officers started the inventory of the equipment warehouses in Djakarta, eventually bringing everything under control and in card files. We sent small teams to assemble AID-provided equipment and put them in operation. One example was a single sergeant first class, equipped with a mobile machine shop, who spent six months outside of Bandoeng (on Java) assembling a huge rock-crushing machine at a quarry. The gravel was badly needed for surfacing roads on Java, but the Indonesians were unable to make the machine operate. The rock quarry was operated by hand labor—literally, hundreds of natives with small hammers pounded on rocks to reduce them to gravel-sized pieces. The sergeant put the rock-crusher into operation, then arranged to put the natives to work hauling rocks to the machine, rather than breaking them up. That way, no one was put out of work because of the "American machine." He also taught a team of Indonesian Army Engineers how to

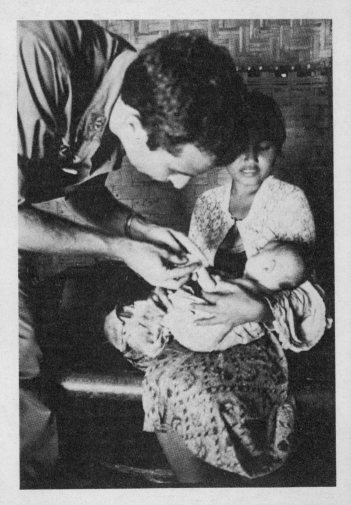

SF medic on Civic Action Projects, SAFASIA, Sumatra, Indonesia, 1971

LTG Lampert in the Outer Ryukyus inspecting one of many Civic Action Projects, SAFASIA, 1971 (USCAR photo)

maintain and keep the machine in operation. At the end of six months' isolation from other Americans, a jubilant SAFASIA sergeant came back to Okinawa with a feeling of having made a genuine contribution to the economy of Indonesia.

The Indonesians had ordered a huge, vertical sawmill, with a circular saw some twelve feet in diameter. An American-made sawmill was provided, and as law required, passed to Indonesian ownership as soon as it was unloaded on the dock. The Indonesians wanted to erect the sawmill in the city of Bandjarmasin, on the southern tip of the island of Borneo (now called Kalimantan). It was needed to furnish boards for the construction of houses in Indonesian military retirement settlements on Sumatra. The Indonesian military get very few "perks" when they retire, but one of them is land and building material in service-sponsored villages located on sparsely populated Sumatra. The sawmill was to provide the needed construction material, but the Indonesians did not have the foggiest notion how to assemble and operate the sawmill. We sent an officer and three NCOs, six months at a time, to that remote and backward city to accomplish the project. Bandjarmasin, whose sole industry is lumber, is situated at the delta of an interior Borneo river that delivers massive teak logs from deep in the island. Men spent their lives perched on high platforms over the river, sawing by hand (and guiding with their toes) six-foot-long ripsaws to produce the necessary planks. There were no modern machine-driven sawmills on the entire island.

The SAFASIA team, with an Indonesian work force of political prisoners, labored for eighteen months to put that sawmill in production. I flew down to attend the inauguration of sawing operations and to honor my soldiers who had single-handedly accomplished so much under dreadful conditions. We watched the huge saw blade cut through logs five and six feet thick, producing rough planks of teak thirty to forty feet long. They had trained a team of Indonesians to take the mill over and maintain it, probably the most difficult part of their mission. I have been told that keeping the blade sharpened is the most difficult part of a sawmill operation, but they even managed that delicate operation and had two Indonesians competent to perform that task. The Indonesians had formed a warm relationship with the team and appropriately honored them with a Chinese feast, speeches, and the self-entertainment they are so adept at improvising.

The Indonesians are the "country boys" of Asia—warm, friendly, and open. They show little of the dislike of foreigners so common to much of the area. As the government is totally run by the military, all government officials, from the president through the ministers right down to the local government, are active military officers, and U.S. military people have no difficulty communicating with them. Though the U.S. State Department, AID, and CIA people in Indonesia resented and feared our U.S. military presence there, there never was the slightest bit of trouble with the Indonesians. To a somewhat lesser extent, third-world governments throughout the world are dominated by military men who feel much more at home with U.S. military men than with our diplomats and bureaucrats. This is a powerful endorsement for future Civic Action programs.

We assembled a sixteen-office Civic Action team that taught an eight-week course to approximately 100 Indonesian officers in the grade of major to colonel. They were district chiefs drawn from all over Indonesia, each charged with the mission of conducting Civic Action programs, as previously described. The first three weeks of the eight-week course were taught in a military school in the beautiful mountain city of Bandoeng.

Hands-on civic action training Indonesian officers on Sumatra, 1971, SAFASIA

They were taught the academics of how to take a census, plan, and prioritize Civic Action projects with systematic goals and objectives. Lt. Col. Clarence Little, commander of SAFASIA's 1st Civil Affairs Battalion, personally led the team and provided it with the spark that his totally enthusiastic personality generated. The U.S. team contained an imposing group of talented engineers, doctors, veterinarians, public health specialists, lawyers, and other professionals—certainly the brightest and best group of officers I have seen projected for Civic Actions deep into the interior of a foreign country. They performed a highly important mission in an exemplary manner. The class was moved to Sumatra to one of the service-owned retiree villages, where the members spread out, planned, and conducted Civic Action missions for the remaining five weeks of the course. The Americans led by example, blistering their hands digging coconut log culverts, erecting flagpoles, building dispensaries, and performing a host of projects the students planned. A census was held in several dozen of the local villages, with surprising results that cast doubt on the official population figures for Indonesia. The U.S. and Indonesian officers actually counted everyone in those villages, then compared their findings with the census held by the village chiefs. Their figures exceeded the chiefs' figures by over 200 percent. Investigation revealed that the Indonesian census counted only *males* of voting age, no women or children. Though most official figures show an Indonesian population of approximately 146,000,000, there is good reason to believe it is over 300,000,000.

To better prepare SAFASIA for Civic Action missions, all of the A Detachments were put through a special school that taught them bricklaying, simple carpentry, how to mix and pour concrete, and other construction skills. There was much good-natured banter from the SF veterans, but they turned to learning the trade with a will; if that was what they had to do to get deployed, then that is what they would do. Shortly after the first cycle of that program was completed, with a half dozen A Detachments successfully graduating, we got a mission in the Philippines that used all six of them for six months. The Philippine president, Marcos, was advocating a widespread school building program and asked the United States for assistance. AID provided the materials, and SAFASIA provided the building skills. We sent a B command and control detachment in overall charge, attached several engineer officers from the 539th Engineer Detachment, and sent them off to the Province of Panay. The Filipinos provided the actual labor, while we stationed one or two SF men at each building site until the construction was finished. They worked under the supervision of their detachment officers and lived together as a detachment—once again, good training for A Detachments. They communicated with the B Detachment by radio; the B Detachment communicated with Manila and Okinawa by radio, thus obtaining communications practice under long-distance conditions. They worked with foreigners in a strange cultural environment, and they worked to achieve specific tasks and goals. The detachment commanders were able to evaluate their team members in a semistress environment to determine their suitability for long haul.

On the rather remote island of Samar, we tried a new approach. The Philippine government of necessity had placed Samar in a rather low priority, and welcomed the opportunity to have help in doing something for it. We sent a U.S./Filipino survey team to circumnavigate the island by road to determine those projects the local provincial officials and mayors wished to accomplish. As part of that survey, we sent a medical team that drew blood samples from among the population in the different locales. The blood samples were sent to the U.S. Army laboratory in Japan, where they were subjected to tests for twenty-five different diseases. Tests revealed no traces of rubella, indicating that German measles had probably never been introduced on the island of Samar. More significantly, it revealed that Samar was very vulnerable to that disease, which is particularly dangerous to the fetuses of newly pregnant women. Supplies of gamma globulin were ordered for treatment in the event that the Civic Action team introduced measles to the island, as at that time there was no available immunization for the disease before detecting its actual onset.

After the survey party returned to Manila, a comprehensive Civic Action plan was drawn up, supplies were ordered, and the Civic Action team organization drawn up to meet the schedule. After a 100-man team consisting of virtually all parts of SAFASIA (SF, engineers, Civic Action veterinarians, intelligence operators, doctors) was put together and assigned tasks, they were flown to the island of Cebu for transportation to Samar on boats of the Philippine Navy. The team fanned out over the island, inoculating hogs and water buffalo, supervising and advising in many road and bridge construction tasks, immunizing the people (and taking more blood samples), building schoolhouses and dispensaries, for which the Philippine government provided teachers and nurses, and generally fulfilling the "wish lists" of the local people. The team remained for six months, though some of the team assignments were accomplished ahead of time, and team members were consequently returned to Okinawa. At minimum cost to the Philippine and U.S. governments, an enormous amount of good was done to that backward island, and great goodwill generated toward both governments among the inhabitants. We also obtained a great deal of intelligence—medical, topographic, cultural, and political—as a result of a concentrated effort to exploit all resources available (with the knowledge and concurrence of the Philippine government, of course). Samar was an example of good Civic Action planning and execution; no project was so sophisticated that the local people could not maintain and man it.

By far the most exotic of all Civic Actions missions was one to the Marshall Islands in the Trust Territory of the Pacific (TTPI). The American Governor-General of the TTPI wanted to do something for some of the more isolated islands, particularly in light of the fact that a referendum to determine the future of that island chain was imminent. The atoll of Jaluit, several hundred miles west of the district capital on Majuro, was selected. Again a Civic Action survey was conducted, a plan and schedule drawn up, a team selected and organized, and equipment and supplies delivered by the ships of the U.S. Navy. Such Navy engineering equipment as a bulldozer, a dump truck, a scraper, and a compressor was put ashore, and the team traveled by air to Majuro and by boat to Jaluit.

Jaluit is exactly what one would picture when a South Pacific atoll comes to mind. Protected by outer reefs, it is a skinny doughnut several thousand to several hundred yards wide, encompassing a beautiful lagoon sixty miles in diameter. The atoll is not continuous, as it is broken by channels to the ocean in a few places. The vegetation is largely tens of thousands of tall coconut trees, as well as tropical fruit trees, flowers, shrubs, and a form of dune grass. It is predominately sandy, and fresh water is scarce. The people lived in several villages, the largest holding approximately 300 people. The women were organized into singing societies, of which there were two in the large village, and they were fierce rivals. Each had its distinctive saronglike highly colorful dresses, and on occasions they wore leis and put flowers in their hair. They sang beautifully in six-part harmony (on those occasions when the men were allowed to sing along).

The Pacific Islands are tribal, with aristocratic chiefs inheriting the position and ownership of most of the land and all of the coconut trees. A chief provided the list of Civic Action projects to be accomplished by the team, and the labor force to work with the Americans. When I flew out in a small seaplane to see the team and its accomplishments, we landed in the lagoon and the plane waddled up on the beach. The entire population of 300 was on hand to greet us with leis, smiles, and hugs; I could barely see over the accumulation of flowers. Jaluit had been fortified by the Japanese prior to World War II, and many of their deserted concrete bunkers remain. The team lived in one bunker and used another for storage, overlooking the beach and surf of the sunny Pacific. That night one of the women's societies, The Society of the Beautiful Flowers, fixed us a feast of turtle steaks, coconut crabs, breadfruit, yams, and coconut cakes, and sang to us well into the night. The native men sat outside the bunker and sang along, but were not invited to participate in the feast.

We toured the completed projects the next day: some eighteen miles of dirt road, a schoolhouse, a dispensary, a dock, and other simple construction feats that were wanted and needed but beyond the expertise of the natives to build. We went turtle fishing in the lagoon with the chief that afternoon and brought back a 300-pound specimen that was the main course for another feast that night. The other women's society hosted that party, though the menu was much the same. When we departed the next day, the entire village once again attended, sang, and waved us off. Civic Action in paradise!

The High Commissioner of the Ryukyu Islands, who was

also my military boss on Okinawa, Lt. Gen. James Lampert, was quick to note the utility of Civic Action projects. In conjunction with SAFASIA, his staff compiled a Ryukyu's Civic Action plan that encompassed all the islands of that archipelago, and provided the necessary funding and construction materials. The plan was for a year-long effort, and was renewed and updated each year. On the average, fifty to seventy-five members of SAFASIA were used at any one time, but they were spread out over the eight principal islands of the 250-mile-long island chain. Twice each year, the High Commissioner and I made a tour of the islands to visit the various projects and see my men at work. At a number of locations, there would be one engineer sergeant with a scraper or bulldozer, patiently scraping out a road through the sugarcane fields, or building a dirt landing strip. One sergeant, alone, on the island of Miyako, moved back and forth day after day to build a 2,000-foot dirt airstrip to give the island access to air travel. After six months' isolation from other Americans, the airstrip was finished and appears on U.S. air charts today under an international airstrip symbol. Others built water catchment projects, fishing docks, culverts, bridges, town halls, and a host of other projects requiring minimal construction, at low costs, and needing only the relatively primitive labor of the Ryukyuans. The little Ryukyuans, particularly on the islands away from Okinawa, had little history of governmental assistance and were appropriately hospitable, courteous, and grateful. In the many months we ran Civic Action projects in close proximity, there was never one incident that reflected resentment, jealousy, or cultural antagonisms. On the contrary, the Ryukyuans and the soldiers of SAFASIA liked one another and mutually benefited from the favorable aspects of the projects and the fine training that was provided by the conduct of Civic Action on-the-ground training.

SAFASIA was not the only Special Forces Group to conduct extensive Civic Action projects. The 8th SFG's "Project Alice" in the Panamanian town of Santa Isabel was particularly imaginative, providing a dispensary, dental facilities, a forty-foot pier, and a potable water system, among other things.

There are many other examples of such projects all around the world. The point is that Special Forces are particularly well suited for such "do-good" projects and the projects are good training for Special Forces. Another point that should be touched on is that an elite unit such as Special Forces needs to be useful as an instrument of U.S. foreign policy if it expects to be kept in the Army's books. Civic Action projects bring the SF's skills out into the open where they can be appraised and, hopefully, appreciated, and that is badly needed.

19. VIETNAMIZATION OF THE CIDG, 1966–1971

The arrival in South Vietnam in 1965–66 of the big American divisions and brigades clearly changed the entire course of the war. The Army of the Republic of Vietnam was placed in a defensive position protecting the majority of the population, while the Americans drove into the interior to engage the major enemy units. The exception to this was the Marine Expeditionary Force in I Corps Tactical Zone, which stayed relatively close to the coast and, together with ARVN, provided population security. The North Vietnamese Army introduced more and more of its divisions, and the grisly game of hide-and-seek commenced. The Americans had tremendous firepower and supporting air power, which guaranteed that they never lost a battle with the NVA, though there were many fierce battles with heavy American casualties and much heavier NVA casualties.

The role of the CIDG changed during those years as they responded to the requirements of the Americans and took up an offensive role. Perhaps the most important change came as it became apparent that the Vietnam War could not continue indefinitely with the large American participation. There had to be a finite and foreseeable end to the Americanization of the war.

All of those in Special Forces were very familiar with the plight of the French Army in Vietnam, which had organized and led battalions of irregular Vietnamese forces, many of them Montagnards, Cambodians, and Meo, for operations in the backcountry against Viet Minh forces. When France withdrew from Southeast Asia, those faithful allies were abandoned to their fates at the hands of the unforgiving Viet Minh. That was bad enough, but the most important aspect of that abandonment lay with the French unconventional warriors who had led the irregulars, had lived with them for years, and who had felt shamed when forced to repudiate their promises and give up the UW role in which they believed so strongly. We wanted to neither abandon our CIDG troopers nor invite bad feelings among the men of Special Forces who had lived with and loved their little strikers. The CIDG program needed a strategy and a plan, both to best support the Americans and to systematically turn over the CIDG program to the Vietnamese.

A look at the locations of CIDG camps in 1966 shows them scattered all over the country, with no apparent single purpose or pattern. The program did grow like Topsy, very much at the whim of the four Vietnamese Corps Commanders, fighting their four separate and relatively unrelated wars. The introduction of the marines in I Corps, as well as U.S. Army forces in II and III Corps, added at least two more separate wars, as the I Force Vietnam Commander in II Corps and the II Force V Commander in III Corps pursued their own aggressive tactics. Of course, General Westmoreland constantly visited both the American and Vietnamese commanders, providing month-to-month guidance, but he had no *command* over the marines, and he had few U.S. ground forces in IV Corps. The 1967 MACV Campaign Plan was intended to provide a centralized strategy for the overall course of the war, and was to be known to everyone, and hopefully, followed by everyone. The initial 1967 Campaign Plan did not set a schedule for the termination of the war, but largely provided for its extension, to include a major increase in ARVN forces.

The 5th Special Forces Group was the only U.S. Army tactical headquarters that had a country-wide perspective of the course of the war, with camps in all four corps areas. The 1967 CIDG Annex to the Campaign Plan provided for two major elements: outlining a strategy for the CIDG camps country-wide, and providing for the phase-out of the U.S. Special Forces and their withdrawal from Vietnam by 1971.

In order to best support the U.S. forces in Vietnam, the plan was to withdraw U.S. Special Forces from all camps that did not support the primary mission of border surveillance, and open new CIDG camps where the border surveillance mission could be enhanced. In 1967, there was to be no reduction in the number of camps or U.S. Special Forces, but rather a reapportionment of the U.S. assets to better support the U.S. war effort. The plan was reviewed and approved by both U.S.

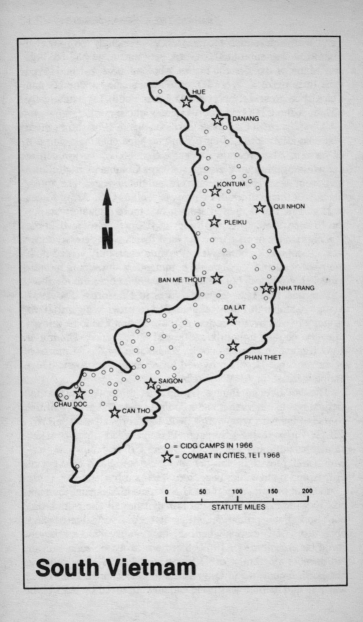

HUE

DANANG

KONTUM

QUI NHON

PLEIKU

BAN ME THUOT

NHA TRANG

DA LAT

PHAN THIET

SAIGON

CHAU DOC

CAN THO

O = CIDG CAMPS IN 1966

★ = COMBAT IN CITIES. TET 1968

| 0 | 50 | 100 | 150 | 200 |
STATUTE MILES

South Vietnam

and Vietnamese senior commanders in each of the four corps before it was submitted to MACV.

Many of the fiercest battles were reactions by the NVA to the opening of new border surveillance camps. The NVA attacked in great strength against Lang Vei in I Corps and Con Thien, also in I Corps. Every member of Captain Cunningham's A Detachment at Con Thien earned a Purple Heart after arriving on site. The camps at Dak To, Loc Ninh, Bu Prang, and Bu Dop also attracted major enemy attention, often for so many days as to be termed a "siege." With the assistance of American troops and air power, none of them fell to the enemy.

The other major element in the plan called for "Vietnamizing" the CIDG camps at the A Detachment level over the period 1967–69. By 1969, there were to be U.S. Special Forces advisors only down to the B Detachment level, but continued U.S. support to all the CIDG camps, then under Vietnamese control. In the following months, the B Detachment advisors would be withdrawn, followed by the C Detachments. By 1970, the only U.S. Special Forces presence was to be at the headquarters and support facility in Nha Trang, with greatly increased participation by the LLDB in those activities. By 1971, the only U.S. participation was to be in the form of supplies and finances provided directly to the Vietnamese CIDG headquarters, much as CIA money was provided to the USSF directly, not through Army channels. That plan was to provide an orderly turnover and phase-out of the USSF *before* the bulk of the other U.S. military presence in Vietnam was withdrawn. To do otherwise would have left us right back where we were in 1965, with vulnerable little groups of USSF spread over the entire country.

Many Special Forces soldiers have wondered why the 5th SFG was withdrawn first instead of last. The answer is that Special Forces planned it that way. General Abrams' dislike of Special Forces may have been gratified by their departure, but he knew about it as early as October 1966, when he was briefed in considerable detail. He fully understood and agreed with the concept. Many of the withdrawn A Detachments were initially retained in South Vietnam to provide useful tasks for MACV, such as the training of Cambodians for the Cambodian Army, and participation and support of the U.S./ARVN incursion into Cambodia in 1970.

Over the period of 1961–71, the SF in Vietnam had built and manned 249 separate CIDG camps and installations for USSF detachments. By 1970, only 49 of them were still active and considered for conversion to ARVN Ranger status. Some 37 of them were selected for conversion, and the strikers given the option of joining ARVN or reverting to civilian life. Most of them opted to become Rangers, a total of over 14,000 well-trained and well-equipped soldiers comprising thirty-seven Ranger battalions. Thus, the CIDG were *not* abandoned, and the USSF who had lived and fought beside them for so many years did *not* become bitter and ashamed. In hindsight, the 1966 plan worked well, though not exactly on schedule.

The above does not imply that the USSF and CIDG from 1966 to 1971 slacked off in anticipation of withdrawal. They fought right up to the day the USSF left in 1971, late in March. The greatly increased offensive operations by the Special Operations, Mobile Guerrilla Forces, and Mike Forces have already been noted in earlier chapters. Invariably, with increased offensive operations, casualties within 5th SFG increased. The majority of the 2,658 Purple Hearts awarded during the war were earned in the last five years.

Although an exception to the generally offensive role of the CIDG, the defensive actions of the CIDG during the Tet Offensive of the VC and NVA in January 1968 proved to be surprisingly successful. CIDG troops were thrown into the battles in many of the cities of South Vietnam, and successfully defended Nha Trang, Dalat, Qui Nhon, Kontum, Ban Me Thout, Chau Doc, and Phan Thiet. Though not trained in urban tactics, they fought extremely well, proving themselves the equal of any Vietnamese soldiers in the country.

Many of the offensive CIDG combat operations were in conjunction with U.S. units. The U.S. units soon learned that the CIDG camps were a valuable source of intelligence, area knowledge, interpreters, and a light infantry force familiar with the terrain. It was not uncommon to have a brigade or battalion base itself on a CIDG camp while operating in the camp's assigned area of operations. The 5th Special Forces Group made a policy of visiting the headquarters of newly arrived U.S. units to tell them of the benefits of using CIDG on their operations.

Last detachment of 5th SFG withdrawn from Vietnam greeted at Fort Bragg, March 1972 (U.S. Army photo)

The Special Forces companies in each corps' area kept close liaison with the U.S. units for their mutual benefit. Many U.S. operations had two or more CIDG companies attached to them for the duration of the operations, sometimes stretching to months.

The most common problem for the CIDG when operating with U.S. units was the tendency of the U.S. commanders to equate the lightweight CIDG companies with the big American companies. Frequently, the U.S. commander would divide up a CIDG company into platoons, and attach a CIDG platoon to an American company for tactical operations. That tactic disregarded the lack of leadership among CIDG platoon leaders, the ratio of American SF advisors (usually two to a company), the number of translators available (usually one to a company), the weapons and equipment of the CIDG, and almost every capability or limitation of the CIDG units. The CIDG were not trained in the "cloverleaf" tactic of moving very slowly through unknown territory. Their sanitation practices were not up to American standards. They did not have the physical stamina of the Americans. They were truly light infantry, in every regard, with definite worth if used in accordance with their training and practices. It took some time to indoctrinate the

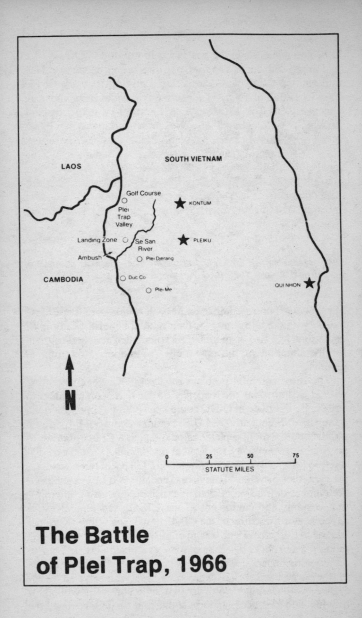

LAOS

SOUTH VIETNAM

Golf Course

★ KONTUM

Plei Trap Valley

Landing Zone

Se San River

★ PLEIKU

Ambush

Plei Djerang

CAMBODIA

Duc Co

QUI NHON ★

Plei Me

N

0   25   50   75
STATUTE MILES

The Battle of Plei Trap, 1966

U.S. commanders on the best ways to employ CIDG.

Perhaps the finest example of cooperation between a U.S. unit and the CIDG was demonstrated during the battle of Plei Trap in the fall of 1966. That battle might never have happened except for Lt. Col. Eleazar ("Lee") Parmly IV who was commander of B Company of 5th SFG, with headquarters in Pleiku in the highlands of central Vietnam. Pleiku was heavily infused with American troops, the most important of which was the newly arrived 4th Infantry Division, commanded by Maj. Gen. Ray Peers (later of the My Lai investigation fame). The American commanders had become very much aware of the combat potential of B Company with its two dozen CIDG camps and over 20,000 riflemen. In fact, Lee had more than bent over backward to put his forces at the disposal of the Americans, in the hope of gaining mutual benefit for his camps, which depended heavily on American relief or reinforcement in the event of heavy attack by the NVA divisions in II Corps.

In the fall of 1966, the high command at MACV had designated four of our camps as priority defense areas against expected heavy NVA attack. While Khe Sanh in the far north of I Corps was the most vulnerable and probable target (surrounded by three NVA divisions), Camp Duc Co in II Corps had long been under pressure from NVA forces, as the NVA 630th Front was located just across the Cambodian border from it. The catastrophic battle of the "Dry Lake Bed" had taken place in August, with four Americans and four dozen CIDG killed in action, just ten kilometers west of Duc Co, on the border. The morale and efficiency of Camp Duc Co had not quite returned to the relatively high level it held before that battle.

The 4th U.S. Infantry Division was still relatively unbloodied, as it had spent most of the first weeks of its arrival building a huge base camp outside Pleiku, and engaging in training-type search and destroy operations in areas not suspected of containing NVA forces. By October, radio intercepts indicated that several NVA regiments had crossed the border from Cambodia and were located in the mountains north of Camp Plei Djerang, just north of Duc Co, but nearer Pleiku and farther from the border. Plei Djerang was an excellent camp with well-trained and well-led CIDG companies. They had made a solid contact in September with about a battalion just north of the camp, but no action was taken by the 4th Division until the enemy had been given every opportunity to withdraw, which they undoubtedly did posthaste. The 4th Division had also been tardy in responding to calls from the Duc Co contingent besieged at the "Dry Lake Bed" battle, so an element of skepticism of the credibility of the 4th Division as an effective relief force had built up among the Americans in B Company.

Lee Parmly was doing much to cement better relations between his command and the 4th Division. He personally attended the rather ponderous and lengthy command meetings held daily by General Peers, and reported as though his was a subordinate unit of 4th Division, which B Company most decidedly was not. However, some of his camps, including Duc Co and Plei Djerang, were in areas of operations that were assigned to 4th Division, which did create problems in command and control.

In September 1966, I visited B Company to make a parachute exhibition jump as a demonstration for Prime Minister Khy's visit with the Montagnards in Pleiku. During the visit, I accompanied Lee to one of the daily 4th Division meetings. They were planning for an operation in the mountains north of Plei Djerang, in the hopes of engaging or displacing the two regiments suspected of occupying that sensitive area. The plan was to put two brigades on line and sweep north, keeping west of Camp Plei Mei, one of the four critical targets designated by General Westmoreland. As the plan unfolded, it became obvious that the sweep would very quickly uncover the left flank of the sweep to a heavily forested area designated on the map as Plei Trap. That area was separated from the area of the planned sweep by a rather sluggish, brown river, known as the Se San River. Plei Trap was thought to contain a portion of the infamous Ho Chi Minh Trail, but no troops, either South Vietnamese or American, had ever operated in the area. After the 4th Division Operations Officer (G-3) completed his brief on the sweep operation, Lee requested the floor and volunteered to place "Task Force Parmly" on the left flank of the sweep, across the Se San and to the Cambodian border to act as a reconnaissance in force, and a trip wire against NVA forces attacking the sweep from the west. He said that he couldn't presume to protect the left flank, but he would provide a force on the ground which the NVA would have to deal with before they could get at the 4th Division. General Peers accepted Lee's offer, and thus Operation Plei Trap was off and running.

I returned to Pleiku about 6 November, to check on the progress of the 4th Division sweep. Since the 5th SFG Mike Force of over 800 rifles was in reserve at Nha Trang, I habitually carefully monitored the progress of any operation that might require the commitment of my battalion. Lee was deep in the process of organizing the Plei Trap task force, and he intended to command it himself. He invited me to join him, and I jumped at the chance of observing Lee in combat. I was his rating officer and needed to know his capabilities from firsthand experience. Lee's company headquarters outfitted me with a tiger suit, a rucksack with poncho, two canteens, rations, and 600 rounds of ammo for my CAR-15. The operation jumped off on the morning of 8 November.

With choppers provided by 4th Division, Lee put his task force into a jungle landing that had been carved out by an engineer company of the 4th Division. As the LZ was late being completed, the landing was delayed until after 1000 hours of a beautiful, clear, cold day. At that time of year in the highlands, it has been known to snow, despite the low latitude. While awaiting the completion of the LZ, teams of gun-choppers roamed over the area. In "slick" command and control choppers with Lee and elements of his command group, we spent several hours reconning at treetop altitude, peering under the trees. We saw a large number of newly constructed earth and log emplacements, widely scattered over the Plei Trap Valley. No other trace of the enemy existed. After the reconnaissance, we returned to Camp Duc Co to refuel and visit the CIDG mustered there for lift into Plei Trap. They were the least reliable of the three companies Lee planned to airlift into the operation, equipped with a motley array of uniforms and headgear—too-large steel pots, baseball caps, or tiger hats with floppy brims. Duc Co, however, enjoyed priority in assignment of first-rate USSF advisors, due to its key location and the fact that an extensive sensitive intelligence net in Cambodia was directed from that camp.

Sfc. James L. Lewis, Jr., was in command of the Duc Co

Jungle Landing Zone, II CTZ, Operation Plei Trap, Vietnam, 1966

Company. Their assigned task was to move directly south of the LZ and block the trail entering Plei Trap from Cambodia, a trail that swung east directly opposite Duc Co and reentered South Vietnam for communications with the southern part of II Corps.

We also visited another company at Plei Djerang, under the command of Sgt. Carlos D. Caro. That was the company our command group would accompany as they moved directly west from the LZ and checked any possible trails entering Plei Trap from that direction. They were a particularly fine-looking CIDG unit, uniformly dressed in smart tiger suits, floppy tiger hats, web gear, and rucksacks; all with bright red scarves tied at their throats. The command element members were also provided with red scarves for instant recognition, and I still prize mine. The third company to be committed to the task force was a Mike Force company from Pleiku, commanded by Lieutenant Jacobelli. It was by far the best unit of the three companies, airborne-qualified and equipped with M-16 rifles. It also had the roughest mission, requiring it to move north and west from the LZ, and recon and block the multiple north-south trails entering Plei Trap from the mountain passes of the north. The Mike Force Company had an extremely competent group of Americans, about half a dozen, including an old Special Forces soldier named Capt. Clyde Sincere, the new commander of the entire Pleiku Mike Force, along in a capacity similar to mine—straphanger and file-closer.

The first unit to land, once the LZ was completed, was the Plei Djerang Company, which was to assume responsibility for security of the LZ. The Mike Force Company landed next and immediately struck out to the northwest to reach its distant objective, initially a grassy hole in the jungle named the "golf course" due to its short, neatly cropped grassy surface. The command group, consisting of about fourteen Americans, including two lieutenant colonels, one major (Buttermore), several captains and lieutenants, and a handful of senior noncommissioned officers, infiltrated between lifts of the various companies. We were joined on the LZ by an even more senior group of officers from 4th Division, including the assistant division commander, Brig. Gen. Glenn Walker, and a brigade commander from the left flank of the 4th Division,

Col. Ralph Young. Coordination was effected for relief and/ or reinforcement in the event that the task force bit off more than it could chew. Fire support was also coordinated, and a forward observer team from 4th Division was attached to the command group.

After the Duc Co Company landed, the Mike Force Company moved out with Captain Sincere and Lieutenant Jacobelli in the lead. Several hundred meters from the LZ, they engaged elements of an NVA antiaircraft company that had been directly in the path of our landing helicopters, but for some unexplained reason had not fired their fifty-caliber machine guns. The Mike Force Company pursued the NVA and captured two of the big machine guns with their high tripod mounts and antiaircraft sights, together with several dozen AK-47s and rucksacks. The task force got its first kills and its most fortunate break only minutes after going into action. It also gave all of us reason to pause and wonder just how many NVA there were in our area of operations. The presence of an antiaircraft company certainly meant the presence of other ground forces, probably at the division level, for the weapons are assigned to the divisional artillery regiment and are not found in the infantry battalion or regiment in the NVA.

The Duc Co Company pushed to the west before turning south, closely followed by the Plei Djerang Company and the command element. We moved in single file through double- or triple-canopy jungle surprisingly free of undergrowth, making movement through the huge ferns rather easy. There was an absence of birds or other wildlife, and the jungle was still. The temperature shortly before noon was in the seventies, and walking was not unpleasant. The column stopped and started several times as the point men checked out dangerous spots on the route of march. About an hour after starting, we stopped for rather a long time, resting on our rucksacks. Suddenly a burst of automatic fire ripped off, to be answered immediately by an even faster burst from an AK-47. The automatic fire was quickly joined by several dozen other automatic weapons, filling the jungle with what sounded like a gigantic firefight. On my stomach, all I could see was several little Yards peering over their carbines off into the jungle. After a few minutes, the firing stopped. We regained our feet, and I walked up the column until I came to a wide trail running across our route of march. The trail was eight to ten feet wide and well worn; at last I was on a major element of the Ho Chi Minh Trail. I found Lee Parmly on the trail to the left, amid grinning Americans and Yards. The point had arrived at the trail at the same time that a small four-man element of NVA had approached from the left. The point men opened fire quickly, reinforced by others from behind them in the column. They killed three NVA, and a fourth unarmed soldier was propped against a tree, being interrogated by a Vietnamese SF captain who accompanied the task force. The soldier was obviously seriously wounded in the chest, but the decision was made to leave him, as we had to move fast to get to the Cambodian border by dark. We could not carry him, and we weren't numerous enough to leave a unit or detail with him. When he learned that we intended to leave him, he asked the Vietnamese to kill him, which was done.

The next few kilometers were relatively easy going, though movement was cautious after that second bit of evidence that our area of operations contained NVA. I am inclined to believe in retrospect that we surprised the NVA, even though they had seen the choppers make repeated landings on the nearby LZ. They were accustomed to American troops who move at a very slow rate, cautiously cloverleafing to both flanks and the front as they crawl along at 600 to 1,000 meters an hour.

We emerged from the jungle into open clearings several times on our march, always a difficult process due to the growth of heavy thickets in areas where there is a break in the overhead cover. We passed through several areas with log and earth dugouts, like those we saw from the air, but all fairly old and not recently used. Finally, late in the afternoon we crossed a stream and stopped in jungle with trees three and four feet in diameter. A reconnaissance patrol was sent out to determine the possible presence of NVA, and finding none, we bivouacked for the night. We lit tiny fires before dark and heated water for our dried rice rations. I slung my tiny CIDG hammock between two huge trees, with a poncho suspended over it for a rain cover. Hanging the CAR-15 on a tree next to the hammock, I climbed in and tried to sleep. I was soaking wet with perspiration from the skin out, and the hammock at first seemed too small to sleep in. Almost miraculously, the hammock seemed to expand until it became quite comfortable, and I slept. Early the next morning, before dawn, I awakened with a thirst and took my two canteens to go and find the stream we crossed. As I left the perimeter, two little Yards grinned at me, shook their heads "no," and made a gesture of pulling their hands across their throats. I moved about fifty yards outside the perimeter, but didn't encounter the stream. I had second thoughts on just how thirsty I was, and returned to strike my hammock. At first light, I discovered something had eaten the finish off my jungle boots and the scabbard of my pistol holster—fire ants, ferocious little fellows much feared in the jungle.

About mid-morning the next day, the Duc Co Company to our south reported that they were approaching a line of log and earth fortifications, and shortly thereafter that they were in a firefight with what seemed to be a company-sized unit. During the rest of the morning, the reports of contact continued with sporadic firing. No one was particularly alarmed, but artillery and air support requests were relayed back to the 4th Division. Shortly after noon, we stopped on a narrow trail for a period of two hours. Lee was not happy about moving away from the Duc Co Company with the only available reserve force. The Mike Force Company reported arriving at its objective on the open dry meadow, and shortly reported that they had evacuated Lieutenant Jacobelli, shot through the abdomen, and the two machine guns. Later they reported ambushing a four-man group of NVA near their perimeter.

While we were stopped, Lee sent out reconnaissance patrols that went as far as the Cambodian border without contacting any enemy. About 1500 hours, an emergency call from the Duc Co Company came in, saying they had heavily engaged the enemy and both Americans were wounded, with several CIDG killed and about a dozen wounded. We immediately backtracked at double time, and reached the rear of the Duc Co Company in about an hour. They were not pinned down, but were psychologically pretty nearly impotent. Our medic bandaged their wounded, and we pulled back north along the trail. There were four Yards KIA and fifteen wounded. The two American SF were not badly wounded and remained with their company. The carrying party went to the LZ, and evac

Author, Gene Deatrick, Lee Parmly. Pleiku, South Vietnam, 7 November 1966

choppers came in for the casualties. The two companies bivouacked together along the trail where the dead NVA medic was left the day before—his body was gone. An ambush party to the north of the bivouac ambushed another party of four NVA, killing one, during the night. No hammock for me that night. I rolled up in the poncho cover and dropped off as though dead.

The next morning we moved to the LZ for another conference with General Walker. My group commander ordered me out of the field, ending my two-day walk in the shade, but not the battle of Plei Trap. That afternoon Lee took both CIDG companies back down the trail and ran into an NVA battalion-sized ambush. Lee acquitted himself very well, though the casualties were fairly heavy, including every member of the command party. An American battalion from the 4th Division relieved the CIDG that night after the NVA surrounded his party. Only American air throughout the night saved his command. Lee got on the radio to the Forward Air Controller overhead and told him to "tell the commander of the First Air Commandos that he has a classmate down here in deep shit." Lt. Col. Gene Deatrick, USAF, had two A-1Es over Lee's position at all times until he pulled out. The Mike Force Company reported it was under attack by another battalion of NVA, and was eventually relieved by the American battalion, after killing several hundred NVA—fifty-eight in one location, by American body count. The battle became an all-American fight after that, as all CIDG forces were airlifted out of Plei Trap and returned to their respective camps to lick their wounds and recover.

Although that battle was seemingly small and insignificant, the results were much greater than credited. It is apparent that the NVA were defending the crossing points from Cambodia where the Duc Co and Mike Force companies found them. POWs stated that they belonged to the 88th NVA Regiment, with a mission to attack the left flank of the 4th Division sweep as soon as it had advanced sufficiently far north. Other NVA forces in front of the 4th Division were to fall back to the north and draw the division into the heavy going of the mountainous terrain. As it transpired, the 4th Division fought the entire 88th Regiment in the original Mike Force "golf course," with heavy NVA and U.S. casualties. The total cost to Lee's task force was one U.S. KIA, twenty-one Yard KIA, ten U.S. wounded, and seventy-five Yards wounded. So ended the battle of Plei Trap for 5th SFG—the battle that almost didn't happen.

In the history of cooperation between U.S. forces and the CIDG, Plei Trap was a classic. The operation was planned and coordinated weeks in advance. The CIDG were assigned their own area of operations, with the understanding that they could not defend it alone, but could provide reconnaissance in force that would make the enemy reveal his presence and intentions. The 4th Division took the CIDG effort seriously and coordinated on the ground as the action unraveled, and responded with artillery and ground support when the CIDG found themselves outmanned and outgunned. The 4th Division sweep would undoubtedly have had a far different outcome if Lee Parmly's offer to guard their left flank had been ignored or refused. The CIDG effort had a far higher proportion of Americans to Yards than the average CIDG battle, with the subsequent stiffening of their combat resolve and effectiveness. The inherent mobility of CIDG units in the terrain they knew best was demonstrated by a forced march of five kilometers in one hour. The limitations of the CIDG, their lack of heavy firepower, their inability to sustain heavy combat for any appreciable period, and their dependence on American leadership, were also demonstrated. Unfortunately, few other American units were as successful in using the undeniable strengths and weaknesses of the CIDG as General Peers's 4th Infantry Division. Lee Parmly ended up in the hospital with a severe case of blackwater fever. Lee also was awarded the Silver Star and the Purple Heart for his role in the battle of Plei Trap.

There are lessons to be learned from the Special Forces/ SOG roles in Vietnam. Both SOG and the CIDG program were devised by Americans, supplied and paid for by Americans, and the most successful operations were led by Americans. The Vietnamese suffered a major lack of leadership at all levels, but particularly noticeable at junior officer/reconnaissance patrol leader levels. The outstanding leadership of USSF NCOs at the CIDG company level and SOG patrol level was a great credit to the enlisted men of Special Forces. They performed dangerous and difficult tasks repeatedly and consistently, with a minimum of recognition and honor, little or no public acclaim, and at considerable cost in blood and sweat. The fact that sixteen of the junior officers and NCOs were awarded the Medal of Honor is only the tip of the iceberg for the thousands of them that led their diminutive strikers and recon team members into situations of incredible peril.

The history of the CIDG program is an excellent example of the right way to fight an insurgent war. The program developed some well-trained offensive light infantry, but never lost sight of the real target of the effort—the people. Some 45,000 Vietnamese, who would never otherwise have been eligible to bear arms, were effectively integrated into the military scheme of things in South Vietnam. That army was about 99 percent riflemen, with a very small Vietnamese support element. There were very few vehicles, only about two dozen cannon, and no extra Vietnamese generals. Of the $120 million or so it cost each year, the vast majority got to the cutting edge to pay, feed, equip, and support those riflemen. The 3,500 (per year) Special Forces men it took to make that program work were almost invisible to the Vietnamese public and did not contribute to anti-American sentiments. The casualties among the Americans were very low, and the same Special Forces men volunteered repeatedly for service with SOG and the CIDG, year after year.

It is very easy to understand why the Vietnamese resented the Americans. With very few exceptions, American commanders were contemptuous of the Vietnamese and would sweep them out of the way in order to accomplish a mission themselves. Many an American Special Forces soldier developed an anti-American attitude, due to humiliating events, slights, and blatant abuse by senior American officers. One of the first ingredients for a counterinsurgency operation is regard for the people that are being secured.

The Special Forces Group is well suited by dint of its flexible organization and high-quality enlisted personnel for the counterinsurgency role. Improvisation and changes were made in the field, but did not cause any major dislocations. The 5th SFG displayed professional and imaginative tactics in the special operations field. The use of mobile guerrilla forces has been tried by other armies waging counterinsurgency, but not by the U.S. Army. The development of the long-range patrol projects filled an obvious need, now recognized in the Long-Range Patrol companies and the Ranger battalions. However, even when the conventional U.S. units in Vietnam had their own organic long-range patrols, they did not employ them beyond the range of covering fires. To be effective, long-range patrols have to be able to work deep, beyond covering fires.

Without the transportation and logistical support provided by all the services, the U.S. Army Special Forces most certainly could not have done it. Without the close air support of the Air Force, Navy, Marines, and Army, many more CIDG camps would have been overrun. The construction of CIDG camps by Army and Seabee engineers contributed greatly to the strength of the camps, although it was a "nice-to-have" and not absolutely essential. The augmentation units of intelligence, engineers, military history, psychological operations, and radio research greatly enhanced the capabilities of the 5th SFG. Of them all, the military intelligence capability was by far the most important, for that is the one field that amateurs can neither do well, nor are they allowed to do well, due to the need-to-know classification systems which few enlisted men or junior officers even know exist.

Despite what many Special Forces personnel and observers believe, the planned departure of SF from Vietnam was one of the best decisions the U.S. Army made during the course of the Vietnam War. That departure was conceived and planned by the 5th SFG in anticipation of the U.S. withdrawal from the war, years before MACV contemplated such an action. One of the unofficial mottoes of SF is "Our job is to do ourselves out of a job." Whether, in fact, that had truly been accomplished is a question that can never be fully answered. The 5th SFG acted on Senator Muskie's recommendation: "Declare a victory and withdraw." If, as some have suggested, the SF were the last Americans to leave Vietnam, the situation would have been exactly as it was in 1965, with small detachments of Americans spread out in numerous isolated locations, vulnerable to attack by NVA large units, and with little hope of relief from the ARVN.

As a matter of conjecture, what might have been the outcome if the 5th SFG, in January 1965, had a 5,000- to 10,000-man Mike Force in being, trained and ready to deploy anywhere in the country to reinforce CIDG camps or other relatively isolated groups of U.S. advisors? Further, what if ARVN *had* to gain the mobility and capability of fighting NVA division-sized formations? A case can be made that it was not necessary to introduce large U.S. combat units if the proper use had been made of Vietnamese manpower. Another case can be made, that if the USSF were not scattered around the country in vulnerable camps, the decision makers in the Pentagon would not have dispatched combat units to Vietnam. Perhaps the lesson to be learned is that the U.S. Army should examine all the ramifications of engaging in a program like the CIDG program before getting pinned down to a situation that is almost irretrievable, except by committing U.S. combat forces. Although it is unlikely that the CIA will be involved in operations in foreign areas soon, the U.S. Army should examine any joint operations under CIA auspices with an extremely jaundiced eye. After being pulled into operations such as "White Star" (Laos), SOG, "Phoenix," and the CIDG program, where the CIA called the tune, prudence dictates caution and very close scrutiny of any bag the U.S. Army may be left holding.

Basically, there was a failure to employ effectively psychological operations throughout Vietnam. While the Chieu Hoy program did result in rather large numbers of defectors who were given an excuse to escape death and destruction, as well as a pass to wave, there was a lack of direction from the top and an absence of usable themes from MACV. That valuable tool in counterinsurgency was left to local commanders to implement.

20. THE FUTURE OF SPECIAL FORCES

Special Forces has been affected, as have all branches of the armed forces, by the withdrawal from Vietnam, the tide of antimilitarism, force strength cuts, and the reduction in overseas deployments. Old antagonists of elite units in general, and of SF in particular, have attempted to do away with the unwanted and obstreperous stepchild. Within Special Forces itself, there were those who, frustrated with the inconclusiveness of counterinsurgency and the loss of Vietnam, reverted to the old guerrilla warfare mission, in conjunction with direct action missions, or ranger/commando roles.

Before going into the question of the future for Special Forces, it is necessary to examine what has happened to SF and what is happening in SF. Of course, there is much that is unknown to this author in both current operations and future plans, so I can only analyze, based on what I see and know, and forecast from the knowledge accrued from many years' experience in SF.

In the late 1960s, the old 10th Special Forces Group was sent home from Germany, lucky to have survived and not been dropped from the books, as the 1st, 3rd, 6th, and 8th SFGs later were. The basic problem is that the Special Forces groups are *strategic forces* designed to pass under the control of joint unconventional warfare task forces when hostilities break out. The 10th SFG was of little interest to the commanding general, U.S. Army Europe, as it could not be counted as "foxhole strength" on D day. When reductions in force are imposed on overseas commands, as they frequently are, the American commander in Europe always has to make hard choices on the units to cut. It is natural that an assigned combat unit, such as a tank battalion or helicopter battalion, is retained over a Special Forces group. Besides, in theory, a long-range aircraft from the United States can infiltrate SF teams into eastern Europe almost as easily as from Europe. The loss of France from NATO denied the traditional deep Special Forces Operational Base west of Paris, far removed from the front. Also, in the past ten years there has been a growing conviction on the part of most informed NATO/Warsaw Pact analysts that a future war in that area will not last as long as thirty days. Thus, the value of guerrilla warfare in Europe, which by nature is a long-term proposition, has allegedly been reduced to negligible probabilities. What was lost by the rotation of the 10th SFG were the advantages of training in a European environment, and the continuous contacts with foreign SF-type units throughout the region. Another fact, known to every experienced army officer and NCO, is that you can never train half as well in the States as you can overseas.

Fort Devens, Massachusetts, is a far cry from the little *kaserne* in the Bavarian mountains. Nevertheless, the commander of the 10th must keep his outfit as well trained as possible, as much on the move as he can, and back to Europe on maneuvers when funds permit. At least the members of the 10th can look forward to occasional tours of duty in Europe with forces that call for SF-qualified men.

Over in Bad Tolz, there is still a remnant of Special Forces Detachment (Airborne) Europe, consisting of a battalion from the 10th SFG (approximately 250 officers and men), only slightly smaller than the entire 10th Group after the 1955 cutback. They continue to maintain close relations with their Bavarian neighbors and take advantage of the incomparable training grounds and facilities that exist in the South of Bavaria. That area is, without comparison, the best prepared unconventional warfare training area in the world, with the local farmers, woodchoppers, and townspeople staunchly behind the unconventional Americans.

In the Canal Zone in Panama, the 8th SFG no longer exists, having been replaced by one battalion (⅓) of the 7th SFG, long stationed at Fort Bragg. There are still many missions for MTTs throughout Latin America, if funds are available, that can be fulfilled by that battalion. With its high incidence of Spanish-speakers, even a battalion can make a major contribution. What will happen as the Panamanians take over more and more sovereignty of the Zone is not known, but the highly political School of the Americas and the SF battalion may not survive.

The 1st Special Forces Group on Okinawa no longer exists. Like the 10th SFG, it was under the command of U.S. Army Ryukyu Islands, but under the operational control of U.S. Army Pacific. When Okinawa reverted to Japan, it too was a political target, due to its wartime missions elsewhere. The demise of U.S. Army Pacific as a major command removed its last protector, and the 1st was demobilized and faded away into the mists of history, leaving, in 1974, only a small SF Detachment in place in Korea. The contacts with the Chinese on Taiwan, the Filipinos, the Japanese Ground Forces, the Indonesians, Malays, and Thais are a thing of the past. Of course its in-place capability as a Special Forces Operational Base on an unsinkable aircraft carrier is also forfeited. Excellent training facilities on Okinawa produced some of the best-trained SF men in the Forces, with detachments combat-ready for UW, direct action missions, and counterinsurgency operations. The numerous training and civic action missions to all parts of the Pacific acclimatized and acculturated the members of the 1st in a unique manner. The 3rd and 6th SFGs were also taken off the rolls, after performing many useful missions in Africa and the Middle East.

As we have seen, the 5th SFG was withdrawn from Vietnam under the leadership of Col. (later major general) "Iron Mike" Healy, the last 100-man increment arriving at Fort Bragg in March 1971. As they marched away to their evacuation airplanes, the first Vietnamese scavengers were already at work demolishing the excellent Special Forces Operational Base at Nha Trang, the work of nine productive years. It is better not to dwell on the ultimate fates of the tens-of-thousands little CIDG strikers and Mike Force heroes, and their tens-of-thousands wives and children. Their remote locations may have allowed most of them to take off their uniforms and meld in with the rest of the Montagnards, Cambodians, and Nungs. Hopefully, the North Vietnamese have as little success in controlling them as the South Vietnamese government had. It is known that there are islands of insurgency throughout the southern portion of Vietnam, including even some ex-VC units. At least the CIDG strikers had several years before the 1975 invasion to think about and provide for the possibility of a North Vietnamese takeover.

Back at Fort Bragg, the 5th SFG and two-thirds of the 7th SFG go about their business as usual. The "Mickey Mouse" menial housekeeping and post details still infringe on more important training, and the vast majority of officers and NCOs with SF experience and know-how have fled into retirement or the conventional Army. There is a pervading dearth of maturity and experience, what little remains being used on MTTs, training committees, and group and Center headquarters. The A Detachments consist primarily of E-3s (privates first class) and E-4s (corporals), some commanded by second lieutenants. There are some experienced NCOs in A Detachments, though too little detachment training to compensate for inexperience takes place. When there is a mission, they scrape together what experienced personnel there are and send them off, thus wearing out the old hands and leaving the newer soldiers still not fully trained or experienced.

There have been various attempts over the years to further reduce the active-duty strength of SF, but it still remains about 3,600 in the three groups. There is another authorized strength of about 5,800 in four reserve and National Guard groups spread over the country, many of whose members have more experience and training than the active-duty groups, and some detachments filled with ex-Vietnam SF veterans are more combat-ready than those at Bragg and Devens.

The modern John F. Kennedy Center for Military Assistance, together with headquarters buildings, classrooms, and barracks, are a great improvement over the scruffy, old, World War II temporary wooden firetraps they replaced. Young soldiers wearing camouflaged fatigues and green berets are seen everywhere, most of them with the half hatflash, denoting non-SF qualification. They look tough and military and move with determination. These are the students in the Special Forces Qualification Course (SFQC). The enlisted men are E-3s, E-4s, and a few E-5s, having come from civilian streets to basic training, to advanced infantry training, to airborne training, and then to the SFQC, without the benefit of any troop experience in a conventional unit. The officers go from their source of commission (ROTC, OCS, or the Military Academy) to officers' basic school, airborne school, and usually a year or two of troop experience before attending the SFQC. Their intelligence is excellent, they are high school or college graduates, and their motivation is good. However, the high standards of the course are such that a majority of them fail to graduate. The authorities are concerned about that high failure rate and have plans to recycle the better washouts to give them a second chance to meet the school's high standards.

The curriculum reflects the present missions of SF: unconventional warfare, direct actions, and counterinsurgency (foreign internal defense operations). A lot of time is devoted to ranger-type training, with many hours of land navigation and patrolling, rappelling, physical conditioning, and raid-type tactics. The physical requirements to enter the school are particularly demanding, with a requirement of forty-five push-ups and forty-five sit-ups in a two-minute period, and a two-mile run in just under sixteen minutes. Unfortunately, the youngsters are conditioned by our society to quit when the going gets tough, and they show a tendency to aim for just achieving the minimums rather than excelling and shooting for the maximums. Of those NCOs who successfully graduate, some 65 percent are said to re-up for a second term of service, while the officers rarely stay around after completing eighteen months' service in SF. The service branches do not like to leave their young officers too long in the SF assignment, for reasons of both branch qualification and careerism.

The commanding general of the Center is pushing the unconventional warfare mission, and rightly so. Training and experience in UW is the flesh and blood of Special Forces. Knowing how to operate as guerrillas is the basis for successful counterinsurgency operations. However, if there are few well-trained A Detachments and UW training opportunities are scarce, it may be somewhat optimistic to stress UW. The UW mission, above all, requires experience, training, and maturity, together with the understanding of the importance of having the people on your side.

Young men who successfully complete airborne training and a rugged ranger-heavy SF course tend to be highly self-confident, cocky, and a bit arrogant. Being "macho" is the opposite of having concern for other people and realizing the need for their support. Direct action missions require supremely confident, highly trained, well-led units to pull them off. Although the UW mission has top priority, the training itself better equips the young soldiers for direct action operations.

A new and long overdue initiative in the Special Forces School is the Army-wide SERE (Survival, Evasion, Resistance and Escape) Training Program. The Institute for Military Assistance is the proponent for this vital program, presently headed by Lt. Col. James N. ("Nick") Rowe. Rowe gained his expertise as a POW in South Vietnam, spending five years and two months in captivity before successfully escaping on his fourth attempt. He did a tour in the Pentagon in Intelligence, worked with the Adjutant General in preparing "Operation Egress-Recap," the plan for repatriation, rehabilitation, and readjustment of Army POWs, and was assigned to the Defense Intelligence Agency. In 1974, Nick resigned from the military and entered politics in his home state of Texas. In 1978, he began training with the 20th Special Forces Group (National Guard) and was on the faculty of the First U.S. Army Area Intelligence School at Fort Bragg, thus maintaining contact with Special Forces and the JFK Center. In 1981, he was recalled to active duty and assigned to the Institute for Military Assistance. He has worked on the development of the SERE Program from its beginning, while also serving the SF School as Assistant Director and Chief of the Field Training Division. He currently is Chief of the SERE Division.

Nick's survival and escape in Vietnam were due largely to his Special Forces training and tours. He spoke Vietnamese and Chinese Mandarin, and had an understanding of the culture, history, religions, customs, and habits of the Vietnamese people. He was able to understand and, at times, exploit his captors because of an ability to anticipate their actions. Nick Rowe opposed the simplification of the Code of Conduct training to "give the Big Four and nothing more." He used the Code as a constant guide during the years of his captivity, but his was the full interpretation of the Code. His close friend, Capt. Rocky Versace, followed the narrow and unbending interpretation of the Code and was executed by the Vietcong, a tragic loss of an outstanding officer.

After the Vietnam War, a DOD Committee reviewed and

revised the Code of Conduct. Article Five now reads, "I am required to give my name, rank, serial number, and date of birth," rather than the original, "I am bound to give *only* my name, rank, serial number, and date of birth." The next line in the Article reads, "I will evade answering further questions to the utmost of my ability." Realistically, after a POW holds out as long as he can on the "Big Four," he must have somewhere to go. He evades answering further questions to the best of his ability. He has not lost, for the real test has just begun. The Army SERE Training Program gives him a tool kit to use in thwarting enemy attempts at interrogation, indoctrination, and exploitation for propaganda.

The SERE course is now taught in twenty-four action-packed days from 0500 to 2200, seven days a week, with one hour in four in the field in practical exercises. In that period of time, the students are given intensive instruction in survival fieldcraft, expedient tools, water and food procurement, planning and conducting evasion, dog and visual tracker evasion, and Code of Conduct-related subjects, including resistance to interrogation/exploitation and escape from captivity. Survival and evasion under varying environmental conditions are studied. Students are taught to survive in desert, tropical, sea, and arctic environments. The medical aspects are stressed in order to emphasize the importance of medical self-aid and self-analysis of physical capabilities. The importance of knowledge of the terrain, language, and culture of the survival area are underlined. Evasion teaches techniques, the penetration of mine fields and sensor barriers, silent-kill techniques, dog and visual tracker evasion, and countersentry techniques. In the resistance field, students are taught communist interrogation methodology (Soviet, Chinese, Vietnamese, Cuban), resistance to interrogation, clandestine communications in the POW camp, and clandestine organization. Under escape, the configurations of various types of POW camps from Stalags to VC "hoochies" are taught, how to break out of them, how to plan for breakout and subsequent escape, how to organize and prepare for breakout, and how to use various extraction means. U.S. Air Force and Navy Combat Search and Rescue Techniques and Equipment are also taught, for the first time tying the three services together in formal SERE training.

One of the goals of the SERE course is to send out mobile training teams to the sixteen active army divisions to train their SERE cadres. Most of Nick's personnel are outstanding NCOs with "ground time" in combat in Vietnam. He wants them to represent SF to the conventional forces and set standards that will attract recruits from among the trained and mature NCOs in those divisions. One of the positive goals of the SERE program is to downplay the macho attitude of the students, replacing it with the quiet confidence that comes from technical proficiency, maturity, and professionalism, and stressing the need for the support and assistance of other people.

Nick Rowe's program should well equip the graduates to live successfully behind the lines in the battlefields of the future. If the SERE program holds true to its promise, the SF will be the military experts on an increasingly important subject, one that has long been neglected, or paid only lip service. Escape and evasion (E & E) has always been one of the submissions of unconventional warfare, but it was one that SF failed to emphasize properly and teach. It looks as though that omission is well on its way to being corrected in a superior manner.

In addition to SERE training, psychological indoctrination and testing is extremely important. Modern psychologists attest to the imperfection of such methods, but even though they may not be scientifically foolproof and might eliminate a few potentially good people, the good man you never get is no problem. The weakling who cracks when the team is committed a thousand miles from home can be a disaster.

What of the future of Special Forces? The past ten years have seen SF lose four of its seven active groups, shrinking down to an authorized strength of about 3,600. That strength can be supported *if* it can attract recruits of sufficient caliber to man its ranks with trained, skilled, mature professionals. A lot of the tired, soft, older SF enlisted men have left the Forces, and, in my estimation, that was needed. However, to have A Detachments composed only of the young, less mature, and inexperienced men severely limits the effectiveness and potential for multi-mission use.

Special Forces has led a very low-profile existence since 1971, and that, too, was needed. It had too high a presence in the Vietnam War and, consequently, paid the price of near-obliteration when its foes took command of the Army. Generals like William Westmoreland, William Rosson, and William Yarborough had (and have) an excellent understanding of the potential of SF and the value to the country and Army that exists in its ranks, but, unfortunately, they are retired now. Fortunately, the present Secretary of the Army, Marsh, and the present Army Chief of Staff, General "Shy" Meyer, also share that belief, and the possibility exists to bring the Forces back to their previous state of competence and professionalism. However, the principal focus of the Army is on armored warfare, with increasingly sophisticated weapons systems coming into the Army's inventory over the next ten years. Special Forces have little potential influence on the modern NATO/Warsaw Pact battlefield. The anticipated short duration of modern warfare seems to preclude the longer organizational times of unconventional warfare, such as guerrilla warfare. However, this does not mean that there is no UW mission for Special Forces.

At the onset of a NATO/Warsaw Pact war, for instance, American pilots will have to operate over Warsaw Pact territory in order to interdict the Soviet divisions moving to the battle area from the Western Military Districts of the Soviet Union. Inevitably, some will be shot down by Warsaw Pact interceptors and surface-to-air (SAM) missiles. Those pilots should have a chance to evade enemy ground elements and rendezvous at pre-specified escape and evasion areas where professionals will take over their return to friendly hands. SF detachments should be inserted into those E & E contact areas to gather, identify, and assist in extracting downed NATO airmen. That mission will have to be performed without support from the local populations, but is within the capability of *well-trained* SF detachments.

SF detachments should also be used for target acquisition and forward guidance deep within enemy lines. The NATO Corps have responsibility for the first 50 kilometers of the enemy's forward area; the Rangers have from 50 to 150 kilometers, leaving the zone from 150 to 300 kilometers for SF. New and sophisticated man-portable guidance systems are available to guide NATO surface-to-surface fires by Pershing II, the extended-range Lance and cruise missiles, as well as air strikes. If the war becomes nuclear, the ADM capability of the SF detachments will contribute "zero-CEP" (completely accurate) emplacement of low-yield nuclear demolitions to create choke points which will pile up Soviet divisions moving to the west and create lucrative targets for NATO tactical nuclear weapons.

SF detachments should also be designated as "stay-behind" teams in West Germany, before the Warsaw Pact ground forces have advanced at the rate of fifty to seventy-five kilometers per day into West Germany. The detachments in Bad Tolz can rapidly be deployed and emplaced in the first hours of a NATO/Warsaw Pact war to take over interdiction of the enemy lines of supply and communications. Some pre-coordination with the German Border Police could result in the linkage of bypassed German forces and the SF detachments to inflict maximum damage on the Warsaw Pact lines of communication, to include the second-echelon divisions following the heavily armored first-echelon attacking divisions. Such a concept will cause the Warsaw Pact armies to devote heavy commitments of manpower to protect their vulnerable rear areas against guerrilla-type attacks. Well-trained SF detachments, equipped with laser target indicators and dependable radios, should have little difficulty in creating the traditional chaos and despair expected of guerrilla forces. Soviet rear area security doctrine addresses this contingency. They are aware of the potential of SF-type attacks, even if the U.S. Army is not.

There are also UW missions in contingency areas outside the NATO/Warsaw Pact area of conflict. The critically dangerous situation between the Koreas does not get much space in the world's media, but daily grows in potential for conflict. The North Korean ground forces have doubled in numbers in the last six years, including hefty new increments of armor and armored infantry major units. The North Korean commitment to special warfare is the largest in the world, with approximately 100,000 men trained for infiltration into South Korea, by sea, air, and ground (to include tunnel warfare). Those troops are targeted for behind-the-lines objectives throughout South Korea where they can control the lines of communication, disrupt the mobilization and movement of reserve units, destroy logistics and ammunition depots, and paralyze South Korea for at least a short period of time. As it is anticipated that the North Korean front-line divisions can penetrate to Seoul in three to five days, their special operations forces do not need to buy very much time.

The presence of some 40,000 U.S. forces in South Korea is an immediate U.S. commitment to the war in the event of North Korean aggression. American planes will immediately be in the fight with rapid air reinforcement from throughout the far Pacific. American soldiers will be committed on the ground, and, inevitably, some will be cut off and isolated. There will be an immediate need for E & E operations to retrieve valuable pilots and equally valuable infantrymen. There will be opportunities for sabotage missions behind North Korean lines, as their road network is sparse and very vulnerable to ground interdiction. Although guerrilla warfare, except by native Koreans, is a remote possibility, certainly the South Korean's seven Special Forces Brigades will be well placed to operate behind North Korean lines. U.S. Special Forces are in South Korea today in reduced B Detachment (company) strength, and should be increased to at least battalion strength, for continuous liaison with the South Korean Special Forces and with forces under U.S. Eighth Army. Stay-behind operations in cooperation with the South Koreans should be planned throughout South Korea, but particularly in the central mountain spine best suited for unconventional warfare. A reserve Special Forces unit should be formed in the Hawaiian Islands to take advantage of the diverse linguistic and racial assets there. Such a unit would provide CINCPAC a strong backup for UW throughout the Pacific, but particularly in Korea. There are many highly trained, experienced SF old-timers retired on Oahu, with multiple language capabilities and Asiatic racial origins that could be vital in establishing such a reserve SF unit.

Similarly, there are UW plans in every theater of operations, and the SF must produce the well-trained *detachments* with area and language knowledge and the expertise to perform successfully all the varied aspects of unconventional warfare. The authorities at Fort Bragg *know* what is required and how to achieve it. The problem of SF is acquiring experienced, trained volunteers, both NCO and commissioned, to join Special Forces. The Forces have to acquire the maturity and experience needed, and stabilize. There is the constant bleeding of those few experienced NCOs on hand to meet levies for SF-designated slots in the reserve SF groups, ROTC cadres, and Recruiting Command organizations. There is talk of ordering experienced SF-qualified NCOs in non-SF-related assignments to return to the Forces or leave the Army. There is talk of creating a Special Forces career field with separate and unique Special Forces Military Occupational Specialties.

Many of the missions undertaken by Special Forces in the past thirty years have been related here. There can be no doubt that SF has been a "force multiplier," an "economy of force" unit that achieves great results with minimum cost in money, equipment, supplies, and manpower. It is not necessary to justify the direct action missions and Foreign Internal Defense operations as missions for the future. Those operations are a result of the great flexibility for a variety of missions that a mature, experienced, well-trained SF unit provides; they are a bonus springing out of the UW capabilities of Special Forces. The *desirability* of direct action missions by SF is obvious, but if the Army wants the *capability* to perform a variety of missions, it must provide SF the resources necessary. The Ranger battalions are superbly trained and ready units for direct action missions. The young SF graduates of the Special Forces School have the potential to become superior rangers, but at the cost of developing a UW capability, however limited.

Special Forces is at a crossroads today. For the first ten years, 1952–61, it was small, quiet, professional, and superbly trained for UW. The second ten years, 1962–71, saw the Forces greatly expanded, highly publicized, and deployed to Vietnam for an eight-year stay. Thousands of men passed through its camps in Vietnam, many of them for repeated tours (all voluntary). The third ten years, 1972–81, saw the Forces greatly reduced in strength, with the remaining groups based on east coast Army posts in the United States. SF became quiet again, and small, and performed well those missions assigned to it, but with increasingly little capability to perform unconventional warfare, as the experienced NCOs and officers left the ranks of SF for assignment and promotion elsewhere. Today, Special Forces is turning upward from its nadir, with limited but increasing capabilities to perform the basic missions. This limitation is not the fault of the present commanders, who understand the current condition and the reasons for it.

Since World War II, assertions have been made repeatedly that the purpose of nuclear weapons is to act as a deterrent, to prevent large-scale war. Small-scale "wars of liberation" have instead been the Soviet's answer to nuclear conflict. Counterinsurgency comes as a natural corollary to such "liberation" conflicts. World War II left the entire eastern bloc hostage to the Soviets. Despite Soviet power and Soviet presence, with no help from the West, resistance to Soviet domination continues with frequent flare-ups. Albania and Yugoslavia are safely outside the Soviet sphere, and dissidence has grown gradually in Poland, Hungary, Rumania, East Germany, and Czechoslovakia. Only Bulgaria has escaped the warm breath of dissident freedom, remaining totally dominated by the Soviets.

In Southeast Asia, reunited Communist Vietnam has exiled some 500,000 of its citizens to Siberian labor camps, a good indication of popular unrest. The old Vietcong insurgents who carried the fight for so many years have been shunted aside by the powerful men of Hanoi, and many have defected to tell their story of harsh oppression. Vietnam has brutally occupied Cambodia and Laos, and thousands of refugees have sought safety in Thailand.

The Soviets have occupied Afghanistan with about 100,000 troops and are engaged in a fierce counterinsurgency war against Afghan freedom-fighters. After many months, this bloody struggle is no closer to resolution. The Soviets also stand poised for massive intervention in Iran and the entire Persian Gulf area. But they have a dilemma, for although they have been supporting Iraq militarily and economically for years, in the current war between Iraq and neighboring Iran, the Soviets are supporting one of the antigovernment factions in Iran.

Central America is seething. Communist guerrillas are seeking to overcome the United States–supported government of El Salvador. Honduras is similarly threatened, as are Guatemala, Costa Rica, and Panama. These all tend to follow the pattern of the Sandinista revolt in Nicaragua, where a pro-United States regime was toppled and replaced by a Marxist state. During this conflict, some 2,000 Cuban advisors and technicians accompanied the Sandinistas. In November 1981,

Cuba's Fidel Castro announced that he had sent "2,000 civilian volunteers" to El Salvador.

If the unconventional warfare assets of the United States were applied in these various countries where oppression exists, or where Communist-supported revolts are under way, favorable results could be expected. Additionally, possibilities for large-scale conventional wars exist in Europe, Korea, and the Middle East which would probably involve commitment of U.S. forces. As part of such action, Special Forces would have their own role to play.

Future wars may last longer than a few weeks, unlike the several Arab-Israeli wars in modern times. Since American national psychology and precepts do not permit aggression against our world neighbors, our military concepts limit our peacetime activities. At the same time, however, our contingency plans must provide enough flexibility to incorporate dissidents into our own military efforts, in the event of war. Therefore, Special Forces missions must be included in any war plans, and these elite troops must be kept in a constant state of readiness for employment wherever and whenever conflict may occur.

A vital part of this preparation involves the intelligence services of the nation operating in peacetime. These services must be of civilian origin, in accord with our historic concepts, but must be available for coordination with the military in both peace and war. There must be a constant sharing of information between these civilian agencies and the military. In prewar planning, cooperation between the two could identify roles, possible missions, and command relationships in wartime. In the next war, petty political considerations must be put aside to permit smooth transfers of authority, responsibilities, and assets.

Apparently, the government is considering these matters seriously, since there is growing awareness of the importance and need for well-trained Special Forces troops. The Army has recently authorized another SF Group, the 8th SFG, which will be oriented toward Latin America. The work of Special Forces men in El Salvador is well advertised in news media, although the number of our troops there is small. One must remember, of course, that mere authorization of a new Special Forces group does not immediately generate a new pool of qualified men. The present three groups all have vacancies which must be filled with trained and qualified personnel, a long and tedious process.

Although the type of publicity that drives a wedge between Special Forces and the rest of the Army is not acceptable, SF will have to go more public if it is to attract the type of recruits it needs. Nick Rowe's idea of exposing the conventional Army to the best of SF by way of SERE mobile training teams is an example of what is needed. Good men are attracted to elite units which satisfy their self-esteem and sense of accomplishment. The old-time SF men stayed with the Forces because they enjoyed each other's company and didn't care much for anyone else. That aspect has obviously been lost in the past ten years, and certainly does not exist among the young troopers that man today's Special Forces Groups. The "brotherhood" of SF can only be restored by forming excellent A Detachments, training them intensively as *detachments*, keeping them together, and employing them as units, even in such demeaning tasks as picking up pinecones or cleaning beaches.

On a higher plane, the SF soldier must know how to deal empathetically and effectively with native populations, and be able to assist them with real understanding and unquestioned expertise. His mission may be the development of a resistance movement in the context of a larger war, counterinsurgency assistance, or clandestine support of a revolutionary movement. He must also be prepared to go it alone and carry out direct action or reconnaissance missions without contact with the local population.

Broad-based training, education, and experience will be necessary, and is available, though often outside the SF system. Officers and senior NCOs in the program need more sophistication in political science and international affairs, as the basic missions of Special Forces are *political*. Some people will come into the program with such polish; others must be sent to civilian schools to acquire it. The same applies to the acquisition of area and language knowledge. Efforts to get good men who already have this invaluable know-how must continue, but they probably will not be sufficient.

Of course, some "career managers" in Washington will still

tell young up-and-coming officers that "SF is the kiss of death," but a small, highly professional organization will attract the type of freethinkers it needs anyway. The opportunist with stars in his eyes who came to Special Forces to get his ticket punched in counterinsurgency, returned to conventional forces, and joined the anti-SF league, has never been of help to the Army overall.

For those who serve in SF, there will be little public recognition, few stars, and no glamor. There will be much hard work, difficult living conditions, long periods away from home, and danger. Satisfaction will come from the private knowledge of being good and being tough, being part of an elite outfit, and from doing important work well. For the nation, there will once again be an organization that is truly "special" to carry out the nation's special missions.

Epilogue

WHERE ARE THEY TODAY?

In early June 1982, the Special Forces Association sponsored a reunion in Fayetteville, North Carolina, of the old-timers who joined the Forces between 1952 and 1959, honoring the thirtieth anniversary of Special Forces. Approximately 400 old-timers and their wives assembled for three days of renewing old acquaintances, honoring the dead, and reviewing the present status of SF. They brunched and banqueted, and assembled before the statue of an SF trooper at Fort Bragg to present a wreath, saluting the fallen. They attended the Gabriel Demonstration and saw a steely eyed A Detachment of mature, language-qualified men expertly explain and demonstrate their skills. The SF HALO Parachute Team dropped into an area about the size of a tennis court, then smartly assembled and saluted the SF Commandant. Everything they saw and experienced was superbly done, demonstrating expert planning and execution by the JFK Center and the committee headed by Herb Brucker.

Col. Aaron Bank was the honored guest and principal speaker at the formal banquet. Still straight and strong, yet gray and lean, he praised the assembled old-timers for their years of devoted, excellent service. All, of course, are retired from the Army, though many of them pursue second careers of surprising diversity. Robert Pezelle paints in oil. Coy Melton owns and operates a nursery. Rocky Nesom flies a plane out of McAllen, Texas. Many work for the huge construction firms with overseas contracts, several of them in Saudi Arabia. Some work for the CIA, many of them overseas. Others work at outside jobs, such as sports-fishermen, park rangers, and hunting guides. Sully Fontaine is employed by the Nevada State Gambling Commission and roams the world checking out the backgrounds of people who apply for gambling licenses. Ex-SFers work in real estate, auto dealerships, bars, and other commercial endeavors, while some are policemen or security guards. Charlie Beckwith owns his own security service in Austin, Texas. "Bo" Gritz works in California at various schemes to liberate U.S. POWs in Vietnam and Laos. Bob Rheault works for Outward Bound in Maine. Frank Dallas is a city engineer for Fayetteville, North Carolina.

A large number have second wives. There is a saying that you can tell old-time SFers by "their sports cars, gold bracelets, Rolex wristwatches, and divorces," which contains more truth than fiction. It was a hard life for the women, and many a marriage failed to survive, for a variety of reasons.

Of course, the men are getting old, with many a bald spot or gray head. Many have physical afflictions derived from years of humping a rucksack and repeated combat tours in three wars. The life of the soldier who moves and fights on foot has never been an easy one. The Vietnam illnesses of malaria, blackwater fever, and "fevers of unknown origin" were and are debilitating, and the effects return periodically long after the first bouts. Many were wounded in the sort of vicious, close-in nose-to-nose fighting in Vietnam characterized by automatic weapons on full fire and hand grenades bursting.

There are many holes in the ranks since 1959. The Vietnam War was responsible for many of those holes, as many of the 544 SF dead in that war were veterans of the 1950s. It is a heartrending sight to see the survivors stand in front of the plaque at the SF Center on which the names of SF dead are inscribed.

"Where's Mazak? Oh, there he is. We served together in the 10th and 5th. He was a good man."

"There is Thorne. So they finally officially declared him dead from missing. I don't believe it."

Time is also taking its toll. The monthly publication of the SF Association, *The Drop*, carries two to four obituaries every issue, most of them from among the old-timers. They were a tough bunch, but mortal nevertheless.

Some have simply dropped out of sight, severing their old SF relations and leaving their old friends. Despite that, the membership of the SF Association is steadily growing, with several dozen chapters all over the United States and Korea. From time to time, an old-timer is rediscovered and comes back to the fold, in from the cold.

They are a grizzled, likable, fantastically experienced bunch of tough old bastards who do not apologize to anyone for the wars they have fought and the things they have had to do. On the contrary, they are proud of themselves, their service, and their country. Above all, they are proud to have worn the green beret.

INDEX

ABOUT THE AUTHOR

A West Point Graduate, Charles M. ("Bill") Simpson spent nine years of his thirty-year military career with the Special Forces. He has taught at the Army War College, written a history of the Middle East, and led Special Forces troops in Germany and Vietnam.

"This account is admittedly written by a man with a deep affection for the SF," he says, "and one who had long service in its ranks. This is not to say that it is entirely uncritical. Mistakes have been made, and I have tried to identify them without bias.

"A lot of it is personal experience. I was there."

Bestselling Thrillers —
action-packed for a great read

__ $3.95	0-425-07671-7	**ROLE OF HONOR** John Gardner
__ $3.95	0-425-07657-1	**DAI-SHO** Marc Olden
__ $3.50	0-425-07324-6	**DAU** Ed Dodge
__ $3.95	0-425-08158-3	**RED SQUARE** Edward Topol and Fridrikh Neznansky
__ $4.50	0-425-08383-7	**THE HUNT FOR RED OCTOBER** Tom Clancy
__ $3.95	0-425-08301-2	**AIRSHIP NINE** Thomas H. Block
__ $3.95	0-441-37033-0	**IN HONOR BOUND** Gerald Seymour
__ $3.95	0-441-01972-2	**AMERICAN REICH** Douglas Muir
__ $3.50	0-441-10550-5	**CIRCLE OF DECEIT** Walter Winward
__ $3.50	0-441-27316-5	**GAME OF HONOR** Tom Lewis
__ $3.95	0-441-47128-5	**LAST MESSAGE TO BERLIN** Philippe van Rjndt
__ $3.50	0-515-08337-2	**DEATHWATCH** Elleston Trevor
__ $3.95	0-515-08415-8	**QUILLER** Adam Hall

Prices may be slightly higher in Canada.

Available at your local bookstore or return this form to:

BERKLEY PUBLISHING GROUP
Berkley • Jove • Charter • Ace
Book Mailing Service
P.O. Box 690, Rockville Centre, NY 11571

Please send me the titles checked above. I enclose _____ Include 75¢ for postage and handling if one book is ordered; 25¢ per book for two or more not to exceed $1.75. California, Illinois, New York and Tennessee residents please add sales tax.

NAME_____

ADDRESS_____

CITY_____ STATE/ZIP_____

(Allow six weeks for delivery.)   422